Sophia Richman

A Wolf in the A

The Legacy of a Hidde. .....
of the Holocaust

*Pre-publication
REVIEWS,
COMMENTARIES,
EVALUATIONS . . .*

"**A** *Wolf in the Attic* is a welcome addition to the literature on the Holocaust. With great sensitivity and insight Sophia Richman allows us to enter the world of child survivors in a way rarely experienced by readers. Her book is more than a Holocaust survivor's tale. It is a story of triumph and resilience. With brutal honesty, Richman takes us through the postwar years—her schooling, her successful efforts to become a psychoanalyst, her marriage, and the tragic health problems of her only child. Her beautiful narrative brings to life the myriad ways in which the Holocaust left an indelible imprint upon the lives of those who went through it."

William B. Helmreich, PhD
Professor of Sociology,
CUNY Graduate Center
and City College of New York

"**S**ophia Richman's book on hidden children is an important document. Not enough has been written about their anguish and courage during the darkest of times in recorded history. Thanks to her scholarly effort, more names and tales will be remembered."

Elie Wiesel
Author, *Night;*
1986 Nobel Peace Prize Winner

"Sophia Richman's *A Wolf in the Attic* presents us with a literal healing from a literal nightmare on the part of a child survivor, one of many who have only recently begun to emerge out of hiding. The book corroborates the frequently ignored fact that massive psychic trauma may show itself years and even decades after the original catastrophe. In it, Richman deals with the unique role of memory in recovery from the traumatic past. She is a tailor of remembering, as she pieces together fragments and pieces of time and place from her past to create a tapestry of her life that feels whole again. One of her most original contributions is the courage with which she demonstrates that mourning and grief are essential to healing connections that were once torn asunder. She shows how she and her family regained the ability to feel out of the abyss of emotional anesthesia, and how they became rehumanized in the process."

Chaim F. Shatan, MD, CM
Clinical Professor,
New York University
Postdoctoral Program
in Psychoanalysis

"Written in a simple yet poignant style, this book is a moving story of a life marked by horror and tragedy but also by an indomitable spirit of affirmation. With her childhood experience of the Holocaust casting its shadow on everything that ensues, the author weaves together an extraordinary tapestry of riveting, vividly portrayed episodes over the course of her life. Accompanying her personal narrative, Richman gives us a philosophy to ponder, articulated in a voice that is at once lucid and passionate. We see its deeply personal origins as well as its specific expressions in day-to-day living and in coping with major crises. The moral challenge is clear: our task is to create and affirm the value of our lives even in the face of the most devastating assaults on our humanity. It is to find a way to love each other, ourselves, and life itself, while at the same time coming to terms with human evil and human tragedy. Indeed, Richman shows us how love and creativity can arise from traumatic suffering and even from our encounters with the abyss. Hearing her story affords us the opportunity to absorb her hard-won wisdom at the same time that we are inspired to discover and express our own."

Irwin Z. Hoffman, PhD
Faculty and Supervising Analyst,
Chicago Center for Psychoanalysis

"Sophia Richman, a psychoanalyst and Holocaust survivor, has written a moving, absorbing memoir that effortlessly interweaves the deeply personal with the historical. Dr. Richman writes with remarkable insight and unflinching honesty about her experience as a 'hidden child' during the Holocaust and its aftereffects. This courageous book inspires readers with hope in the capacity of the human spirit to free itself from the hidden ghosts that haunt all of us. This is one of those rare books that will touch professional and lay audiences alike."

Peter Shabad, PhD
Author of *Despair*
and the Return of Hope;
Northwestern University
Medical School,
Chicago, Illinois

More pre-publication
REVIEWS, COMMENTARIES, EVALUATIONS . . .

"**A**n intimate memoir of tragedy and triumph, *A Wolf in the Attic* is an engrossing and haunting narrative that documents the hand of evil reaching across time and generations. Sophia Richman, a psychologist and psychoanalyst, writes naturally, subtly, powerfully, absorbingly, and with unusual insight as she describes the psychological impact of her family's experiences in the Holocaust and its shaping character on her own psyche and on the personal choices that she made in her life. This book speaks clearly and decisively about the ongoing devastation of the Holocaust on children and children's children. It speaks too about the power of understanding, memory, and interpersonal relations to mitigate the vicissitudes of trauma, and of the incredible human will to prevail over the worst horrors and to move on with life and spirit."

Lewis Aron, PhD
Director, New York
University Postdoctoral
Program in Psychotherapy
and Psychoanalysis

"**A** *Wolf in the Attic* is a brave, honest, and compassionate work that is written with clarity and power. It should be mandated reading for those interested in the relationship between childhood trauma and adult functioning. An impassioned and earnest writer and expert psychoanalyst, Richman offers hope to other survivors, an invaluable tool for clinicians, and an accessible and fascinating volume for general readers. Richman weaves the myriad particulars of her involved and rich life and leaves the reader engaged, informed, and awed by the resourcefulness of the human spirit. While the reader may not agree with all the interpretations offered by Richman, none would question the long-term impact of the Holocaust on the lives of survivors or the talent of this sensitive and compassionate writer."

Judith L. Alpert, PhD
Professor, Department
of Applied Psychology,
New York University

The Haworth Press®
New York • London • Oxford

A Wolf in the Attic
The Legacy of a Hidden Child of the Holocaust

THE HAWORTH PRESS
New, recent, and forthcoming titles of related interest

Celebrating the Lives of Jewish Women: Patterns in a Feminist Sampler edited by Rachel Josefowitz Siegel and Ellen Cole

Jewish Women in Therapy: Seen But Not Heard edited by Rachel Josefowitz Siegel and Ellen Cole

Jewish Mothers Tell Their Stories: Acts of Love and Courage edited by Rachel Josefowitz Siegel, Ellen Cole, and Susan Steinberg-Oren

The Use of Personal Narratives in the Helping Professions: A Teaching Casebook edited by Jessica K. Heriot and Eileen J. Polinger

The Body Bears the Burden: Trauma, Dissociation, and Disease by Robert C. Scaer

Holocaust Survivors' Mental Health edited by T. L. Brink

Women's Encounters with the Mental Health Establishment: Escaping the Yellow Wallpaper edited by Elayne Clift

The Holocaust: Memories, Research, Reference edited by Robert Hauptman and Susan Hubbs Motin

Another Silenced Trauma: Feminist Therapists and Activists Respond to a Woman's Recovery from War edited by Esther D. Rothblum and Ellen Cole

A Wolf in the Attic
The Legacy of a Hidden Child of the Holocaust

Sophia Richman

The Haworth Press, Inc.
New York • London • Oxford

The Haworth Press, Inc., 10 Alice Street, Binghamton, NY 13904–1580

Author's note: Some family members' names have been changed to protect their privacy.

Ritsos, Yannis; *Healing.* (Translated from Greek by Edmund Keeley.) Copyright © 1991 by PUP. Reprinted by permission of Princeton University Press.

Cover design by Marylouise Doyle.

Library of Congress Cataloging-in-Publication Data

Richman, Sophia, 1941-
    A wolf in the attic : the legacy of a hidden child of the Holocaust / Sophia Richman.
        p. cm.
    ISBN 0-7890-1549-8 (alk. paper)—ISBN 0-7890-1550-1 (alk. paper)
    1. Richman, Sophia, 1941- 2. Jewish children in the Holocaust—Ukraine—L§'v—Biography. 3. Holocaust, Jewish (1939-1945)—Ukraine—L§'v—Personal narratives. 4. Holocaust survivors—United States—Biography. 5. L§'v (Ukraine)—Biography. 6. United States—Biography. I. Title.

DS135.U43 R537 2002
940.53'18'092—dc21

                                                                                2001024337

In memory of the thirty-five members of my extended family
who perished in the Holocaust.

With gratitude to those who rescued me from the same fate.

In appreciation for the chance to restore life
to the broken branches of my family tree.

I dedicate this book to my husband Spyros,
whose unwavering love has sustained me,
and my daughter Lina,
whose courage has been my inspiration.

CONTENTS

Foreword   ix
Spyros D. Orfanos, PhD

Preface   xiii

Acknowledgments   xvii

Chapter 1. Fragments of a Lost World   1

Chapter 2. Scrambling for Life   11

Chapter 3. Excerpts from Hell   19

Chapter 4. Escape   37

Chapter 5. Hidden in Plain Sight   45

Chapter 6. In Death's Shadow   55

Chapter 7. Refugees   61

Chapter 8. Lost and Found in America   75

Chapter 9. Struggles and Triumphs of Adolescence   85

Chapter 10. The College Years: New Avenues and Dead Ends   97

Chapter 11. Illusions of Freedom   107

Chapter 12. Gathering Strength   117

Chapter 13. On My Own Again   127

Chapter 14. Healing Relationships   139

Chapter 15. The Life Thread   151

Chapter 16. The Hour of the Wolf   161

Chapter 17. Out of Hiding   167

Chapter 18. Secrets and Secretions   177

Chapter 19. The Wolf Strikes Again   189

Chapter 20. Invisible Scars   207

Chapter 21. Coming to Terms   219

Epilogue: Ghosts of Galicia   229

Bibliography   239

Foreword

I thought I knew the story. I had visited the camps, read the history, seen the documentaries, and listened to the music. As a very young boy, I absorbed my mother's description of how inhabitants of Ereikousa, her small island on the Ionian Sea, had hidden four Greek Jews during the war. Knowing and loving Sophia for close to three decades, I heard fragments of the story often. In reality, I knew little of the story.

Sophia would share her fragments of memory with me especially when we traveled. Geographical transitions often bring out our hidden anxieties. At first, her memory fragments were like faint murmurs from far away; then, over the years, the murmurs became audible. The memories always spoke in a compelling manner, yet they would stop abruptly, as if some sharp psychic door had slammed. Over time, the stories emerged with greater frequency and detail. They became textured and tragic. But still, they were unintegrated, like musical phrases without a melodic line, without rhythm, harmony, or bridges. I did not know that her memories had been frozen. I did not know that her lack of clarity was protective. Ironically, it was after a tragedy had turned our world upside down that Sophia began to write. She wrote in a burst of creative integration that lasted close to a year.

Each day of that year, and often at night, Sophia could be found upstairs writing on her Macintosh computer. At times, I wondered if she preferred writing to other interests—including me. She actually loved the process of writing. She hated *not* writing. I think I envied her driven self-analysis. Following the completion of the first chapter, I expected her to lose enthusiasm. I was wrong; no creative blocks occurred. True, she was sometimes insecure about revealing a certain family secret—she did not want to hurt others. Yet her internal muse insisted on remembering, integrating, and writing.

We know that writing about traumatic experiences has been found to be beneficial in some instances. Written expression about traumatic or stressful events seems to benefit both somatic and psychological health; the research on this is clear. The theory behind the research findings proposes that writing encourages the creation of a structured narrative out of previously unstructured sensory fragments. It is as if writing about emotions forces the encoding of traumatic memory into narrative language. The American psychiatrist Harry Stack Sullivan once explained that the goal of psychotherapy is to organize one's experience. I believe that writing organized Sophia's emotional and cognitive experiences and has been therapeutic for her. This is not surprising for most. What is of interest, however, is that the writing followed formal psychotherapy and psychoanalysis for Sophia. I am not suggesting that the "writing cure" be substituted for the "talking cure." I believe that writing helped Sophia integrate new understanding with prior self- and worldviews. No doubt, a complex relationship exists between writing and healing. Dangers are inherent in any expressive writing activity or self-analysis. The isolation of this exercise may allow for aspects of the story to be ignored, denied, or discarded if they do not fit the conscious frame of the writer. I sense that Sophia navigated these dangers with the courage and the skill of the seasoned psychoanalytic voyager that she is.

A psychoanalytic treatment is never complete. It may have a profound effect on one's life, but it is never a final product. At best, it is a process of inquiry, of reflection, and of learning. Sophia learned her lessons well—sometimes lessons that her teachers (her analysts) were probably not even aware of. As the words cascaded from her open heart, found their way to her feminine hands and onto the keyboard, and subsequently were transformed via computer binary system onto the printed page, the memory fragments emerged in a single eloquent voice. It is a voice, I am ashamed to admit, I did not know she possessed.

This memoir is the crystallization of a conscious and unconscious undertaking. Sophia has probably been working on this since she was a toddler. She has found her mode of expression. Perhaps the reader will be impressed, as I was, with her narrative tone. Narrative tone is more than a matter of personal style and particular language. In Sophia's case, it is an all-encompassing sensibility that is honest, forthright, and ironic. No longer a frightened little girl, Sophia's tone is mature. She knows what her search has been about. It is about her memory speaking, and it is about the choices she made and continues to make. It is about concretizing the catastrophic and the particular.

Sophia's voice tells the story of what happens when a hidden child of the Holocaust grows up. This is an account we rarely see in the Holocaust literature. It is about the aftereffects of trauma. It is about the personal difficulties of a young woman fighting to forge an identity in the midst of a world that wants to forget. It is about a clinical psychoanalyst with unusual tact and talent. It is about a wife and a mother. It is about integrating memories in our fragmented and unforgiving information society. It is *not* about a victim.

Holocaust derives from the Greek *olokaufston,* "whole burnt." The term was not much used until reintroduced by historians during the 1950s to denote the mass murder of the Jews by the Nazis in the war of 1939 to 1945. Although I can place the word *holocaust* in etymological context, I cannot at all place the experience of the Holocaust in any rational or psychological context. Neither does this memoir try to offer a rational explanation. It does try to evoke one person's unique experience. In so doing, Sophia is following in a long line of Holocaust writers, but she has created something new. She is, as British psychoanalyst D. W. Winnicott might put it, in union with the past tradition of writers but also separate. Her originality is that her story is not over when the trauma is over, nor is it over when the healing is almost complete, nor is it over when great emotional depth has been reached. We know how the story ends, but the story is never really over. Sophia's originality can be found in the blending of psychology and social awareness with a clear philosophy of life. Her originality can be found in how she develops meaning in the context of untrustworthy gods and human uncertainty.

Horrible evil awaited Sophia and all other Jewish children during World War II. She and the thousands of children who were hidden escaped a grim fate often by luck. Sophia's story is many things; it is also a story of chance and choice. The moral climate of her early years did not allow for much choice. The personal courage of her adult years, however, insisted on choice and responsibility. She took this stance and acted often in the context of serendipity and even meaninglessness.

Sophia's story is, and I am not sure she would agree with me, also an act of revenge. Like the triumphant woman in a Modern Greek poem, Sophia walks into her vineyard having expelled the small-spirited, the psychoanalytic illusionists, and the dealers of death. Her very act of writing torments ignorance and malignancy, wherever it may be. This memoir is a quiet story about the victory of the forces of life.

The totalitarian regimes of the past century that created so many victims are now mostly, but unfortunately not completely, gone. Yet we continue to suffer their aftereffects.

Organized evil, however, is not limited to totalitarian regimes. In this new century, we are dealing with terrorist networks that create overwhelming horror of the sort which struck the United States on September 11, 2001. While thousands of innocent civilians were killed, we have yet to calculate the psychological effects on the surviving families and children. Who will calculate such effects for us? Who will calculate the effects on our human right for freedom from fear, despair, and amnesia? The traumatic consequences of terrorism during peacetime are probably different than those of war. Nevertheless, on both a political and personal level, we recognize all too well the intergenerational transmission of trauma, the handing down of unintegrated and inaccessible feeling states. The story you are about to read will give you a firsthand psychological account of what it means to have survived a hidden childhood. In and of itself, it is an act of coming out of hiding. In other words, it is an expression of freedom.

Spyros D. Orfanos, PhD

Preface

The dream begins:

I have to catch a plane or boat to some distant destination. I haven't allowed myself enough time to pack all my stuff. I desperately gather my clothes and things. Time slips away. I'm racing against the clock.

When the dream ends, it's never clear if I've managed to complete the task. Ready or not, the journey begins. This recurring dream has become frequent in the past few years. What am I trying to tell myself? I am a psychoanalyst who acknowledges the wisdom of dreams. For over thirty years, I have worked in this field, and I know from both sides of the couch that much of what goes on within us is outside of our awareness. Dreams can reveal certain elusive truths about our inner lives. To understand a dream, we must know the dreamer and the significant issues in the dreamer's life.

I am a survivor of the Holocaust, one of the remaining witnesses to the events that took place more than fifty years ago in Eastern Europe, when the Nazi death machine was running rampant. As a Jewish child born during the Holocaust, I spent my earliest years living in hiding in a geographical area that had been a part of Poland until the outbreak of World War II.

Children, the future of the Jewish people, were special targets of annihilation. Out of the 1.6 million children living in Europe in Nazi-occupied territories, 1.5 million perished. In Poland, the survival rate was even lower, a staggering one half of one percent. We survived against great odds, most of us in hiding. After the war, our trauma was minimized. We were constantly reminded of our good luck to be alive. We were told that because we were spared the concentration camps, we were not considered genuine survivors.

For many years, only the grown-ups were given the responsibility of testifying to the horrors they had lived through. But now, as these adults are dying out, we, the children who were told, "You were too young to remember," are given the torch of memory to carry and pass on to future generations.

Remembering is a precarious task for those of us who survived as very young children. It is easy to challenge our hold on the past. At its best, our memories consist of fragmented images disconnected from time and place—memories without context, fading with time. We were vulnerable to the attempts of adults to influence our perceptions of what transpired when we were too young to understand the meaning of the events taking place around us.

In their attempt to shield me from suffering, my parents encouraged me to forget what I had witnessed. The assumption that young children are not affected by traumatic circumstances because they don't understand them is naive at best. The story of my life is a testament to the long-term and often subtle impact of a traumatic childhood. This memoir is an attempt to understand the ways in which those early years have shaped my life and to come to terms with them.

For many years after the war, I complied with my parents' injunction to forget the past. I did not consider myself a survivor. I was numbed emotionally to the events of my childhood. I did not hide my Holocaust history; I simply treated it as irrelevant. The price of forced forgetting is that individual parts remain secluded and unavailable to experience life fully. Sometimes those unacknowledged aspects of experience are reenacted in behavior that has lost its essential connection to its source and therefore appears strange. One can't mourn what one doesn't acknowledge, and one can't heal if one does not mourn. After years of remembering to forget what I remembered, I discovered within myself a profound desire to know. My internal change corresponded to a shift in the climate around me concerning the Holocaust.

Typically, survivors face the past with great ambivalence. The responsibility to preserve the memories coexists with the impulse to forget; we are perpetually suspended between concealment and disclosure. For many years following World War II, the balance was decided in favor of concealment and reinforced by a society that did not want to know the gruesome details. Then, about thirty years after the Holocaust, the climate began to shift toward disclosure and remembrance.

After years of silence, both of my parents decided to reveal the details of what had happened to our family during the war. My father published a book about his life in a concentration camp, and my mother agreed to be interviewed by the Yale Fortunoff Video Archives for Holocaust Testimonies. Their documentation validated some of my earliest memories and enabled me to reconstruct the events of the war years. I am most grateful to them for providing me with a way to restore my own personal history, fragmented by the trauma of war and by its aftermath of migration and displacement.

Having lived with secrets and mystification for a good part of my life, I now place a premium on getting the story straight. With that end in mind, I find myself paying particular attention to dates and names, and, for the most part, I follow a chronological sequence in my narrative. Furthermore, for the sake of authenticity, I quote passages from my parents' accounts of life during the war years. Identifying the names of relatives gives me an opportunity to memorialize them. There are no headstones marking the passing of those who perished; I don't even know the names of many of my dead cousins. No one is left to mourn them. It is as though they never existed. By including them in this memoir, I found a small way to preserve their memory.

What is the journey the dream I recurrently have refers to? The use of the word "journey" to describe one's travel though life has become a cliché. In my case, however, I have traveled literally from distant shores. As a refugee, I knew the anxiety of leaving a familiar place under pressure, regardless whether I was ready or not. For me, the image of a journey is a personal as well as a universal symbol. So what is the meaning of the dream? Because of its timing, I think it refers to the commitment I made to write the story of my life. For several years prior to the dream, I had been planning to embark on this new venture but always managed to postpone it. The dream highlights the sense of urgency about the task at hand. Soon, the last survivor will be gone; our numbers are dwindling. Not much time is left to tell our stories.

What does one pack for such a journey? How do you sort out from a full life the relevant and meaningful from the superficial? How does one prepare for the travel? Do I have the necessary "stuff" to embark on such a long journey? Do I have enough talent for this ambitious endeavor? Do I have enough knowledge about my past or sufficient understanding about myself?

There are other concerns. There is the delicate matter of self-disclosure. In our culture of open confession, we are encouraged to share our private thoughts and feelings with a curious public. The success of the talk show format suggests a hunger for intimate details about people's lives—the more sordid, the better. But for a psycho-analyst, it is a more ticklish matter. Our training warns us that self-disclosure has complicated consequences that must be understood if we are to be helpful to our patients. When our patients also become the readers who learn our most private thoughts and feelings, we have no way of gauging the impact of revelations disclosed in a published book.

For me, an added implication exists: writing a memoir is one more major step in coming out of hiding. Perhaps for this reason more than any other I must put my reservations aside and realize my promise to myself.

Since I began to write, the journey dream no longer recurs. It doesn't need to. The story that follows is its fulfillment.

Acknowledgments

First and foremost, I wish to acknowledge my husband Spyros D. Orfanos, a witness to my self-discoveries, who shared in the joy as well as the pain of the process. I'm deeply grateful for his enthusiastic support and generous help throughout every phase of this project from its conception to its birth. He encouraged me to write the book, patiently read and reread every line with a critical eye, and applauded the final product.

Heartfelt thanks to Lina Orfanos, my loving daughter, for allowing me to tell her story within mine and for letting me know that she is proud of me for writing this book. Her willingness to expose intimate details of her life for the sake of this memoir is a testament to her courage and her generosity of spirit.

I am indebted to my parents, Leon and Dorothy Richman, who, before their deaths, provided me with details of what happened to our family during the war years. This memoir could not have been written without them to pave the way. I miss them and deeply regret that I cannot share this achievement with them.

Special thanks to Frank Stiffel, a survivor from my hometown, who carefully read the first draft of the manuscript. His painstaking attention to editorial details and his astute comments were invaluable. His intimate knowledge of the culture we both came from was critical in verifying the accuracy of facts about prewar life in Lwów.

Michael Chernilevsky, my guide and translator in Ukraine, went beyond the call of duty in negotiating Ukrainian bureaucracy during my two visits to the land of my birth. He helped me immensely in my quest to give substance to places from my early childhood that had previously existed only in memory.

I give my gratitude to Marion Landew, a gifted teacher, editor, and friend, for her editorial help, her guidance, and her unwavering support. Other friends who read early drafts of the manuscript and gave me insightful feedback include Rena Bernstein, Julie Blackman, Mitchell Dinnerstein, Linda Garofallou, Barbra Zuck Locker, Cate

Miller, Helen Neswald, Felice Swados, Brenda Tepper, and Joan Zuckerberg.

Acquaintances with contacts in the publishing world who offered helpful suggestions include Rick Balkin, Yannis Fakazis, William Helmreich, Marc Jaffe, George Zimmar, and Sandy Choron, who represented me for a time. Sandy's personal interest in the subject, her belief in its value, and her hard work on my behalf were very much appreciated.

It has been a pleasure to work with my publisher, The Haworth Press. Bill Palmer, Publications Director and Vice President of the Book Division, was the first person there to recognize the potential in the book proposal and gave me the chance to turn my vision into a reality. Everyone on the staff has been amazingly responsive, especially Joshua Ribakove, the Manager of the Copywriting Department, whose competence, patience, and good humor always made it easy for me to turn to him for guidance. Marylouise Doyle, who designed the book jacket, encouraged my collaboration so that she could create a cover that I would love. I appreciate her attitude as well as her talent.

The preparation and publication of this volume was in part made possible by a grant from the Memorial Foundation for Jewish Culture. My thanks to my friend Felice Stokes for encouraging me to apply for the fellowship grant, and my appreciation to the Memorial Foundation for acknowledging the importance of this work.

HEALING

The nights passed very darkly.
Great cries ran in the wind.
The next day we didn't remember a thing.
There was a deep hole left in time.

There where the wolf had nestled in,
a pothole remained, spread with warm wolf hair.
Now a sheep could lie down there.

Yannis Ritsos

POLAND (1939-1945)

——— Boundary of Poland up to September 1, 1939
- - - - German-Russian border, September 1939 to June 1941

SOPHIA RICHMAN GENOGRAM

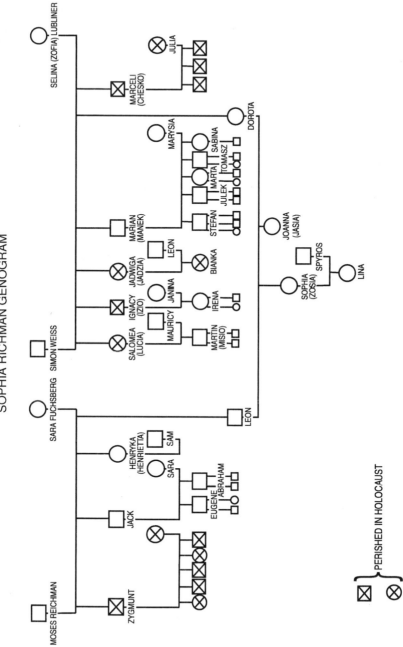

PERISHED IN HOLOCAUST

Chapter 1

Fragments of a Lost World

My parents met toward the end of 1936 through an ad in the personals. I would have thought that finding a mate through newspaper advertising was a modern invention of our alienated times, but apparently it was also an option for middle-class Jews living in Poland. The story was told to me by my father, who rarely spoke about the past, at least about such personal matters, and it was confirmed rather sheepishly by my mother who was obviously embarrassed by the way she had acquired a husband.

They were living in Lwów, a large urban city in the southeastern part of Poland. My mother, Dorota Weiss, known by friends and family as Donia, was an attractive, bright, vivacious young woman of thirty-three, dangerously close to becoming an "old maid." My father, Leon Reichman, a serious, intellectual young man of thirty-five, was beginning to be concerned about finding himself a wife after having concentrated too long on his studies.

Leon found Dorota's name in the Polish-language Jewish newspaper in an advertisement placed there by my worried grandmother, Zofia Weiss. Her husband Simon had died in 1933, and my grandmother felt the weight of responsibility for the welfare of her six children. They had all married and settled into parenthood except for her youngest daughter, Donia, who was recovering from a broken engagement and a broken heart. Donia was the brightest and most charming of the sisters, but, according to my grandmother, she was too educated for her own good. "Men don't like women who are too smart," my mother used to say to me when I was an adolescent. I'm sure she had heard those words from her own mother. My grandmother had reluctantly agreed to send her daughter to college, but now her fears were coming true: Donia was over thirty and unmarried. So she decided to take matters into her own hands and, without consulting Donia, put her name in the local Jewish newspaper and waited for an attractive prospect.

Leon Reichman saw the ad and decided to investigate further. He was a fastidious man, inclined to be suspicious. He carefully interviewed acquaintances of my mother's to make sure she would be fitting as a wife. Apparently finding her reputation unblemished, he agreed to the match.

For Donia and her mother, Leon Reichman must have seemed the perfect choice. He was Jewish, educated, not bad looking, and, most important, ripe for marriage. My mother was grateful and ready to overlook certain flaws. The fact that he came from a little *shtetl* outside of Lwów and was not as assimilated as my mother's family were things that could be overlooked. Having renounced the religious roots of his *shtetl,* he considered himself a Jew in cultural terms rather than religious ones. He was a thinking man, an intellectual; she was particularly impressed with his knowledge of thirteen languages. By the time he came into her life, both of his parents had died, eliminating the possibility of in-law problems. He came from a respectable family. His father, Moses Reichman, a barber, had also been a *felczer* (a physician without a medical degree) in the little town of Tluste; his mother, Sara, had been a midwife. She had given birth to nine children, of whom only four survived into adulthood. My father was the youngest. His older brother, Zygmunt, had five children and had remained in the *shtetl*. His other two siblings, Henryka and Jack, had emigrated to America in the 1920s.

My father's political convictions may have been harder to overlook. He was sympathetic to communist ideas and had been jailed for his convictions because membership in the communist party was outlawed in Poland. Furthermore, because of his strong antireligious feelings, he made two demands before agreeing to marry my mother. They would be married by a judge in a civil ceremony, and she would renounce her Jewish identity publicly. Marriage was very important to her, so she complied. A public announcement renouncing her Jewishness appeared in the local newspaper, and, on January 16, 1937, two days after my father's thirty-sixth birthday, they were married in a civil ceremony.

Perhaps there was less opposition than may have been expected to my father's antireligious sentiments. My mother came from a family who considered themselves more Polish than Jewish. They did not speak Yiddish among themselves; they did not live in a Jewish community; and two of her three brothers had intermarried. Ignacy (known as Izio), the oldest, was a physician who married the daughter of a Ukrainian Greek Catholic priest; Marian (known as Manek) was a chemical engineer who converted to Catholicism in the 1920s, changed his surname, and married a Polish Catholic. After thus changing his identity, he cut off contact with his family of origin, presumably so that he could keep his Jewish roots hidden from his children.

There were many secrets in my mother's family. It has taken me years to sort out the truths, half-truths, and lies. In fact, I owe my life to my mother's great ability to distort and dissemble, for I have no doubt that it was her acting skill that helped us to survive the Holocaust by living as Christians. The problem for me was that my mother was equally successful in distorting reality when our lives no longer depended on it. Her desire to look good in the eyes of others and her unusual capacity to figure out what people wanted to hear combined to make her a master of mystification. With her easy smile as her calling card, she could manipulate and control her way out of most situations.

A combination of factors makes it difficult for me to recount the events leading up to my entry into the world in January 1941. In their desire to protect themselves, my parents spoke little about the world they came from—to talk about their lives before the war meant to face the enormity of their losses. It is my impression that, in spite of the anti-Semitic atmosphere surrounding them, they loved the city of Lwów and considered it their home. This was the place where my mother was born and had spent many years of her life until the war displaced her. She had all of her schooling there, including college, where she majored in biology and expected to become a high school teacher. She had many friends, Jewish and Polish, and was well liked. Her relationships with family members were loving and warm; she was particularly close to her father. The family led a middle-class existence. Her father owned the apartment building that the family lived in, and he also had a dry-cleaning business that provided him with a good income. After he died in 1933, my mother's oldest brother, Izio, became the father figure. As a well-respected gynecologist, he was financially successful and apparently helped to support his siblings; my mother adored him.

After her college graduation, Donia found herself unable to get a job in her profession. The quotas in existence at the time made it difficult for Jews to find academic positions. She capitalized on her love of music and the many years she had studied the piano, turning to private piano lessons as a source of income, which was how she was earning her living when she and my father met.

Raised in the *shtetl* by hardworking and not very generous parents, my father earned money by tutoring fellow students throughout his school years. He wanted to become a physician, but the quotas my mother encountered were also a barrier for him. It was even more difficult for a Jew to become a doctor unless he studied abroad; my father could not afford such an option. So he turned to banking as a career. After obtaining a degree from the Commercial College of Foreign Trade in Lwów, he found a job in a local bank and worked his way up to an executive position.

Leon, or Leouche, as he was called by friends, seemed to have had a fairly good social life before the war. Looking at old photographs, I see a smiling young man surrounded by friends at a mountain resort. This is not the withdrawn, bitter man I knew all my life, but I suppose the psychic damage he sustained during the war was irreparable.

Mountain and country resorts figure prominently in family albums. Apparently, residents of Lwów frequently took vacations in the mountains surrounding the city.

Lwów, located in the province of Galicia near the Carpathian Mountains, was a beautiful city with a long and rich history. Founded in the Middle Ages, it was the seat of many struggles between conquering groups. With each new ruler, its name changed as well as its official language. In the late eighteenth century, when Poland was partitioned among Russia, Prussia, and Austria, the southern part was annexed to the Austro-Hungarian Empire under the name Galicia. Its capital, Lwów, was renamed Lemberg. When Poland regained control of the area after World War I, Polish again became the official language, and Lwów regained its name.

For hundreds of years, Lwów had been a center of Western culture. Its sophisticated architecture and cosmopolitan boulevards were reminiscent of some of the great cities of Western Europe. In fact, it was often called the Vienna of the East. Medieval churches and ancient palaces as well as gardens and monuments decorated the city. The winding cobbled streets and red tile roofs added a charm to this most picturesque place.

By the 1930s, Lwów was the third largest city in Poland. It was home to three major groups, the Poles, the Ukrainians, and the Jews. The Jewish community was one of the oldest and largest in Europe. On the eve of World War II, the Jewish community of Lwów numbered about 109,500 people, one-third of the city's population. It was a thriving community with its own schools, synagogues, a Jewish hospital, and a Yiddish theater. A short film produced as a travelogue in 1939 depicts Jewish life in Lwów. Stylishly dressed people are filmed promenading through Lwów's market squares and walking purposively in the Jewish commercial district. The city projects an aura of prosperity. Trains, cars, horse-drawn carriages, and bicycles crowd its busy streets. The old ghetto, the heart of Jewish Lwów on the eve of the Holocaust, is teeming with life. It is eerie to watch those citizens of Lwów captured on film, unaware of the magnitude of the tragedy that is about to befall them.

Not that one could feel safe in those times. Most people were well aware that, in Germany, Hitler was preparing for war. Shortly after they married, my parents began their efforts to leave Poland but once again ran into those daunting quotas. In her testimony recorded in 1984 by the Yale Fortunoff Video Archive for Holocaust Testimonies, my mother says:

> We tried already to emigrate to the United States because my husband had a sister there, but the quota was always. . . . We had to wait twelve or fifteen years, so we just had to go on. But we knew what is coming because, you know, in Germany it started much earlier, in '33 already.

So they went on with life. They returned home from a memorable honeymoon in the resort town of Krynica—a honeymoon that was more exciting than they bargained for. What began as a romantic holiday turned into a nightmare. My mother's poor sense of direction was legendary; or perhaps my father was mesmerized by his new bride. Whatever the problem, they managed to get hopelessly lost in a deep forest for several terrifying days and nights. Finally, exhausted and hungry, they were found and rescued.

Upon their return to Lwów, Donia and Leon were faced with a major decision. Should they have a child? After all, my mother's motivation for marriage was primarily influenced by her desire for mother-hood, and, at her age, she had little time to postpone it. On the other hand, the precarious political situation in Europe was a serious deterrent to bringing a child into the world. So the decision was made to postpone parenthood, at least for a while.

In the meantime, my mother found a way to satisfy her strong maternal needs by directing her love toward her siblings' children. By this time there were many nieces and nephews. Even her youngest brother Marceli, nicknamed Chesko, had three sons. The children she was closest to, however, were those of her two sisters. Lucia's son Martin (known as Misio), who was born when my mother was just eighteen, was her favorite. He was a handsome boy who spent a lot of time with the extended family, particularly after his father's death in 1936. The year that my parents married, my mother's second sister, Jadzia, gave birth to a baby girl, Bianka. After several years, Jadzia was abandoned by her husband, who moved to Finland and left little Bianka to be parented by the males of the extended family.

Another way that my parents met their nurturing needs during their childless years was to adopt a puppy. Mikush was a black miniature pinscher with a sweet disposition, except for one little quirk. For some reason, he would go crazy when he heard a particular piece of music on the piano. His frantic barking would make it impossible for my mother to continue playing. Stories such as these give me the impression that there was laughter and lightness in the life of my parents before my birth. The depressed parents I knew had suffered too much in the following years to play and laugh lightheartedly. Mikush had a short life and a terrible end. I never had a chance to meet him. He disappeared one day and later was found dead. My parents suspected that he was poisoned by a neighbor. Perhaps the barking that made my parents laugh did not seem so amusing to their neighbors; or maybe Mikush's demise was a case of anti-Semitism. My parents did not live in the Jewish section of town; the majority of their neighbors were Polish and Ukrainian. For the most part, they got along with them, but the undercurrent of anti-Semitism in prewar Poland was an inescapable fact of life. Whatever the cause, the untimely death of little Mikush seemed a portent that foreshadowed the horrors to come.

Another very painful event for the Weiss family was the death of my maternal grandmother in April 1939. This was to be the last "natural" death in our family for years to come. My grandmother was one of the lucky ones to die before the *Shoah* and thus to be spared the greatest of sorrows—to watch her children and her children's children murdered.

The first of the countless unnatural and premature deaths in our family occurred in 1939 at the start of World War II. In September, the Germans attacked Poland and bombed Lwów. My aunt Lucia, then forty-eight years of age, was struck by a bomb fragment in her apartment. Her adolescent son, Misio, was visiting a neighbor downstairs, and Lucia, home alone, bled to death.

The anticipation of war had finally materialized; the Jews knew that they were in mortal danger. According to my mother's account, my father wanted to escape eastward toward the safety of the little town where he was born and where his older brother still lived. Because they expected that only men would be in immediate danger, Leon headed east alone and my mother remained in Lwów with her family. As things turned out, the Germans did not enter Lwów at that time, and my father returned. Shortly before Germany had invaded Poland, a nonaggression pact had been signed with Russia. A clause in that document called for the partition of Poland. Once the war began, the Germans proceeded to occupy the western territory; the eastern part of Poland fell under Soviet domination. And so, for the inhabitants of Galicia, the Russian occupation began.

In his youth, my father had been a communist sympathizer, and I assume that he was not sorry to see the Russians arrive on that day in September 1939. First, it must have been a great relief to realize that the Germans were not taking over Lwów. Also, he believed in the Soviet ideology. He appreciated the antireligious stance, the presumed equality of people, and that, at least officially, anti-Semitism was outlawed under Soviet law. However, I'm sure that it did not take long before he realized the discrepancy between the rhetoric and the reality of communism. By the time I knew him, my father was strongly anticommunist. Whenever he heard someone extol the virtues of communism, he would say, "They should live in the Soviet Union and then tell me how wonderful it is!"

Once again, Lwów underwent a name change. Now it came to be known as Lvov, and Russian became the official language. Political repression was the order of the day. Bewildered citizens lost the freedoms they had been accustomed to in democratic Poland. Suddenly, basic civil rights were taken away; people could no longer work where they chose, speak freely, or travel. A Soviet passport for purposes of identification had to be carried at all times. Speaking against the state was punishable by exile. The inhabitants of Lwów lived in fear that a minor infraction would result in deportation to Siberia or Kazakhstan. The irony of this situation is that no one realized at the time that those deported were the fortunate ones. For the Jews of Galicia, deportation during the Russian occupation meant a better chance for ultimate survival.

With the start of the war, thousands of people fled from the German-occupied part of Poland to the east, taking refuge from the Nazis. The population of Lwów swelled to about 700,000, including about 180,000 Jews. With the overcrowded conditions and political repression, life was not easy for the residents of Lwów. But as bitter as life was under the Soviet occupation, it was clearly the lesser of two evils.

At some point during the occupation, my parents decided that since life was unlikely to change for the better in the near future, it was time to have a baby. And so, on a cold January night, I was born in a makeshift hospital, a two-story family house requisitioned by the Russians and converted into a maternity ward. My father wanted to name me Selma, but my mother insisted that I was to be named after her mother. After all, tradition was on her side, since a first daughter was typically named after the nearest deceased maternal relative. My birth certificate, a translation from Russian, begins with the phrase "Proletarian, of all nations, unite" and lists me as citizen Zofia Leonivna Reichman, born on January 28, 1941, in Lwów, USSR.

I have always had difficulty answering the simple question, "Where were you born?" If I answer "the USSR," the questioner usually looks confused. If I explain that the USSR refers to what was once the Soviet Union, the next question is: "Do you speak Russian?" "No,". I answer. "Polish is my native language." "So you're Polish?" "No," I say, "not really. I'm Jewish." "But what nationality are you?" And around and around we go. Since the territory of my birth is now Ukrainian, I sometimes say, "I'm from Ukraine." "So you're Ukrainian" is the conclusion. "No, I'm not." In an effort to avoid the confusion and still be accurate, I occasionally say, "I was born in Eastern Europe" and hope that it won't lead to the question, "What part of Eastern Europe?" Even passport bureau personnel have difficulty identifying my country of origin. Recently, when I attempted to renew my U.S. passport by mail, I received a phone call informing me that there is no such place as Lwów, USSR. If I wanted a new passport, I needed to list another place of birth. We settled on Lvov, Ukraine. It felt alien to me, like someone else's identity. A simple question such as "Where do you come from?" has no simple answer for those of us who have been up-rooted by historical circumstances.

My birth was a joyous event for my parents despite the fact that Dorota was a bit disappointed to bring a girl into the world. "Life is easier for boys," she would say to me, years of resentment resonating in her voice. She looked me over with her critical eye and decided that I was not as beautiful as her sister's child. I did not even compare favorably with her next door neighbor who had an infant girl my age. In fact, she was so embarrassed by my looks that when she took me for a walk in my carriage, she made sure I was on my stomach and my funny little face was hidden from the view of curious passersby. Dorota was very concerned with appearances, and this new little extension of herself disappointed her. Undoubtedly, it was this exquisite attunement to appearances that ultimately helped us to survive. As for the blow to my self-esteem, in all fairness I must report that she always made sure to tell me that, before long, her ugly little duckling had turned into a beautiful baby.

The Russian occupation was soon to come to an end. In retrospect, the two years under Soviet rule were not all that bad. Galician Jews had gained more time to survive the ravages of the Holocaust, and they experienced a more gradual transition into a malignant foreign dictatorship.

In June 1941, when I was just five months old, the worst fear of the Polish Jews was realized. Germany invaded the Soviet Union, and life under the Nazi death machine began.

Chapter 2

Scrambling for Life

The German invasion of Lwów in late June 1941 brought panic to the Jewish population. The invasion was sudden, and most inhabitants were unable to flee. The Soviet army pulled out of Lwów and headed east, taking very few civilians along. One of the lucky ones was my cousin Misio who, having joined the Communist Union of Youth during the occupation, was now inducted into the Soviet army. Since he had lost his mother at the start of the war during the bombing of Lwów, Misio now had no responsibilities to keep him in town. When the troops left on June 28, he left with them.

Not all citizens of Lwów were dismayed by the new developments. Ukrainian nationalists who hated the Russians were happy to see them leave. Having been led to believe by German propaganda that Hitler would help them establish a united and independent Ukrainian state, they cheered the arriving troops. It would take several months before they learned that the invading Germans were not to be trusted. As soon as the Germans arrived, the Ukrainians launched a four-day pogrom against the Jews. The rampage by the Ukrainian militia and bands of Ukrainian toughs was encouraged by the Nazis whose goal was to stir up further hatred of the Jews. During the early months of German occupation, thousands of Jews were beaten, dragged to prison, and killed. Those spontaneous riots were followed by more systematic operations referred to as *Aktionen* (actions) by the Germans. Throughout the summer of 1941, actions against the Jews continued and led to a general state of panic.

Many tried to hide from the Germans and Ukrainians who searched Jewish homes. My parents desperately tried to keep my father hidden. In her videotaped testimony forty-three years later, my mother recalled how she concealed my father during one of those home searches by the Ukrainian militia.

> It was just a nightmare. They came to search for men. I was hiding my husband under a table that had doors. They didn't find him that time.

The new labor law instituted by the Germans required every Jew aged fourteen to sixty to work for them. Anyone who could not present a work certificate from a company sanctioned by the Nazi authorities was inducted into forced labor. Since the goal was to brutalize Jews while benefiting from their free labor, the work assigned was backbreaking toil. SS vans cruised city streets and seized Jews for work. Jews were easy enough to spot: besides the terror in their eyes, there was the blue Star of David on a white armband that they were now forced to wear.

After his near encounter with the Ukrainian police, my father realized that trying to hide was futile; he decided to take action and find a job in a German organization. In army-related work, the Jews received a token wage; more important however, was that such work provided them with the certificate that would protect them from being seized and forcibly thrown into camps at the mercy of their captors. The work card stated that the recipient was employed and was not to be assigned to any other job or seized by the police. This protection was extended to members of the immediate family.

On the outskirts of Lwów, on Janowska Street, was a car repair shop for military vehicles that was converted into a work camp run by Obersturmführer Gebauer of the SS. Polish men worked there voluntarily and earned good pay. But Jewish men were forcibly brought there every morning by the SS and Ukrainian policemen to provide free labor. A few Jews, like my father, actually applied for work there in search of that much-desired work certificate. My father hoped that his fluency in the German language would help him land a desk job rather than the backbreaking work assigned to the poor Jews snatched from the streets.

That is how my father ended up working at the Janowska camp, the largest of about a dozen or so labor camps set up by the Germans in the area around Lwów. At that time, late August through October of 1941, Janowska was designated a labor camp, which meant that workers would arrive early in the morning, put in a long and grueling work day, and leave in the evening to return to their homes and families.

The pay that such work provided for Jews who worked there voluntarily was minimal. To obtain money for food, my mother began selling family possessions to our gentile neighbors. Prior to the war, my parents, members of the Jewish middle class, had managed to accumulate some material goods, such as attractive furniture and jewelry. Those items were in jeopardy because of the economic war that was being waged against the Jews. Theft was commonplace; Germans would enter Jewish homes and help themselves to whatever they desired. Official plunder came in the form of fines imposed on the Jews because of their "responsibility" for the destruction of the city. After all, if it wasn't for the Jews, there would be no war, according to German propaganda.

With my father employed at Janowska in the late summer and early fall of 1941, we seemed to be temporarily safe. Continuing actions brought police to our door, but the valued work certificate protected us. At some point during this period, my mother hid my four-year-old cousin Bianka under our bed in a wicker suitcase. Danger permeated the air. I often wonder how the incredible anxiety experienced by my parents, particularly my mother, affected my early development. As she struggled to survive, she attended to the basic needs of her infant. She nursed me even though she herself had barely enough to eat. As was typical with her own upbringing, she was preoccupied with toilet training me at a very young age. As soon as I was able to sit, she placed me on a little potty, affectionately named *najcio* (a derivative of *nocnik* or chamberpot), and waited for me to produce. Apparently, I would sit for long periods of time on the little potty placed on the kitchen table as she encouraged me to fill the potty. Perhaps these universal activities normalized her life to some extent and kept her sane. She used to call me *moje słoneczko,* my sunshine, a name that captured the light in those days of darkness.

In early October, a ghetto was set up by the Nazis to segregate the Jews of Lwów and allow for better control over that doomed population. The most rundown section of town, Zamarstynowska and Kleparowska Streets, without municipal sewage or water facilities and with almost no electricity, were chosen as the site of the ghetto. All Jews were expected to move into the ghetto from other parts of the city by the middle of December. Before my parents could contemplate this new turn of events, a dramatic development took place in our lives.

It was a change that no one expected. On October 31, 1941, my father reported to work as usual. By noon, when registration came to an end, the sound of an alarm resounded through the grounds. All Jewish workers were ordered to gather in the middle of the yard, and hundreds of Germans and Ukrainian police surrounded the area. Shortly before this date, the camp had been encircled with barbed wire and a couple of barracks had been built. Now, a lookout tower was erected, equipped with powerful search lights and manned by SS guards armed with automatic rifles. Suddenly, the Janowska work camp had become a concentration camp. From that time on, Jews were no longer permitted to leave the premises; all contact between the Jewish workers and the outside world was cut off.

Gentile workers, however, were free to continue as before—that is, to return home at the end of each day. Sometimes they would bring news about Jewish inmates to relatives. It was my parents' Ukrainian neighbor who brought the news of my father's imprisonment to my mother that first day. She was distraught by the news, and I developed a mysterious high fever. Mother was convinced that the shock had poisoned her breast milk and caused my sudden illness. Although her specific theory about the bad milk may have been faulty, she intuitively knew what researchers are confirming today: that trauma is transmitted from mother to infant.

Now we were alone, prey to anyone who chose to harm us. Danger lurked everywhere. One day, the Jews in the apartment building where we lived at 33 Maczynskiego Street were rounded up in an action. Our ground-floor apartment became the central place where our neighbors were herded together before being hauled onto trucks waiting on the street. My mother held me in her arms. A Ukrainian policeman and a German Gestapo officer were in charge. The neighbors filed past us; we were the last to go. From my mother's arms, I leaned toward the young German soldier and touched his face. My mother shrank with terror. She had heard of the sadism of policemen who used Jewish babies for target practice. Miraculously, this soldier was different. Maybe my Aryan looks (my fair complexion and light hair) made it easier for him to have compassion; maybe I reminded him of his own baby. He smiled and responded warmly to me. When the Ukrainian tried to shove us out of the apartment to the waiting trucks, the German put his hand out and pushed my mother back, "No," he said, "this one stays." Germans were in charge, so the Ukrainian obeyed. Our lives were momentarily spared.

This close encounter with deportation highlighted the danger that we were in. My parents had ignored the initial call to move to the ghetto, and, after December 15, 1941, the ghetto option was closed. So here we were, my mother and her one-year-old, living in a forbidden neighborhood in constant danger of being taken to a concentration camp. Through the neighbor who acted as a go-between, my father urged my mother to leave the city and find a hiding place somewhere in the suburbs.

My mother could not turn to her extended family for help. Each of her siblings was scrambling for life in his or her own desperate way. Her brother Manek, who had converted to Catholicism in the early 1920s, had been employed by a German armament firm as a chemical engineer and somehow had managed to get out of the country, first to Rumania, then to Hungary, and eventually to take refuge in England for the remaining war years. Manek had left his Catholic wife and three children behind in Warsaw. The situation was undoubtedly precarious for them as well. German laws defined a Jew on racial rather than religious terms, so conversion did not provide automatic amnesty for him or his children.

Her oldest brother, Izio, who was also married to a Catholic woman, continued to work in a small neighboring town, but his situation was as desperate as ours. It was just a matter of time before he would be picked up by the Gestapo.

Her sister Jadzia was also working on finding a hiding place for herself and her four-year-old in a suburb of Lwów. It was more difficult for Jadzia and little Bianka to pass as Christians as they had the "misfortune" of looking Jewish. In contrast to dark Bianka, I was a blond, blue-eyed baby with fair skin and could easily pass for a Polish toddler, a perfect cover for my mother. With such a baby in her arms, my mother's authenticity as a Christian was not likely to be questioned. Her flawless Polish would help with the deception. So going into hiding as a gentile was a likely possibility. The problem was to find documents to substantiate our new identity.

My mother had a number of close gentile friends, among them Stasia Drabicka. The two were linked by music. Stasia played the cello, and, before the war, they frequently enjoyed playing duets. Stasia was a Catholic, and she was related to a priest. As a member of the clergy, Stasia's uncle was in a position to provide papers that could help my mother with her escape plan. Asking gentiles for this kind of help was a very risky business. There were severe reprisals for those helping Jews. Gentiles helping Jews risked death or deportation for themselves and their families as well. Furthermore, for Jews seeking help, the question of trust was of paramount importance. In those desperate times, a gentile acquaintance might betray her Jewish friend. My mother was confident that Stasia could be trusted. Mother was generally a good judge of character, but what about Stasia's uncle, a man she had never met? The Catholic church did not always act in charitable ways. True, some priests and nuns saved Jewish lives; but others chose noninvolvement or, even worse, sold out their Jewish neighbors.

The choices were limited: pressure was mounting daily. The goal of the extermination of European Jews had been decided on in Berlin at the end of 1941. In January of 1942, around the time of my first birthday, the conference on the "Final Solution of the Jewish Question" authorized the extermination plan. In March 1942, the Nazis began liquidation actions in Lwów. Over 15,000 people were taken for "resettlement," the euphemism for deportation to Belzec, the death camp north of Lwów where people were murdered in gas chambers.

The plan for going into hiding had to be carefully implemented. Stasia's uncle provided the birth, baptismal, and marriage certificates of a deceased Catholic parishioner, Maria Oleszkiewicz, born in 1908. My mother's 1903 date of birth was close enough. It was arranged that I would be baptized as Zofia Oleszkiewicz. We had our new identities. Now we had to find a place to live where no one knew us. It was generally believed that hiding in a small town was safer than remaining in the city, where police searches were a constant fact of life in early 1942 and where it was possible to run into an acquaintance who could betray you. The outskirts of Lwów seemed a good choice as a hiding place because it would allow us to remain relatively close to my father. There was always the distant hope that he might be freed or find a way out of Janowska.

Leaving Lwów would be no simple matter. Even a short train ride to the outskirts was fraught with terror. Jews were forbidden to travel. Extreme caution was therefore necessary; the Jewish star would have to be removed. Railroad stations were crawling with informers who preyed on Jews and either brought them to the Gestapo for a reward or blackmailed them. Many obstacles had to be overcome, but first was the most important concern of finding a place of relative safety. Again, Mother turned to trusted friends.

Her childhood friend Jerzy Huppert was a Jew who had converted to Catholicism in the 1930s. He lived in Zimna Woda, a village located about nine miles north of Lwów, with his wife and two adolescent daughters Marysia and Krzysia. Jerzy also had a mistress in the town who lived with her parents. Ewa Donikowska was in her early thirties and was in love with Jerzy; apparently she was so much in love that she was willing to risk her own life to help him rescue his desperate friend Donia and her baby. She agreed to take us into her home without her parents' knowledge of our Jewish identity. Her courageous act of rescue was a testament not only to the power of her love but to the strength of her character as well. I suspect that Ewa Donikowska had that rare quality found in people who are willing to defy convention and live their lives on their own terms. Having an affair with a married man in a small town under the close eyes of her parents suggests it; saving the lives of two individuals she did not personally know confirms it.

My mother sent word to my father that she was leaving town and sent him a picture of me taken at a photography studio in Lwów. A chubby toddler standing awkwardly next to a teddy bear belies the reality. I had no toys. I was hungry. I was a Jewish baby marked for death, with no teddy bear of my own to comfort me.

On a spring day in April 1942, Ewa went to the railroad station in Zimna Woda, not far from her house, and met the train arriving from Lwów. A brunette with large frightened eyes clutching a toddler in her arms emerged. Ewa reminded herself that she could no longer think of this woman as Donia, Jerzy's friend. She must remember to call her Maria. One slip of the tongue could mean death, not only for herself, for Jerzy, and for Donia and her baby, but for her own unsuspecting parents as well.

Ewa brought us to her home and introduced us to her parents as Maria Oleszkiewicz and her little girl Zosia. The retired bank director and his wife were pleased to have a tenant to rent their upstairs apartment and did not question the authenticity of Maria's story. She presented herself as a Polish woman of limited financial means separated from her husband when he was inducted into the Polish army. She claimed that she did not know of his whereabouts after he had been taken prisoner by the Germans. This loss of husband explained her sad eyes and anxious manner; the Donikowskis were satisfied as to our legitimacy.

One other close friend of my mother's knew of our whereabouts. He was a central figure instrumental in our rescue. I heard his name often as I was growing up but did not learn until much later that Tadeusz was the man who had broken Donia's heart when he ended their engagement many years before my father came into her life. My mother never acknowledged the nature of their relationship; I learned of it after she died, from a relative who was unable to tell me the reasons for the breakup. I can only speculate that the differences between them made marriage problematic.

Tadeusz Witwicki was a Polish Catholic and the son of landed gentry. His father, a renowned psychologist, was a professor and the author of the text that was used for psychology courses at the local university. Tadeusz and my mother had met at the university. They remained friends even after the love affair was over, and he played a significant role in our rescue. Apparently, he knew the Donikowskis from before the war and was well respected by them. His frequent visits to our apartment provided us with an air of respectability and authenticity. Who could possibly suspect that a man such as Tadeusz would associate himself with a Jew?

Those connections with her past life must have been very precious and meaningful to my mother. In just a few years, she had lost some of the most significant people in her life. She barely had had enough time to mourn her mother's death when suddenly she was confronted with the tragic loss of her sister, Lucia. Now her husband had been taken away; she was left on her own with a small child. With fear as her constant companion, she had to be vigilant at all times; her life and that of her child depended on her ability to maintain a false identity. Only with Jerzy and Tadeusz could she be herself.

Thus began our precarious life in hiding.

Chapter 3

Excerpts from Hell

My father chose the title *WHY?* for a book describing his experiences at the Janowska concentration camp. Presumably his choice of title reflects his struggle to bring meaning to the senseless brutality he was exposed to daily during the year and four months that he was imprisoned there. The question "Why?" comes up again and again in the works of survivors. "Why did this tragedy happen to our people?" "Why did God allow this to happen?" "Why did the world not intervene?" "Why did I survive when stronger, brighter, more deserving loved ones perished?" There are no answers to these questions, but the imperative to find meaning is so strong that it will not be silenced.

Primo Levi, the Auschwitz survivor who eloquently wrote about his wartime experiences, observed that in the camps the hunger for understanding was as prominent as the hunger for bread. He calls this hunger "curiosity." I feel that the term *curiosity* doesn't begin to capture the desperate drive to make sense of the unbelievable, the unnatural, and the shocking. The need to understand, under such conditions, is the intellect's attempt to master overwhelming emotions. It's a way to bring some order into chaos and to stave off madness.

Experts on the subject of trauma recognize the universality of such unfathomable questions in the face of tragedy. Judith Herman, a psychiatrist who has extensively explored the aftermath of violence, writes: "Survivors of atrocity of every age and every culture come to a point in their testimony where all questions are reduced to one, spoken more in bewilderment than in outrage. Why? The answer is beyond human understanding." Herman notes that thought alone is not enough to reconstruct a sense of meaning; the injustice must be remedied by some form of action. For Leon, it was writing a book.

This chapter is an attempt to give voice to my father's struggle to find meaning in his life through a recounting of the brutal events that took place at Janowska.

Leon Reichman was a scrupulously honest man. Unlike his wife Donia, he never embellished the truth. He seemed unconcerned with the impact his words or actions had on others, for he was not especially interested in being liked. He did not have any of the pretensions of his wife; status was not important to him. He did, however, care about material things; one always had the sense that he worried that he would never have enough. His tendency was to hoard and save. Perhaps he always expected a bleak future. As it turned out, he had good reason to be pessimistic. In fact, it was probably his mistrust that helped him to survive. While others around him were eager to believe the Nazis when they promised relief with words such as, "This is the last action" or "If you pay this fine, the hostages will be released," Leon realized that those were ploys to make the Jews more compliant. He was never lulled into a false sense of security.

Another characteristic that served him well during the war years was his meticulous, compulsive nature. He was a man of detail. His documentary account of daily life in Janowska is testimony to this ability to note and record minute details. He listed the names of Nazis and their victims; he used their own words in German. His work is difficult to read; it is not great literature. Sometimes he gets lost in the details, but at all times he is dedicated to providing the reader with an honest and accurate account of what life was like in Janowska. Through his writing, Leon bears witness to the crimes of the Nazis. His determination to tell the world about what he saw gave him the will to live and provided his life with meaning. He strove to be objective in his account rather than to share his personal experience of the events. This attempt at objectivity was doomed to failure: How can one be objective in a situation where one is witnessing the sadistic torture of human beings? Emerging from the pages of his book is a profound rage. Missing is his own overt personal feelings and observations that could have enriched his narrative. I suppose that his rationale was that in the eyes of the world, a subjective account would have less validity than an objective one. He was aware that people might question the truth of his observations. After all, who could believe the unimaginable horrors that he witnessed? I expect he was less aware that the mantle of objectivity also enabled him to keep his own feelings of despair at a safe distance.

Following are some excerpts of the work he wrote about his life in the Janowska concentration camp. Initially, he kept notes on scraps of paper he managed to steal from the workshop to which he was assigned. Later, after his escape from Janowska, he turned these notes into a structured manuscript. The manuscript was written in longhand in Polish and was not translated until the early 1970s. He finally published his book in 1975. *WHY? Extermination Camp, Lwów (Lemberg) 134 Janowska Street, Poland.*

He begins his account by describing the motivation that eventually led him to end up in the most infamous concentration camp in Galicia. On Janowska Street, a major road leading northwest from Lwów, was a factory for manufacturing grinding machines. Before the war, the factory at 132-134 Janowska Street was under Jewish ownership. Then, in 1939, it was nationalized by the Soviets. With the German occupation of 1941, the SS set up armament workshops on the site. The Jews considered a work card for the Janowska factory valuable because it protected them and their close families from arrest during roundups.

> It was absolutely essential to start looking for a job. Under the rules of the military authorities, the consequence of not reporting to work was the death penalty by a firing squad. On the other hand, going to work was taking your life in your own hands, since from the moment the German army had marched in, Jews were placed outside of the law. Considering the mortal danger involved, it was advisable to be taken to the place of work by a Ukrainian escort, one of those guys wearing armbands and blue-yellow rosettes, whose lifelong dream was to see the German army marching in. Those dreams, and all the hopes about "liberation" that came with them, were blown away to nothing in no time, as it took just a few months before many Ukrainians were thrown into prison.

> It was imperative to start looking for a job because the Ukrainian militia went from house to house, dragging people out to "work." From this type of work quite often people never returned home. So where was the best place to work under such conditions? There, of course, where a job certificate was respected by many authorities.

So then, it was considered a lucky break when someone found a job with the SS itself. People were saying that the safest place to be was in the lion's jaws. The SS institution carried a business name: "D.A.W." (German workshops for armament equipment). (p.2)

The little security that my father felt was lost when Janowska became a concentration camp, as this passage reflects with great detail.

. . . during the roll call, after the day's work had been finished, the leader of the workshops, Obersturmführer Gebauer, whose headquarters was located in Lublin, first made sure that all exit gates were blocked off, then made the following statement: "As of today and until further notice, you'll stay right here. No more going home. You'll get room and board here. Nothing will happen to you if you follow instructions and comply with the rules. If you don't, you'll get a thrashing. Anyone who tries to escape will be shot."

That was on October 31 of the year 1941. There were about 200 of us. They marched us into the barracks which we had built ourselves. There were two of those barracks. In one of them fifty Jews had already been locked after they were caught on city streets by SS men and brought into the D.A.W. The camp on Janowska Street had become a fact.

This was the birth of the Jewish forced labor camp, which was patterned after the concentration camps of Dachau and Auschwitz. As far as the discipline was concerned, the rigor of Janowska 134 [the number of the factory on the site] matched the others in every respect.

The tragedy, to an extent never recorded in the history of martyrdom, had begun. Hell on earth—hell in the literal sense of the word—had come into being. (p. 4)

Each of the eighty-six chapters of my father's book describes in detail the conditions of camp life and the brutal incidents that took place daily during his incarceration. This camp earned the reputation of being one of the most savage concentration camps in Eastern Europe. The commandants in charge were known for their brutality and sadism. As he describes situations of torture, Leon's tone is filled with bitterness and sarcasm. His rage fills every page. The constant sarcastic references to the so-called advanced German culture speak to a bitter disappointment with a society he once greatly admired. When Eastern Galicia was part of the Austrio-Hungarian empire at the turn of the century, German was the dominant language of the region. My father was fluent in the language and well versed in the poetry and literature. It was in German that he chose to express his loving feelings to my mother on the occasion of her birthday. He appreciated the music of Bach and Beethoven. He attributed organizational talents and special spiritual qualities to the German character. In short, he respected and admired the culture. The barbarism of the Nazis was totally unexpected.

> Since the bulk of statements made by the fascist dogs weren't always kept, and quite often failed to materialize, statements made by camp SS men were not to be taken literally and at their face value. However, when Gebauer made the threat that anyone trying to escape would be shot, the story was not the same. Perhaps it was because there are even worse penalties than the death penalty by a firing squad.
>
> And so, when the first incident of a failed escape attempt occurred, at the evening roll call we were treated to a cultural spectacle which bore witness to the high degree of "culture" of the show organizers. The super-bandit degenerate Gebauer asked two SS men to assist him, and the three of them joined in meting out the punishment and executing the sentence which read: "50 lashes over the bare body."
>
> Now, the reader must not think that this type of punishment was less cruel than death by a firing squad. The SS bandits were well aware of this fact. Being hit with fifty rubber clubs over the naked body was tantamount to having your kidneys knocked off and, as a rule, death followed in a matter of weeks after excruciating pain.
>
> The fury of Obersturmführer Gebauer as he kept coming down with his whip on this poor man was indeed unbelievable. He was straining to the utmost to intensify the man's pain to the limit. We had a demonstration of the first sample of sadism by that degenerate and then, after he had satisfied his barbarous instincts, he said, "Now you know us and you know what to expect," and since that was only the first escape attempt, they waived the death penalty. However, in case of another escape attempt, five of us would be shot. (p. 6)

My father proceeds to describe the living conditions in the camp at this early stage of its existence.

> Here's how it was; black, bitter coffee in the morning; warm water, which was our so-called soup for dinner; and in the evening— coffee of the same ilk as the morning breakfast, which was supplemented by 1/16th of a loaf of bread to last for four days. (p. 9)

Two separate barracks were used for sleeping. One barrack housed the craftsmen, the other those without specific skills—the laborers.

> We had planks for beds and straw for the planks. The barrack housing the craftsmen was better constructed, since sawdust had been pressed in between the wallboards to make it warmer than the other barrack. The 1941 winter was early and severe and since laborers were fewer in number than craftsmen, the laborers' barrack was so cold at night that people were unable to sleep there. But it was more than room and board that made people risk their lives and attempt escape from the camp.
>
> The camp was not ready at all to receive the hostages in a number of respects. No kitchen had been built and readied to put out the proper quantity of meals. There was no water, no washing facilities, no bathing facilities. (p. 11)

There were no toilets in the barracks. One distant outhouse served the entire camp. It could only be used during recess hours in the morning and in the evening. It was forbidden to go out during the night to use the toilet.

> . . . such a trip often involved risking one's life. For this reason everyone got himself a bottle or a pan to take care of his needs. It happened quite often that an open pan or a vessel without a tight-fitting lid would turn over in one's sleep and tilt its contents onto the fellow sleeping in the lower bunk and pour a stream of urine down. The depth of human depravation under such living conditions is best attested by incidents involving biological needs. It would happen, for instance, that an inmate who did not have his own bedpan used his canteen to urinate. Then he'd wash it out and use it for coffee. (p. 50)

Some, like my father, recognized that one's physical appearance could preserve one's life. Nazis reduced their prisoners to a level of degradation that made them seem less than human. It was easier to destroy someone who seemed subhuman. Also those who looked healthier were more likely to remain in the workforce and therefore stay alive. So the prisoners found ingenious ways to give the impression of cleanliness.

> Whenever we got up in the morning and the ground was covered with a white shroud of snow it was a blessing—at least we could use the snow to wash ourselves. We didn't need it for shaving; for that we used some of the coffee left on the bottom of the canteen. Coffee was our substitute for warm shaving water.
>
> It was absolutely essential to shave, because that was the only way we could give the impression that we had washed. (p. 18)

Leon describes an incident in which four men were taught a lesson in cleanliness by being subjected to a public bath in the outdoors in below-zero temperature.

> That was Sunday. We came back from work. (Work was done on Sundays, too.) The snow squeaked underfoot. The frost nipped at our ears. As we crossed the gate which represented a sort of border between the camp and plant areas, a monstrous, terrible sight unfolded before our eyes; four naked bodies. One of those poor men was immersed in a vat of water and next to him an SS man diligently and zestfully performed the duties of a bath attendant, using for this purpose a scrubbing brush. Two of the other victims quivered and shook from the cold, and we didn't know whether they had had a bath already or were about to have it. The fourth victim lay on the dry snow and was rolling in it. He bled profusely. Perhaps he resisted. (p. 19)

Pneumonia, which resulted from these "exemplary" baths, took the lives of every one of these men within the week.

The high mortality rate of 75 to 80 percent during the initial period of incarceration was due to hunger, cold, ruthless beatings, and a typhus epidemic brought on by the horrendous living conditions in the camp.

As a child, my father had had typhus. What seemed to be an unfortunate illness at that time turned out to be a lucky break. Because of his exposure to the deadly disease in childhood, he now had an immunity to the illness that killed so many of his fellow inmates.

Drastic measures were necessary to fight the typhus epidemic. When a quarantine failed to achieve the desired results, the camp authorities decided that the inmates needed to be brought into the city to the public baths on Balonowa Street where they could be disinfected and deloused.

> It was a typical winter morning. The streets had plenty of snow on them. We marched under guard like lepers. We knew that the Jewish streets would be aroused the moment the news reached them that we were coming. . . . When we reached the Jewish streets crowds of people surrounded us from all sides, keeping up with us and growing in number. The street was full of turmoil. Fathers and mothers recognized their sons; children recognized their fathers, wives their husbands, sisters their brothers. (p. 65)

At this point, my father relates a personal incident involving my mother, but in his attempt to be impersonal and "objective," he writes about it as if it happened to another inmate.

> One detainee's wife [my mother] almost got into grave trouble; as she walked alongside with her husband in our procession . . . she was pushed into the rows of the marching inmates by the escorting Ukrainian militia man. She had not noticed that the armband with the Star of David had slipped off her shoulder, and that she was walking without it. A Jewish person showing up on the street without the band stigmatizing her as a member of the Jewish population faced grave punishment. While arresting the woman the militia man could not leave his post as an escort, and so he pushed the woman into the midst of the marching camp prisoners. So there she was, among us. Luckily her husband managed to push his way through the rows and slip her an armband which he happened to have on him. In the confusion that was created by the ever-growing crowd following us, and since the escorting militia man's attention was drawn to the pressing crowd, the woman managed to slip away to freedom. (p. 65)

A few inmates seized the opportunity created by the march through the city streets to slip away; Gebauer decided to stop the bath and disinfection in town. Typhus continued to rage. Gebauer tried a new measure.

> He chose fifty people from among the old inmates and ordered that they be given passes for fifteen days. From that day on, the fifty lucky guys were to line up for work separately; then, following a check of their number, they would go home and report back to work at seven o'clock in the morning. (p. 71)

My father was one of those lucky guys. Those passes came as a complete surprise. The emotions that followed his return home surprised him as well.

> Having been crushed by the living conditions that existed in the camp, we had been so dehumanized and our feelings were so deeply suppressed that our unexpected return to our families failed to produce the joy we had thought we would experience. . . . Although each one of us had been dreaming that his joy would have no end the moment he rejoined his dear ones and saw them and the good old surroundings, we were simply incapable of emotion and helpless to rejoice. The same syndrome occurred to our families. (p. 75)

The feeling of apathy gradually faded, and Leon began to feel alive again.

> After two or three days a person literally changed his appearance. He became someone else. In short, he became human again. (p. 76)

It is noteworthy that Leon remains impersonal even as he discusses his feelings about the reunion with his loved ones. For instance, there is no mention of the infant who in his absence had changed dramatically into a toddler. My first birthday had come and gone. I had learned to walk and had begun to use words. Here I was, a concrete representation of life moving forward. What did that confrontation feel like for a man surrounded by death, emerging from hell?

The passes were due to expire on March 15th, two weeks after being issued. Leon's greatest fear was that the pass would be withdrawn prematurely. It was. In the typically arbitrary style of the camp administration, the passes were taken away after just one week.

One of the most difficult aspects of camp life must have been the lack of predictability about one's fate. No hard and fast rules existed about anything. Death came at the whim of the persecutors. A sudden change of mood could unleash their brutality. One could be randomly chosen during morning roll call because a stranger had successfully escaped during the night and the commandant had decided to take the lives of five or ten other inmates as retribution or warning to others contemplating escape.

The lack of control over one's fate was an existential reality that created unbearable anxiety. Some gave up struggling for life and joined the ranks of the living dead—"the Muzulmen," as they were called. Others, like my father, refused to give up the struggle. He used his intellect to make sense out of the nightmare. He never stopped asking questions. Throughout his text are numerous historical references as he tries to place these times and events into some meaningful context to better understand the calamity.

He reflects on slavery in ancient times and compares it with his situation.

> At those times one could buy a slave as if he were a thing, then sell him, beat him, or even kill him. But a slave was in a situation much more favorable than ours. He represented a concrete asset; he was merchandise which had a price. His master, to whom he belonged, had to take care of him if he wanted to get use out of his slave, out of his labor, and if he didn't care to use him for any reason whatsoever, he had to make some effort to have this slave well-fed in order to be able to sell him. (p. 123)

Gradually, the inmates became aware that the true purpose of the camps was extermination of the Jews rather than exploitation of their labor.

During the spring of 1942, heightened actions in the city brought greater numbers to Janowska. Major changes took place as the camp went from a forced labor camp to an extermination camp. A new commandant, Untersturmführer Willhaus, arrived, the facilities grew, and the number of inmates went from the hundreds to the thousands. The newly constructed barracks could accommodate as many as 20,000 prisoners. Living conditions deteriorated further.

The rapid rate of growth in the camp population affected the development and maintenance of friendships among prisoners. A sense of camaraderie was one of the few experiences of camp life that could sustain an individual during these hard times. In the evenings, after work, men would discuss the political situation and find some comfort in sharing feelings and ideas with one another.

> It was possible to develop some friendship at the start of camp living, either because of sharing a job in the workshop or because of sharing a bunk or for any other reason . . . you became intimate with those newcomers. You assisted each other during that oppressive and dismal period of life, in a material and moral sense. Were it not for that community, who knows how soon you would have broken down under the burden of the chains of the terrible camp prison?
>
> Later, however, because of the constant fluctuation, and particularly because of the typhus, the circle of friends with whom you shared your thoughts, to whom you revealed your feelings, related events from your past, and, in short, who were linked with you by a spiritual and moral intimacy, grew narrower and narrower. (p. 93)

By the summer of 1942, the Nazi killing machine was well in place. Daily, men, women, and children were brought in truckloads from the city and its neighboring towns. Those who were able to work provided a supply of fresh labor to take the place of workers worn by starvation, exhaustion, or disease. Others, unable to work because of illness or age, were liquidated as soon as they arrived or put on trains bound for Belzec, a more efficient killing center equipped with gas chambers and crematoria.

> Murders in the camp, murders and plunder in the city, murders in the ghetto. In the camp they murdered men and boys; in the city they slaughtered men, women, and children, or, the men were detained in the camp and the women and the children were slain in bestial fashion—murdered or sent to Belzec. The Gestapo men and their Ukrainian assistants smashed infants' and small children's heads by tossing them against walls, fences, or posts. . . . What was mankind capable of? To grasp all of it was impossible. The horrible visions would bring you to the brink of insanity. (p. 178)

It must have been a great relief for Leon to know that his wife and child were no longer in Lwów. It had proved wise of him to urge Donia to find a hiding place for herself and the baby, and it seems that they had gotten out just in time. It was an unselfish act on his part; it meant that from now on, survival would be more difficult for him; he could no longer rely on the occasional package that Donia had managed to smuggle into the camp through the Ukrainian neighbor. Nevertheless, he knew that this was her only hope for survival.

At first, camp inmates were not aware of executions taking place in an area adjacent to the camp called the "Sands." In this sandy, hilly area, thousands of people were shot and buried in mass graves. The Nazis, masters of subterfuge, took care to hide their murderous deeds. Perhaps they were afraid that at some point the inmates would rebel; rebellion would interfere with the efficiency of the killing machine. When, for a brief time, my father was assigned to work outside of the workshop, he learned of the mass executions and witnessed people being led to their deaths by the "Askaris" (non-German auxiliary police). The shock of initially learning about the systematic executions was soon replaced by a sense of numbness and resignation.

> We found out that last night eighty detainees were shot. Figures did not impress us any more, particularly when we did not witness those mass executions. We accepted the news with a sort of resignation. We only knew that it was terrible news, but still it was no more than a figure, statistics. Even when I watched certain incidents, I suddenly realized that I had hardened. (p. 121)

Maintaining one's humanity in this dehumanizing environment was a major challenge for everyone. Camp life seemed to bring out the bestiality of the oppressors. It was as if some evil force dormant in them was unleashed and out of control in this environment. In civilian life, men like Gebauer and Willhaus must have been human beings with frailties but not the monsters they became at Janowska. Gebauer, who came from Berlin, was handsome and aristocratic in his demeanor. He had a pleasant melodic voice and dark deep-set eyes that gave the impression of an intelligent inner life. Initially, if he was in a good mood, he showed some interest in prisoners who were educated and intelligent, asking them questions about their accomplishments in civilian life. His mood, however, could swiftly change, and he was known to crack his whip or pull out a revolver without a second thought. It was said that his favorite method of murder was strangling.

The practice of murder developed into a habitual pleasure for the SS men at Janowska. Willhaus enjoyed himself by firing at live targets; without any warning, he would fire into a crowd of prisoners. It has been reported that his wife as well would show off her marksmanship to her guests by shooting inmates from her porch.

In the spring of 1942, the position of deputy to Willhaus was filled by Untersturmführer Rokita. This man's physical appearance also made a favorable impression. He was described by survivors as having a "sweet face." His round facial features gave him the appearance of mildness. In civilian life, he had been a musician and played in an orchestra. Before long, the inmates realized that Rokita's appearance belied his brutality. His revolver never left his hand, and he seemed to enjoy using it.

Rarely among the SS existed men who showed some compassion toward the prisoners and did not engage in the brutality that was the norm at this camp. At one point, Gebauer was replaced by a new deputy.

> His deputy, Untersturmführer Junghans, was a man of a completely different caliber. He was one of a very few among the SS, and although those very few could not save the whole lot, they were evidence of the fact that even among SS Germans there were people harboring humane feelings. (p. 120)

Under his command, conditions at the D.A.W. improved, and the workshop where my father was assigned became a refuge from the deteriorating conditions of the remainder of the camp. This respite was brief, however. Gebauer returned, and once again sadism reigned supreme. In time, the SS men became wilder and meaner. In a chapter that he titled "Hell," my father describes a scene reminiscent of Dante's *Inferno*.

> A starless night. It is so dark that you can't see your hands in front of your face. A horror hangs in the air, and spreads on the ground like a shroud. A horror envelops us from every side and permeates our hearts, turning us into creatures who are not formed in God's image.
> We are in the heart of hell.

Bricks, beams, boards. They march. No, this is no march; this is a convoy of slaves, dragging their aching feet behind them, dead-tired, their necks bent. Pressed down by the heavy loads of the beams, they plod by twos, by fours, or sixes, carrying the boards on their shoulders, their heads tipped to the side, or in their outstretched arms, they carry bricks stacked one on top of the other. They drift like ghosts in the direction of the huge square to the left of the camp. They are passed quickly by ordered columns trotting from the opposite direction, driven, urged on by the cracking whips and by the roars of the savage Askarises.

They are weird, frightened figures, tattered people hustling in panic to get to the rail yards as quickly as possible in order to load themselves up with heavy burdens. Why? Because those loaded and yoked are not inflicted with the blows of cracking whips wielded by their degenerate oppressors. And at the end of the road, SS men with carbines on their shoulders form a row, spaced a few steps from each other; there they stand at the section of the road behind the first gate. Across from the unloading square they are bunched more closely, gripping their clubs in their hands. This is the third group of this eerily busy camp road, at this late hour of the dark night. And behind them there is the fourth group; unfortunate figures, tied to posts and roadside stakes—once human beings, now rending the night air with their terrible moans. Although it is dark, we can catch a glimpse of those martyrs who suffer excruciating agony, not knowing why. This nebulous nightly glimmer turns into a malevolent, forceful, dazzling, and blinding glare of this terrible hell on earth. (p. 205)

My father's references to hell are purely metaphoric. He didn't believe in an afterlife or follow any of the tenets of the religion in which he had been raised. From his youth to the end of his life, he identified himself as an agnostic and harbored strong antireligious feelings. To my knowledge, after the war, he never set foot in a house of worship or observed any of the Jewish holidays. Yet apparently his relationship to Judaism was more complicated than one would expect from his philosophy.

During the Hitler regime, when he was branded with his Jewish identity and literally forced to wear it on his sleeve, Leon seemed to reconnect with his religious roots for a brief time. Perhaps he was able to find some solace in the rituals of his childhood.

One of the most moving sections of his book describes Yom Kippur at Janowska. I have reason to believe that my father considered "Day of Judgment" to be his most important chapter. He felt that this piece of writing, more than any other, communicated the tragedy of the times. When, shortly before his death, he attempted to publish a paperback sequel to *WHY?*, he included this chapter in its entirety in the book proposal.

> The day was September 20th, the Day of Judgment. But not in the sense of any atrocities—not this time. The twentieth day of September that year was the Jewish Holy Day the Day of Judgment, the day when Jews usually spend the whole time praying, begging God for forgiveness of their sins, for a better New Year, and religious Jewish women in houses of worship tearfully pray for health for their husbands and children. On this day religious Jews fast, remember the dead, and recite a special prayer for them.
>
> The Day of Judgment in the camp was quite different.
>
> From morning to evening, instead of being dressed in festive clothes, we wore filthy, torn rags, and worked and labored under the cracking and lashing whips wielded by our savage oppressors, yet most of us declined to accept any meal until evening. In the evening both barracks on the former D.A.W. territory turned into houses of worship.
>
> It seemed that at no other temple at no other time in history did people pray so zealously as in the camp on that holy day of Yom Kippur, the Day of Judgment. There were no women, but the crying was so loud and occasionally so spasmodic and the sobbing so pitiful and so sad that you might say it was not a house of worship but a hall of mourning. The barracks groaned, sighed, sobbed, cried, wept, and resounded with a plaintive accusation elevated to the feet of the Eternal, imploring Him for mercy and grace. The weeping tore the collective heart apart. Like a fiery column a flaming glow rose from below, as if trying to pervade space by its sound of despair and waken the conscience of that God of Mercy.
>
> Would the God of revenge, the ruler of the destinies of this world, the creator of human happiness deign to avert the terrible evil and that horrible punishment that touched every one of those wretched human beings?

> People who witnessed torture and torments, massacres and atrocities, who watched every day—perhaps even callously—as other people died, now were overcome by tears, like little children. They supplicated forgiveness for their guilt and sins. Had they indeed been so sinful to deserve such a cruel fate? Had these people committed so many sins that this terrible atonement was to redeem them from those sins? (p. 220)

A Jew among Jews, Leon shared in the collective mourning. The ritual observance of Yom Kippur gave the grief-stricken inmates of Janowska a chance to express their blocked emotions and to feel human once again, even for a brief moment in time.

By the fall of 1942, Leon had managed to hang on for more than a year in a place where the average life expectancy was counted in weeks. It's a mystery to me how this man, forty-one years of age, no longer in his physical prime, did not succumb to the conditions of camp life. He was one of the old timers. He knew the score. He had no illusions. He had come to the conclusion that the only way to save himself was through escape. He waited until the time was right. Perhaps the events that took place in the fall of 1942 solidified his decision. On September 31, another of his fears was realized; there, among the newly herded Jews arriving in a transport, was his brother Zygmunt with one of his three sons.

> I had seen the terrible wave rolling out farther and farther into the country and I had realized that any day it would reach the locality where my brother and his family lived. I had felt the approaching horror; I knew it would be upon me one day and say to me: here I am. And here it was.
>
> My brother and his son were brought to camp from their distant town. His other son had been detained in a camp near Tarnopol for a number of months. His youngest son had perished during the war in 1939. His wife had been taken away and only his daughter was left at home. What would happen to her? Would the next "action" engulf her in the Holocaust, too? (p. 226)

By mid-November, both my cousin and my uncle were dead. My cousin, whose name I shall never know, was probably clubbed to death or hit by a bullet on a Sunday in October of 1942. My father describes his brother's last days:

At the beginning he was keeping afloat somehow, but he harbored no illusions about the nature of the camp. Right from the start he maintained that this was not a labor camp but an extermination camp. He worked in the city. In just a few weeks he changed immensely. When I saw him one day, squeezed in a line for dinner, I noticed that he did not look like my brother Zygmunt any more. He had aged tremendously. He seemed shrunk and his eyes had a sad, indifferent look in them; my heart bled. Sometimes he seemed to be absolutely determined to get his dinner portion, which would indicate that he still wanted to live.

On November 14th, following several days of frustrating inquiries, I found him right at the roll call. He had changed completely, but I did not think that I was seeing my brother for the last time. Perhaps he did not think so either. Darkness was descending on the square. We were shivering from the cold, having been made to stand for hours at the roll call. My brother's hands were swollen from the cold. I took off my gloves and gave them to him. I had another pair in the workshop. He complained that his stomach hurt him. We did not have too much time left for a long conversation because of the threat of death by shooting, or at least a terrible beating, which awaited anyone found not near his column. (p. 263)

The next morning, Leon learned that Zygmunt had died during the night. Less than three weeks later, Leon made his daring, courageous escape from Janowska.

Chapter 4

Escape

Escape from Janowska was dangerous and nearly impossible. But that fact did not keep inmates from trying to flee. In the early stages of camp life, when they still had some hope of freedom, escapes were less frequent. In those days, many still believed the slogan "Work will set you free," the lie perpetrated by the Nazis and inscribed at many concentration camp entrances.

In the early days of his incarceration, Leon was still grappling with the irony of having entered that "hell on earth" of his own free will. It made no sense to him that people who had voluntarily reported to work and whose labor was useful for the German war effort would be imprisoned and tortured. Only later, when he realized that the goal was extermination of the Jewish population, did he truly grasp the hopelessness of his situation.

Perhaps Leon was tempted to escape when he was given a pass to return home that brief week in March. Yet he must have realized that there was no place to run. Plans to go into hiding took care and time, and the suddenness of his visit home did not allow for preparation.

As time went on, and the death machine was firmly in place, it became more difficult to escape. Punishment for failed escape attempts was severe. Even in a world where torture and death were daily events, the punishment for escape attempts stood out for its unmatched brutality. Escapees who were caught would be executed by methods that resulted in a prolonged and painful death, such as hanging from a gallows upside down with hands and feet bound or tied naked by barbed wire and left outdoors to die. In the hierarchy of death, there was either a quick, merciful death, such as a bullet in the back of the head, or an excruciating, agonizing one, such as that awaiting the inmate who was caught trying to escape.

Retributions for escapes were fierce. When a prisoner escaped, the lives of others were taken—ten, twenty, as many as the commandant's whim dictated. Fellow workers in the same brigade would be chosen at random to satisfy the aggressive lust of the SS. Sometimes, members of the inmate's family would be hunted down, brought to the camp, and murdered. When an inmate successfully escaped, he knew that he was jeopardizing the lives of others.

Then there was the problem of where to flee. Jews with shaved heads and prison garb were easy to spot. After the countless actions, the entire Jewish population was forced into the ghetto. It was forbidden for nonresidents to enter the ghetto without a special permit; there was an elaborate system of checks at the gates. Besides, by the end of 1942, there was talk about turning the ghetto into a julag (a work camp). For Jews who managed to escape, there was no place to hide unless they had non-Jewish friends on the outside who could help. Despite all of these considerations, attempts to escape never ceased and instead increased in number as time went on.

> People kept trying to save themselves in any way they could, whenever and wherever, regardless of the militia and police, regardless of the observation towers and the dazzling searchlights, and such a state of affairs aroused our bestial enemies into a frenzy.
>
> Thus a period was ushered in which was marked by an increased escape incidence on the one hand, and by an increased rate of executions on the other hand, casting a mortal fear over those who remained, tearing our otherwise frayed nerves into shreds. (p. 168)

To weed out those prisoners who were too ill or infirm to work, the SS would conduct a weekly "race" in which inmates had to run, often loaded down with beams, bricks, and boards on their backs, for long distances. Those who stumbled or fell behind were condemned to death. Leon realized that his death was only as distant as the next selection. The longer he delayed, the harder it would be to escape.

> Why shouldn't one flee, when a camp inmate had to demonstrate his racing ability at a review . . . as proof of his working ability?

> Why shouldn't one flee, when on September 3rd, one hundred seventy-five people were shot?
>
> Why not flee, when new observation turrets were constantly being added, and machine guns were mounted on each one of them? (p. 207)

At that time, Leon's wife was in hiding, relatively safe for the moment. After the death of his brother and nephew, no close relatives were alive in Lwów who would be endangered by reprisals for his escape.

In that life of captivity, the only remaining freedom was how one faced one's death. One could choose to die fighting, praying, or pleading; one could face death with terror or with courage. Or one could risk everything and escape. Leon decided to take control over his own life. He would not begin the new year in Janowska.

The book my father wrote about life at Janowska ends without any mention of his escape. In his effort to keep the account impersonal, he leaves out one of the most interesting aspects of his experience. Years later, he decided to write the details of that escape. Excerpts from his unpublished manuscript follow.

> The year 1943 was to be a decisive one in my life. It meant, for me, the slight chance of surviving or an almost-certain death. Death was not terrible to me; I was not afraid. I used to look into the eyes of death not every day, but every instant. . . . It was the way of being killed that I was afraid of.

Leon did not tell anyone about his plan to escape. His close friends had perished by that time, and he decided that he was better off keeping his plan secret. Even when the subject came up a day or so before his actual escape, he did not let on.

> One day a man who worked in the offices of the camp said to me: "If you want to save your life, you must risk your life." He did not know that I had already made up my mind some time ago and prepared every detail of every step to make my escape a success.

Leon's position as a storekeeper in an electromechanical workshop gave him access to a pair of overalls. This piece of clothing turned out to be crucial in his escape plan. Not only would it cover the yellow patches that marked him as a Jewish prisoner, but it would also help him pass as a civilian workman once he reached the outside.

On the second of December, a Wednesday, Leon set his escape plan in motion. First, he told his assistant that he would remain in the workshop while the other workers went to lunch. He would join them a little bit later.

> This was the first phase of my escape. It was 12 o'clock noon. Just the time when the camp prisoners would leave the D.A.W. accompanied by armed guards for the campgrounds, where the so-called "lunch" was given out. I considered this the most favorable moment to escape, because it was in the minds of the SS the least expected time to try a possible escape.

The camp was situated very close to a dense forest on one side; on the other side was a Christian cemetery. Campgrounds were surrounded by a high barbed-wire fence. Since most of the escapees headed for the forest, the guards in the watchtower were more likely to point their machine guns in that direction. Leon reasoned that since no one would expect an escape to take place in broad daylight into a cemetery with its vast open space, this would be his best chance for a successful escape.

> The guard on the nearest observation tower was just having his lunch. He was busy. The moment I was waiting for had come. As soon as he turned around, I jumped over a high fence on the west side of the camp and found myself on cemetery ground.
>
> It was of course a very risky undertaking to jump the fence. It often happened that the SS or Ukrainians were hiding there and would pick up the escapee. A terrible death with tortures awaited the victim.
>
> On this day no SS or Ukrainians were there.

Leon was extremely lucky on that day. Not only were there no Nazis in sight, but there was a funeral taking place in the cemetery, and, in his civilian clothing, he could mingle with the mourners without attracting attention. When the funeral ceremonies were over, he left the cemetery with the crowd. In the pocket of the overalls were the precious notes—his diary—that he had been faithfully keeping to document the atrocities he had witnessed.

Donia had provided him with the address of the Drabickis, Stasia's parents. Once again, her friend Stasia from the conservatory was to play a heroic role in saving our lives. It had been prearranged that should my father ever have an opportunity to escape from Janowska, he could find shelter at the Drabickis.

Leon walked through the streets of the city in a terrified state. The forty-five minute walk from the cemetery to the house on K Street where Stasia's parents lived seemed like an eternity to him. Finally, toward the end of this very long street, stood the Drabickis' house.

> I rang the bell. Mrs. Drabicka opened the door. I told her who I was. She knew that I was supposed to come in case I succeeded to escape. She said okay, come in.
>
> There I stayed only four days. After four days I had to leave, because they were afraid to hide me. It was understandable.

Hiding a Jew was an offense punishable by death. It is to the Drabickis' credit that they were willing to keep my father, a stranger to them, for four days. They contacted Tadeusz Witwicki, my mother's Polish friend, who knew exactly where to find us.

Late in the evening, under cover of darkness, Tadeusz and my father set out together to walk the nine miles that would take them to Zimna Woda.

> It was wintertime, snow to the knees. We started to walk. He walked before me about ten yards. It was a very clever precaution: If they would have caught me, he was safe, not having anything in common with me. It took us several hours to arrive at the place where my wife lived.

When they arrived in Zimna Woda, they headed to Jerzy Huppert's house. It was not safe to appear at the Donikowskis'. My father could never pass as an Aryan and therefore was better off out of sight. He stayed with Jerzy and his family for several days until they were able to work out a plan.

The plan was that my mother would come at nighttime to fetch him and take him back to the Donikowskis when they were asleep. She would take him upstairs to our apartment and hide him in the little attic attached to the kitchen.

I stayed in the house of his family for two days. After the two days, my wife with our little daughter in her arms came to see me and took me to her lodgings late at night. I got into the attic without the owners of the house seeing me. I started a life of nonexistence.

The attic was a small room without a window; only a few cracks in the roof allowed some daylight to enter the space. It was accessible through a small door in the kitchen. One had to bend down and practically crawl to enter. In this space, my father spent almost two years of his life.

In the meantime, the situation at Janowska deteriorated further. From other survivors of that death camp who wrote their memoirs, I have learned about the increasing brutality that took place and culminated in a massacre of the Jewish inmates on May 26, 1943, about five months after my father's escape. Out of the approximately 10,000 inmates who were there at that time, more than 7,500 were murdered in the "Sands."

The massacre in the camp was staged to make room for work detachments from the Lwów ghetto immediately following its liquidation.

As the Allies advanced and the Nazis began to realize that the war might be lost, they created a brigade specifically to hide their crimes at Janowska. This "death brigade," as it was called, was established in June 1943 and was comprised of selected inmates remaining at the camp after the May massacre. Its task was to exhume corpses from all the places of slaughter near the ghettos and camps and set them on fire, thereby obliterating the evidence against the Germans.

Final liquidation of the camp took place in November 1943.

It has been estimated that 300,000 to 400,000 Jews passed through this infamous camp. At least 200,000 were murdered in the "Sands" and in the nearby forest of Lesienice.

The carnage that took place in the vicinity of Lwów was so great that even the notorious Nazi Adolf Eichmann made note of it. The prosecutor at his trial asked him, "And you were not bothered by being the great expeditor of death?" He answered:

It bothered me more than anyone can ever imagine. For example, I remember once driving through the outskirts of Lemberg [the German name for Lwów] and seeing something I had never seen before—namely, a fountain of blood. I passed a sight where Jews had been shot sometime before and apparently as a result of the pressure of the gases from the bodies, the blood was shooting out of the earth like a fountain, and that had to happen to me of all people! And I was still considering an entirely different solution for the Jews. I then asked my superior for the first time to get me a different assignment because I was not the right man for these things.

Whether or not one believes Eichmann when he says that he was sickened by this gruesome sight, his testimony speaks to the magnitude of the massacres that took place in the vicinity of Lwów. It is noteworthy that even Eichmann, the monster who implemented the liquidation of the Jewish population in Poland, considered the murders in these parts to represent the ultimate of horrors, unforgettable and shocking.

Chapter 5

Hidden in Plain Sight

"Stay away from that door!" Mamusha *(Mommy) said. "Don't look there; don't go near it. There's a mean, hungry wolf in there, and if you open the door he'll get out and eat you up." I look at the door nervously and keep my distance. After awhile, I get used to it but never feel safe.* Mamusha *goes out a lot, and she won't let me come with her. One day,* Mamusha *isn't there, and I'm all alone. I go to my little* najcio *(potty) and, just as I sit down on it, that dreaded attic door begins to open. A shadowy figure comes out. It's not a wolf; it's a strange man. I've never seen him before. I'm terrified.*

I don't remember what happens next. I know that, in time, the man becomes familiar. He comes out of the attic once in awhile to be with me and Mamusha. *She's not scared of him, so I figure it's all right, even though I know something is wrong there.* Mamusha *reassures me that there are no more wolves to worry about. But she says we have to keep a big secret. Never, never tell anyone about this man. Eventually (I don't remember when specifically), I call the man* Tatush *(Daddy).*

This, my earliest memory, has always been available to me. In later years, my parents put it into a context. Desperate to keep the fugitive's presence in the attic a secret, even from their toddler, they had created an ingenious lie. The wolf, a commonly feared creature in those parts of Eastern Europe, was the perfect threat to stop a curious child from exploring. It also provided a cover story for Leon's resounding snoring and the creaking floorboards overhead.

I was about two years old when my father suddenly opened that door and revealed himself to me. Mother had gone out of our little apartment to take care of some business or other. She often left me alone when she went out to do other people's laundry or to the market to sell the candies Mrs. Donikowska taught her to bake. If she had some qualms about leaving a two-year-old alone, she probably reassured herself with the knowledge that my father was nearby to keep a watchful eye on me. With the attic door slightly ajar, he could see me and protect me in case of emergency. But he *was* the emergency on that morning when the dreaded door suddenly opened. Apparently, my parents failed to recognize the traumatic impact of such an event on a toddler who had been repeatedly warned of the dangerous animal lurking behind the attic door.

Forty years later, in a videotaped interview, my mother spoke about her perception of my experience regarding my father during our years of hiding.

> Even my child didn't know. She knew that there was something wrong there. I said, "Don't look there. There is something very dangerous there; don't go there. . . ." She saw him sometimes, but she didn't say. He watched her. Sometimes I had to go to make some money to wash linen in the neighbor's house, so she was all day by herself. First, she was playing with some boxes on the bed—she didn't have any toys—and then, my husband said, she threw everything on the floor and she went to the door and she was standing at the door, waiting, waiting . . . and she knew . . . she saw him sometimes when he went out to stretch. I don't know what she was thinking.

The long-term psychological impact of our living situation was not of uppermost concern for my parents; they were overwhelmed and struggling with staying alive at all costs. Besides, they comforted themselves with the illusion that because of my young age I was unaware and would not remember the events taking place. Without awareness and without memory, they reasoned, there would be no trauma.

> I was thanking God that she is so young that she didn't know much about what was happening. . . . All the time I said, "Thank God that she doesn't understand what is going on." I wanted to shelter her somehow, to shield her from these terrible experiences.

The notion that children growing up in wartime who were too young to understand what was going on around them would not be affected by the events is naive at best. In fact, the lack of understanding, the confusion, compounds the trauma.

Outside of the little apartment, my mother played her role impeccably. Maria Oleszkiewicz, with her ready smile and warm manner, was liked by everyone. She was an honest woman who took good care of her little girl. She was a good Catholic who went to Mass every Sunday. She made sure to leave her door unlocked to show the world that she had nothing to hide.

Maria was a poor woman with little means to support herself and her child. She had arrived in Zimna Woda with just one little suitcase packed with some of her husband's suits, a camera, a set of binoculars, and a few pieces of jewelry, including her engagement ring, a watch, and her mother's bracelet. Ewa helped her by selling these items when she took her regular trips into the city of Lwów. Mrs. Donikowska, also eager to help out, taught Maria to make candy, which she then brought to the market in town to sell. Maria was ready to take on any work; she was happy to wash laundry or mend clothes; she was grateful for whatever jobs the neighbors were willing to offer. People were impressed with this hard worker who never complained. My mother believed that our poverty also helped with the image she was trying to create. The stereotype that "Jews have gold" certainly did not apply to her. No one envied Maria.

Life in Zimna Woda was difficult. Even if we had not been fugitives, the war itself was hard to bear. First, there was an ever-present gnawing hunger that the meager rations could not satisfy. Mother nursed me for as long as she could, but she was so undernourished herself that her milk was diminished and, by the time I was eighteen months old, she gave up on breast-feeding. Bread was the staple of life in those days, but rations limited its availability, even if one had enough money to buy it. I have been told that one of my first words was *chleb,* the Polish word for bread. Apparently, I was always so hungry that I could barely contain my excitement when I saw anyone carrying bread and would squeal, *"Chleb! Chleb!"* I have a memory of reaching for a package of butter left lying on the table and finishing all of it while my mother busied herself in the kitchen with her back to me. To this day, I remember her shriek when she discovered that a week's ration of butter was gone. Perhaps I haven't forgotten this incident because mother rarely got angry; it was memorable when she did.

The winters in Poland were very cold. The little stove in the room, the main source of heat, barely kept us warm. It had to be fed endlessly with wood. The Donikowskis showed Maria how to get branches from the forest and break them up into kindling for the stove.

Outdoors, the cold nipped at my fingers. With envy, I eyed the children who were lucky enough to have mittens. Sometimes the Donikowskis' grandson came to visit. He was the child of their second daughter, Ewa's sister. A room upstairs next to ours was kept empty for the family's occasional visits. He was a sweet little friend, about my age, and we liked to play together. I liked him in spite of my envy of the mittens that kept his hands warm and of the toys he always brought along.

After my father's escape from Janowska, and his presence in the attic, life was even harder for my mother. Besides the terror of possible discovery, which now increased immeasurably, practical concerns were abundant as well. Food obtained on ration cards had to go further as there was now another mouth to feed. No running water in the apartment meant that my mother had to lug containers from a well in the garden. Then my father's biological needs had to be taken care of, for, of course, he could not use the hall bathroom.

As for my father, life was difficult in a different way. Trapped in a small, dark room, cold in winter, unbearably hot in summer, he could not face the light of day, except through tiny cracks in the roof. Outside he could see dogs playing and felt jealous of their freedom.

At night, when everyone slept, he quietly crawled out of the attic and was able to stretch his legs and spend some time with Donia. This is the time he would read to her from the manuscript he fervently worked on during the day. Writing his story gave him a purpose and provided his life with meaning. It was a way to work through the trauma that he had recently endured, and it gave him an opportunity to share his experiences with Donia. He wanted to make her understand what he had been through and, as a result, to feel less alienated and alone with his pain.

Tadeusz, who was a frequent visitor, would bring Leon books and occasionally mathematical problems to solve to keep his mind occupied. In time, as he felt safer, my father began to spend more time in the kitchen, away from his dark, cramped hiding place, but always poised to disappear through the attic door should he hear the sound of unfamiliar footsteps. The attic was a relatively safe haven; however, since it was a storage place for the Donikowskis, it was possible that the landlady could decide to come upstairs to get some of her old things out of storage in Maria's absence. The latter, eager to communicate that she had nothing to hide, never locked her door when she left the apartment. An unexpected visit from the landlady was always a dreaded possibility. Prepared for the worst, Leon made a hiding place within his hiding place by piling up boxes and rags in a corner. His caution was borne out.

> And it so happened that one day—my wife was not home—I was sitting in the kitchen. From the kitchen there was an opening to the attic. Suddenly, I heard somebody walking up the stairs. Silently, I bent down and crept through the small opening leading to the attic that belonged to the owner of the house, pressed myself to the wall where I had my prepared ahead cover in case of need. The lady stepped in and started to look for something in boxes of old junk. I held my breath in. It lasted only a few minutes. She left without noticing anything unusual.

My mother describes another close encounter with danger that took place around that same time.

> On the same floor (as our apartment) there was a room where the son-in-law of the owners stayed sometimes on the weekends. One day in June, it was a glorious Sunday morning, I got dressed in my best summer dress, which was washed and starched numerous times. I dressed up my child—she was two-and-a-half years old—and we went to church.
>
> When we left, Dad [Leon] quietly and carefully came out from the dark attic and sat in the kitchen which was filled with the warm sunshine. He must have been dozing off, because he didn't hear the son-in-law approaching our door. The young man was tall, and he could see through a glass panel in the upper part of the door.
>
> When we came back from church, the owner and her family were sitting as usual on the porch. Right away, I felt some change in the family's behavior. I sensed it because I was living all the time in terrible tension and fear of discovery. In fact, I was right to sense a change; they asked me, "Who is the man in your apartment?" Without missing a beat, I answered, "He's an

acquaintance of mine who ran away from the Germans and begged me to let him stay until dark when it will be safer for him to get home a couple of miles away, shielded by darkness." It was a believable story because at that time Germans took Poles into forced labor; many tried to run away because they were fed very poorly.

I quickly went to my apartment under the pretext of preparing a meal for him, but, in fact, I wanted to hide my fear and confusion—always in fear, that was the way of life.

Another instance of quick thinking happened one morning when a knock at the door brought an unexpected and most unwelcome visitor. It seems that an SS officer passing through the town needed a place to stay overnight and found lodging with the Donikowskis, right on our floor, in the room next door where Ewa's sister and her husband occasionally stayed on the weekends. When the unfamiliar knock came, my father had no time to get to his usual hiding place. He jumped into a wardrobe and hid behind the clothes. My mother answered the door in terror. Apparently, all the officer wanted was to borrow a little mirror for shaving. He looked around, smiled at me, and left.

I wonder what that was like for me, a three-year-old, to witness these bizarre goings-on; to see the panic on my parents' faces, to watch my father disappear into a closet, and to observe my mother's terrified expression suddenly shift as she assumed an air of nonchalance before opening the door to a stranger. How confusing that must have been; terror was in the atmosphere I breathed.

One of the most frightening moments for my mother was the day that the SS came to Zimna Woda in search of Jews who might be hiding there. They combed the neighborhood, going through each house checking papers. My mother stood on the porch with a neighbor watching the Germans in their search. The neighbor commented, "I can always tell a Jew; they're not hard to spot." My mother thought that this was the end for us. She knew that if the Germans took her to Gestapo headquarters, she would not be able to withstand questioning. The SS went to the house across the road, then to the one next door. Miraculously, they somehow missed the Donikowski house.

Donia grew used to the anti-Semitism around her. Thinking that she was one of them, her neighbors felt free to express their opinions. Mrs. Donikowska once said to her:

"They didn't kill many Jews. You see, they are all hiding. You'll see after the war how they will come out like mushrooms after the rain. That was not enough. Whatever was happening was not enough for them," My mother said bitterly. I saw how the Germans took the Jews from the town. They held hands. They took them to the forest. My heart was bleeding . . . and I had to stay and look, with these Polish women standing next to me, and I couldn't say a word.

One day, my mother was at the marketplace when she ran into someone who recognized her, a worker who used to deliver coal to our apartment in Lwów before the war. He confronted her without hesitation and said, "*Where* is your armband, Mrs. Reichman?" Somehow, she managed to lose him in the crowd. She was so shaken by this experience that forty years later she was unable to talk about it. In her testimony, she begins to recount the incident to the interviewer but interrupts herself and manages to change the subject.

Our second winter in Zimna Woda, typhus made its macabre appearance at the Donikowski house. Both our landlady and her daughter contracted the disease. Friends stayed away; no one was willing to care for them except for my mother. Putting aside her fear of this highly contagious disease, my mother attended to mother and daughter. Fearful of bringing typhus home to me, she washed her hands with disinfectant until they were raw. The disease killed Ewa and spared her mother.

In spite of my mother's devotion and her unusual courage in the face of this highly contagious disease, Mrs. Donikowska let Maria down when she needed her most. In the fall of 1943, my mother discovered that she was pregnant. Apparently my father did more than just read his manuscript on the nights when he came out of the attic. As I lay sleeping, they shared the bed in the other room. The withdrawal method of birth control they used was not reliable, to be sure, but Donia had not menstruated since the beginning of the German occupation, and she was convinced that she was infertile. Obviously, she was wrong.

This pregnancy was a calamity. How would she, a single woman, explain this situation? Would Mrs. Donikowska, a proper, conservative Polish Catholic woman be sympathetic? She was not, even after Maria explained that Tadeusz, who was identified as the prospective father, had the intention of marrying her after the war. With a coldness unbefitting a woman who owed her life to Maria's care, she ordered her to move out immediately. This time, there was no Ewa to intervene for her. Perhaps the loss of her own daughter embittered Mrs. Donikowska; perhaps the idea of another woman giving birth when she recently lost her own child made the prospect of pregnancy too painful to bear. Whatever the reason, Mrs. Donikowska showed no compassion.

But another neighbor, Mrs. Bilowa, did. This woman, a widow, had grown very fond of Maria and her little girl. She offered her own house. "You can come and live with me," she said to Maria. She seemed to welcome the company; the idea of having little ones around actually appealed to her. Of course, Mrs. Bilowa had no idea that she was getting more than she bargained for. Somehow, some way, my father had to leave his hiding place and find a new one.

An ingenious plan was worked out by my parents. One evening, my father accompanied us across the street, his profile hidden by the suitcase he carried on his shoulder. Both landladies believed that Maria had enlisted the help of a man she had met at the market to carry her belongings and help her with the move. Houses in Zimna Woda were similar to one another. The layout of the new apartment was just about the same as the one they moved from. Up the stairs were a room and a kitchen with an entrance to the attic. My father had a new hiding place.

Another experience forever imprinted on my memory took place in this second house during our time in hiding.

The sun is streaming through the window. I sit at a large table. Tatush *sits across from me. We hear steps outside of the door.* Tatush *is very scared. He motions to me—he puts his hand on his lips. I know he wants me to keep the secret. The woman outside asks me if I'm alone. I lie; I say yes. She goes away.*

My father wrote his version of this experience:

> One day when my wife went to the village for shopping . . . I was sitting in the room with our little daughter. Somebody knocked at the door. It was the landlady with her dog. She asked my daughter, a two-and-a-half-year-old kid, "Zosia, who is there with you?" I shook my head giving a sign to my daughter that nobody is with her.

Apparently, at barely three years of age, I understood the importance of keeping the secret of my father's existence. On that day, the wrong answer could have cost all three of us our lives. Those years in hiding have left their legacy. From time to time, in certain circumstances, I experience an inhibition in speaking that I believe has its roots in a time when words uttered out loud had the power to save or destroy.

On May 25, 1944, two months before our liberation, my little sister Joanna was born at home with the help of a midwife. Jasia (her nickname, pronounced *Yasha*) was a frail baby and not much to look at, as far as I was concerned. I didn't like her from the start. She was the reason I had been separated from *Mamusha* for the first time in my life. Even though Marysia and Krzysia took care of me, I was very upset. I always liked spending time with them; they played with me and made a fuss over me, but this time I didn't want to play. I was so afraid that I had lost my *Mamusha* forever.

My memories of Zimna Woda end here. I don't remember the liberation. Perhaps it was anticlimactic. In her testimony, my mother speaks about the young Russian boys with rifles who followed on the heels of the fleeing Germans. These young boys hardly looked like conquerors who defeated the powerful, ruthless Nazis.

> The Russians liberated us . . . we saw the Germans fleeing. One came to us and asked for a suit of clothes. He wanted to throw out his uniform, but she [the landlady] didn't give any to him. She said she doesn't have any. They wanted also to somehow escape. Then came little young boys, maybe fourteen, fifteen years old with machine guns on a string, and they asked for some food and water. That was in June or July of '44.

My parents chose to leave Zimna Woda quietly, without revealing their true identities to anyone. I imagine that they left at night so that they did not have to explain my father's presence. As far as Mrs. Bilowa was concerned, one day, Maria and her two children disappeared. Emaciated and crawling with lice, with a practically empty suitcase in hand, the four of us boarded a train back to Lwów.

Chapter 6

In Death's Shadow

With the Russian liberation of Lwów, we were freed from Nazi terror, although the war continued to rage in other parts of Poland. The task ahead was to find housing, work, and to try to put the pieces of our fragmented lives back together. The Donats, a couple who lived on a large street in the center of town, offered us lodging in their apartment building. Mr. Donat was an acquaintance who had worked with my father before the war. It was good to realize that there were still people around who did not shy away from us, the wretched Jews, who crawled out of hiding with nothing to call our own.

Our apartment, on the third floor at Czajkowska Street, was large and bright—at least that's how I remember it. There were several rooms, lots of open spaces, probably because of the scarcity of furnishings. I slept in my own bed. My little sister had a makeshift cradle in another part of the apartment, near my parents' sleeping quarters.

This little sister was no fun. She got too much attention from my parents, especially my father, who seemed partial to her. He spent a lot of time walking her around the apartment trying to calm and soothe her; she was frail and sickly and cried a lot. I felt betrayed by *Mamusha,* who was supposed to be my ally. I resented the boring job that she assigned to me: I was to sit by the cradle and watch over Jasia to make sure that the summer flies wouldn't disturb her sleep. The nerve of *Mamusha!* Didn't she realize that I wanted to get rid of this little intruder, not to make her more comfortable? When I objected, *Mamusha* tried to convince me that I was fortunate to have such a responsible job—a privilege due me because of my big sister status. I did not believe her, but *Mamusha* did not relent, so I obeyed; I had become used to doing exactly as I was told.

Perhaps Mother didn't know what to do with me. There wasn't much to keep a four-year-old occupied—no toys, no books, no children around to play with. Besides, she had plenty on her mind. First, she was preoccupied with attending to the essential concerns of life, such as finding work to feed and clothe the family. Then she was faced with the devastating losses of the last few years. Who was left alive after the storm?

Lwów, the beloved city of her birth, was a graveyard. Most of the Jews of Lwów had been annihilated. According to one official account, of the 150,000 to 160,000 Jews registered before the German occupation, only 823 had survived.

Mother learned from her sister-in-law that Jadzia had perished with little Bianka in the town where they were hiding out as Aryans. Bianka had been ill, and Jadzia had left her at home to get some medication for her. It was past the curfew imposed by the Germans, and she was picked up for questioning, recognized as a Jew, and never heard from again. Bianka remained alone. In her testimony, my mother recalled:

> . . . they chased out the child in the street . . . for a couple of days the child was just going from one house to the other, and then they [Nazis] took her. Such a beautiful child, five years old. She was dead.

My uncle Izio, my mother's older brother who had remained in the town where he was working as a doctor, was murdered in the early years of the war. He had not gone into hiding and was picked up by the Gestapo, beaten, and shot. Many years later, with anguish in her voice, my mother told me that Izio's wife Janina had come to her and begged her to hide him. Donia knew the risks were too great to hide both her own husband and her brother while she remained out in the open on false identity papers. Despite her love for Izio, she had refused. Bitter feelings remained forever between the sisters-in-law. Tormented by guilty feelings, each held the other responsible for Izio's death. Since Izio's wife was Ukrainian and the daughter of a priest, my mother felt that she was in a better position to protect him. She resented being asked for an impossible request that made her feel helpless and guilty.

After the war, Janina and her daughter Irena went to live in Zimna Woda. By then we had left the little village. Janina became the teacher in the elementary school and remained there until the early 1950s. Our paths never crossed again. It was only after Janina's death many years later that contact was reestablished between Irena and my family.

My mother's youngest brother, Marceli, his wife Julia, and their three young sons had been deported from Lwów and were never heard from again. We could only assume that they ended up in Belzec, the death camp where so many other relatives met their bitter end.

Of my mother's five siblings, only Manek, the brother who had converted to Catholicism many years before the war, was left alive. At the war's beginning, he had escaped to England, leaving his wife and three small children in Warsaw. After the war, he returned to Poland and collected his family. We later learned that he moved them to Oswiecim, the Polish name of the infamous Auschwitz.

It is hard to imagine that any Jew, even a converted one, would choose to live in the town where millions of his brethren were murdered, a place that had become synonymous with horror. The reasons given had something to do with work opportunities, but I can't help wondering if deeper psychological reasons influenced this man to settle in Auschwitz. Perhaps it was his way of doing penance among the ghosts of his people. His son Tomasz was born there in 1946. After a year or so, the family moved to another city in Poland and continued to grow. My cousin Sabina was the last of our family to be born in my generation.

Although my father had been witness to the death of his brother Zygmunt and one of his sons at Janowska, the fate of Zygmunt's wife and four other children remains unknown.

Taking an inventory of deaths, my parents found a total of thirty-five relatives from the immediate family wiped off the face of the earth. Uncles, aunts, cousins—gone forever. Not to mention friends and more distant relatives. How were my parents to mourn such profound losses?

They threw themselves into life. My father found a job as a senior economist with a firm in Lwów. My mother placed my sister and me in a day care center and found work as well. We settled into a routine. I even began to like Jasia a little more. She was more interesting now; she recognized me, cooed, and giggled. A vivid memory of Jasia remains.

Tatush *is holding her in his arms, she looks over his shoulder at me and giggles heartily. I am crawling on the wooden floor, rolling an*

empty spool of thread, a makeshift toy discarded from Mamusha's
sewing. I like making Jasia laugh.

Mrs. Donat was a portrait painter, and she decided to paint my picture in oils. The idea was exciting until I realized what was involved
in being an artist's model. Mrs. Donat expected me to sit very still for
what seemed to be an eternity. Each day, I would climb down the
flight of stairs to her apartment and dutifully sit for my portrait. It was
worse than sitting by Jasia's cradle and shooing flies away. I became
a cranky model and a very restless one. Eventually, Mrs. Donat re-
signed to continue her work from a photograph of me, and I was freed
from my brief modeling career. The painting was very successful, an
excellent likeness. Today, it has a prominent place in my living room
over the piano. I believe it is a testament to my parents' desire to preserve memory and affirm the living at a time when they were surrounded by shadows of death.

The day care center was a terrible place to be in. Jasia was relegated to a floor with infants in cribs, while I spent my days with other
four-year-olds. I remember many children and few caretaking adults.
I liked playing with the children, but I missed *Mamusha* desperately.
One day, she came to pick me up during working hours. When she
learned that I was involved in some activity, she left. I never even
knew that she had come until she told me of it later that night. I was
distraught. I had been longing for her to come; my wish had been realized, as if by magic, and I had missed her. The disappointment of a
missed opportunity haunted me. For many days after that, I was
superalert to the possibility that she might come again. But she never
did.

At some point during the year that we were there, the institution
became the object of scrutiny by the authorities. A little boy, one of
the younger ones, fell out a window. The staff was accused of neglect.
Bars went up on the windows. My parents considered taking us out,
but, to my disappointment, decided against it. Finally, death did release us from that institution, but not the death of a stranger.

Whooping cough, a childhood respiratory disease, became rampant in our day care facility. There were no vaccines against it. Both
my sister and I contracted it. I soon recovered my health, but frail little Jasia did not. Although I have no memory of being ill, I have a
clear mental image of the morning I learned of her death.

I wake up and see Mamusha *and* Tatush *sitting next to my bed. They are both crying. I have never seen* Tatush *cry before, so I know something terrible has happened. "Jasia," Tatush says, sobbing, "is dead. She was very sick, and she died during the night. Your little sister is gone."*

That was July 10, 1945, less than fourteen months after her birth. She never even learned to walk, this frail baby born in hiding. Years later, my parents would refer to me as an "only child," as if denying her existence. I too thought of myself that way. Another destructive family myth made me responsible for my sister's death. Jasia, it was told, had contracted whooping cough from me. While I, the stronger child, had survived it, she, the fragile one, had fallen victim to it.

The war had ended in May, a couple of months before Jasia's death. Another memory from that time and place is the excitement attending the news of the war's end.

We are on the balcony of our apartment, watching the celebration in the street below. People are shouting and dancing. There is music playing, a parade in the street. My parents are happy; everyone is excited.

Now that the war was finally over and Jasia was dead, my parents decided to leave Lwów as soon as possible. After liberation, Lwów had been annexed to Soviet Ukraine according to an agreement between the Soviet Union and the Polish Republic. For a brief period, residents of Lwów were given an opportunity to choose their citizenship. They could remain in Lwów, or Lviv as it was now called, and become citizens of Soviet Ukraine, or they could emigrate to a Polish city and become citizens of Poland. Like many other Jews, my parents preferred Polish citizenship. During the occupation of 1939, they had become disillusioned with the Soviet way of life; the Russian language was alien to them as well. But most important, they were eager to leave the city of their youth with all of its painful memories. In September 1945, two months after Jasia's death, we joined the mass exodus out of Lwów and headed to the small industrial town of Chorzów in western Poland.

By leaving Lwów when we did, my mother missed a reunion with Misio, her beloved nephew who had joined the Soviet army at the start of the German occupation. He returned to Lwów just one month after our departure. Within the year, he met and married Olga, a young Russian who had been sent to Lwów to work. It would take years, and the help of the Red Cross, before we reconnected with Misio and his new family. Also, many years were destined to pass before I would finally meet my Uncle Manek—the only "real" (by birth) uncle I would ever know.

My father's second brother, Jack, who had emigrated to America in the 1920s, met an untimely death in 1945 at the age of fifty. His sudden death of a brain aneurysm was tragic but at least his loving family was at his side when he died. He lies in a proper grave with a headstone and a loving inscription, while my other poor uncles, victims of the Holocaust, are in mass graves somewhere in Eastern Europe. No family is left there to mourn their passing.

The most exciting event that I remember before our departure from Lwów in September of 1945 was the discovery that I had an aunt in America. After the war, my father's sister Henryka (now called Henrietta), who had followed her brother Jack to America in the 1920s, desperately searched for any relatives left alive in Eastern Europe.

She found us through a refugee organization and sent us a telegram. The telegram was followed by packages. There was something in those gifts from America for all of us, even a stuffed toy for me, a big yellow bunny. I vividly remember the events and feelings surrounding the arrival of the first package.

I can barely contain my excitement. But it is short lived. My parents sell my bunny and most of the contents of those packages. But worse yet, I find myself in trouble. For some reason that I still don't understand, Mamusha *tells me to keep the packages a secret. No one is supposed to know about the bounty coming from America. One day, right after a package has arrived,* Mamusha *and I visit a neighbor. In my enthusiasm and excitement, I blurt out the secret. No sooner do I get the words out than I realize my indiscretion. I am mortified and frightened. For most of those early childhood years, I had been well schooled in keeping secrets. How could I have slipped? I realize that* Mamusha *is disappointed in me. I vow to be more cautious in the future.*

Chapter 7

Refugees

I have no memories of the Polish city that became our home after leaving Lwów and crossing the border. Not a single image remains from the year that we spent in Chorzów in the district of Silesia in Southwestern Poland. I know only that we were there from October 1945 to October 1946 on Hajducka Street, number 11. I know this because some documents and letters bear that address, papers that I found in my parents' apartment after my mother's death in 1992. That I remember nothing of our stay in Chorzów is particularly striking because I have such vivid memories of earlier times dating back to my second and third year of life. Yet the place where I celebrated my fifth birthday is totally absent from memory.

In the summer of 1993, I decided to visit Eastern Europe and retrace the path of my early childhood years. Chorzów was the last stop on my retrospective journey. Accompanied by my husband, my survivor friend Rena, and a translator, I arrived in the small industrial city of Chorzów, an hour or so west of Kraków. I hoped that my visit would jog my memory. At least I had a specific address to pursue.

Chorzów turned out to be an unattractive town lacking color and charm. The ambiance was gray; the buildings and shops had little character. I'm sure that we were the only tourists in town; who could possibly find interest in that polluted industrial city? We easily located Hajducka Street in the old section of Chorzów. Under the nameplate affixed to a corner building, a discoloration indicated that another nameplate had recently been removed. We learned that in the 1950s, during the communist takeover, the street name had been changed to a Russian one. With the recent fall of communism in Eastern Europe, Hajducka Street had gotten its old name back. I realized that had I come in search of my home in Chorzów just one year earlier, I wouldn't have been likely to find it. When we arrived at number 11,

I stared blankly at an undistinctive three-story building. We tried the front door; it was locked. Nothing sparked my memory. I was disappointed. I had come all that way to look at an apartment building that could have been in Queens, New York, for all it meant to me. Worse yet, I had dragged along to that unmemorable place three other people who had better things to do.

To salvage something from the trip, we took some photographs in front of the building. At least we would have a memento for the photo album marking a stop on our refugee journey. Apologizing to my companions for wasting their afternoon, I prepared to return to Kraków where we were staying. Elizabeth, our guide and translator, said, "Not so fast; let's see if we can find some people who lived here right after the war and may remember your family." I wasn't optimistic, but I humored Elizabeth. This tiny thirty-something Polish woman, who looked like an elf and spoke beautiful English, had an air of determination about her.

She darted in and out of local shops asking around, in search of someone who may have been living in the area in the mid-1940s. This search led nowhere, but, undaunted, Elizabeth suggested that we ring a doorbell on the panel next to the outside door and try to get into the building. A list of nine names faced us. "Which bell should we ring?" I asked timidly. Elizabeth thought for a moment then said brightly, "There's one German name here; during the war, many *Volksdeutsche* [Polish citizens of German origin] settled here and some remained. Let's try this one." All the other names were Polish. The name Krautwurst certainly sounded German. I didn't quite grasp Elizabeth's logic, and, given the circumstances, I did not expect a warm reception from someone with a German name. But she seemed confident and we had nothing to lose, so I agreed.

Elizabeth rang the bell. After a brief conversation through the speaker phone, we were buzzed into the building. We entered a dark lobby; it did not look familiar. We climbed up a flight of stairs, and a door opened on the first floor. A pleasant-looking silver-haired woman who seemed to be in her midseventies looked the four of us over. Suddenly her eyes met mine, and she stared. As Elizabeth spoke, the woman's eyes were riveted on me. Suddenly, she exclaimed with great emotion, "Zosia, *moja* [my] Zosia!"

She not only recognized me instantly but seemed to remember a great deal about me and my parents, for we had rented a room in this very apartment in 1945. The fact that she recognized me after forty-seven years was amazing but plausible; I have often been told that because of my "baby face" I don't look all that different from my childhood photographs. What was incredible, however, was that by some strange act of fate we had managed to ring the one doorbell that could bring back a piece of my childhood history.

Mrs. Krautwurst warmly invited us all into her apartment, and we sat in her kitchen as she reminisced. The room was bright, immaculately clean, and decorated with numerous religious pictures of Jesus and other Catholic images. There was a prominent cross on the wall. She was obviously a religious woman. I still had no memories of her or of the apartment. The place seemed small, and I imagine it must have been quite cramped with four adults and one child living in three rooms and sharing a kitchen and a bathroom. She showed me the room where the three of us had slept. It was totally empty except for a big steamer trunk. I found no clues to my life there.

The coincidence seemed so astounding that there were moments that I asked myself, "Could she be making this up?" But as she described my parents and my childhood personality, I could no longer doubt that she was a voice from my past. She recounted an incident in which I assertively had reacted to her husband's teasing. When he changed the words of a song I had just learned, I announced, "You're teasing me, sir, and I won't stand for it; I'm going to my room!" And off I went in a huff. My husband laughed and said, "It sounds like Sophia; she hates to be teased."

Mrs. Krautwurst described me as a friendly, bright child, very attached to my mother. She remembered my father as distant and formal. He worked long hours and kept to himself. "I never saw a man who seemed so uninterested in his child," she said. My parents had frequently argued about money, with my father blaming my mother for spending too much. This was certainly consistent with the parents I knew.

Apparently Mrs. Krautwurst and my mother shared good moments together; they were fond of each other. They spend a lot of time in the communal kitchen chatting over the stove. Despite their friendship, however, my mother deceived Mrs. Krautwurst into believing that she was a Catholic married to a Jew. It was interesting for me to learn that, after the war, my mother continued to hide her Jewish identity.

The Krautwursts were childless and, as it turned out, would never be able to conceive. Perhaps that was why Mrs. Krautwurst had such fond memories of the little girl who came to live with them after the war. As we talked, from time to time she exclaimed with emotion, "I can't believe that I have lived to see the day when my dear little Zosia has returned. I'm so sorry that my husband is no longer here to see you."

Mrs. Krautwurst told me that when my family left abruptly in 1946, she was heartbroken. She had become attached to us and felt a great loss at our sudden departure. It seems that plans to emigrate out of Poland were kept secret by my parents; we left Chorzów without giving our landlords much notice. Within the following year, the couple received a letter from my mother that included a little drawing of a duck from me. I do remember a duck-drawing phase. "Yes," I said to myself, "I can trust Mrs. Krautwurst's memory; it's intact."

At the end of our visit, we promised to write and to exchange photographs. I wanted to give Mrs. Krautwurst some money, but she refused. We had noted on our trip that, because of the poverty in Eastern Europe, people gladly accepted dollars when they were offered. Mrs. Krautwurst was the first person to decline our offer; she insisted that my visit was gift enough for her. Still, I felt the need to thank her for her generosity. In town, we purchased a crystal vase, filled it with a bouquet of beautiful flowers, and brought it to her.

As we left her apartment, I was filled with a strange mixture of feelings. I felt the euphoria of having rediscovered a little piece of my history. I also felt a sadness, a realization that I was not likely ever to see this woman again. As she waved good-bye from her window, my companions waved back, but I found myself unable to turn for a last look.

We got in our car to return to Kraków, and as I tried to conjure up Mrs. Krautwurst's face, I realized I could not, try as I might. Her image had already vanished from my mind. Other faces appeared before me in her place. The face of the woman we had met several days before, the one who had been instrumental in rescuing my friend Rena, kept intruding. No amount of effort could bring Mrs. Krautwurst's face back. At that moment, I realized that my earlier experience of separation was being reenacted there and then. Just moments after leaving the Krautwurst apartment, once again I experienced the force of repression. It felt like forgetting a word, a word that was "on the tip of my tongue." Only now it was a face that refused to come to mind.

Why had I not repressed earlier events in my young life? Why only Chorzów? Perhaps because I was torn from a secure, loving environment unlike anything that I had experienced prior to that time. After the traumas of my early childhood, I had finally arrived at a safe haven only to be torn away once again. Maybe this time the pain of separation and loss seemed too great to bear, so I blocked out the Krautwursts and anything associated with them. Now, as I was leaving Chorzów once again, I was reliving the earlier experience, blocking it out of my mind.

I never saw Mrs. Krautwurst again. We corresponded for awhile; a couple of years later, a relative of hers wrote to inform me of her death. I consider myself most fortunate to have encountered her when I did. It was an unexpected gift.

While we lived in Chorzów, my aunt in America had been working hard to help us obtain a visa to the United States. In spite of her husband's objections, she had decided to provide us with an affidavit, a document declaring that she would accept responsibility for us if we were unable to take care of ourselves once we became residents of the United States. My Uncle Sam, her second husband, afraid that we would become a burden on him, tried his best to dissuade her from her commitment. But Aunt Henrietta, a strong personality who had no one left in the world besides her younger brother and his family, would not be dissuaded. So Uncle Sam set his worry aside temporarily, figuring that with the stringent quotas against immigration to the United States, he did not need to be concerned about our arrival, at least for awhile. In fact, he was right. It took another five years before America would accept us in 1951.

In the meantime, my parents tried different ways to get out of Europe. Some of their friends went through Germany into the displaced persons camps and then on to the United States, but my father was adamant about avoiding Germany at all costs. Another option that was open to refugees like us at the time was South America. With Henrietta's help, we obtained an entry permit to Paraguay. I think Paraguay was merely a way out of Poland for us, for we never actually set foot on its soil. On the way to Paraguay, we stopped in Paris. We somehow managed to remain there for the next five years on a temporary visa while we waited for the American visa to become a reality.

I have a memory of a long, overnight train ride, sleeping on a little suitcase, changing trains in the middle of the night, Russian soldiers in uniform. Perhaps that was part of the journey to Paris; perhaps that happened earlier on our way to Chorzów; I can't be sure. No one is left to validate parts of my childhood, so I must rely on fragments of memory.

I do, however, remember a great deal about my life in Paris. At first, we moved into a hotel room, then another; then, in the winter of 1946-1947, we settled into a little apartment on the Left Bank near the Seine. We spent several years on a narrow winding street named Rue de la Huchette, right off of beautiful Boulevard Saint Michel. Current tourist guidebooks refer to Rue de la Huchette as one of the most famous streets on the Left Bank. Some of the buildings there are so old that they must be propped up by timbers to prevent them from collapsing.

We occupied the top floor of number 11 Rue de la Huchette, a six-floor walk-up. According to Mother, the building was about 700 years old. The windows of our garret faced the rooftops of Paris and offered a clear view of Saint-Severin, a Gothic church built in the thirteenth century in a style similar to Notre-Dame, the famous cathedral a few blocks away across the Seine.

The romantic connotations that this picturesque section of Paris holds for the tourist meant nothing to me as a six-year-old living in squalor. The building was dark and run-down. A steep flight of misshapen stone steps led to our garret. The apartment consisted of a single room with a partition that separated the kitchen area from the living and sleeping space. We had no electricity, only gas lights, and no running water in the apartment. My mother lugged pails of water daily from a faucet located on the floor below us. There were two public bathrooms to accommodate all of the tenants, one on the third floor and one on the ground level in a courtyard. Those stinking dirty toilets were the stuff of nightmares. The bathroom was a small, poorly ventilated, dimly lit room, with a large hole in the ground at the center from which an unbearable stench emanated. On either side of this hole there were footholds designated for standing on. The goal was to squat over the hole, carefully aim, and take care of one's biological needs as quickly as possible, without falling in. Since I tended to be constipated—and who would want to release the contents of one's bowels in such a disgusting place—I spent much more time in that room than I wish to remember. One of the great fears of my childhood was that I would slip and fall into that cavernous hole.

Despite those living conditions, it was a happy time. Life was hard, but the terror was over. My parents concentrated on rebuilding a life. My mother had some talent for sewing; she decided to work at home. She took a dressmaking course, purchased a sewing machine, and began a new career. My father found work as an accountant. I began school.

My happiest memories of those early years in Paris revolve around school. Not only did I love to draw and write, but I liked to be among other children. Despite the language barrier, I managed to communicate pretty well. My mother, an expert in the friend-making department, would urge me to approach children playing in the park and introduce myself. Because I was a bit shy, her method was hard for me. At some point, I discovered my own technique. I remember a day in school when I realized that smiling was an easy way to connect with people. I practiced the art of curving the corners of my mouth upward and grinning, smirking, beaming. I practiced it as I practiced my new name: they called me "Sophie" here, with an accent on the last syllable. It sounded strange, but that was the way it was to be. Zosia, my real name, had to remain at home.

One of the teachers from the upper grades took a special liking to me; she would visit me in my classroom and sometimes take me to hers. Her students, taking their lead from her, made a fuss over me. I never understood what she saw in me, but I enjoyed the attention. Looking back, I wonder if she felt sorry for the little refugee child who needed special care. Photographs of me taken at that time show a skinny, pale little girl with sad eyes and a very serious demeanor.

Perhaps my mother had told her our history. Or maybe the perceptive teacher could see for herself that I was a nervous child. At some point during the Paris years, I developed an annoying mannerism, a tic. Whenever the urge to release tension overcame me, I repeatedly blinked my eyes and wrinkled my nose. The strange little movement seemed to have a life of its own, appearing and disappearing mysteriously without my volition. The more I tried to control it, the more it controlled me. That sign of inner distress gave me much grief and troubled Mother as well. For me, it was an embarrassment; it made me different from other children. For her, it must have challenged the notion that she so tenaciously clung to, that her child had emerged from the inferno unscathed.

During our first year in Paris, we had a visit from my Aunt Henrietta. This was an exciting event. I had always envied other children who talked about their sisters, brothers, aunts, uncles, cousins, grandparents. I had no one—that is, until my Aunt Henrietta arrived. And she was not just any aunt; she was my aunt from America, the place that brought stars to the eyes of my parents every time it was mentioned. Aunt Henrietta came bearing gifts, the most special one was a big doll with beautiful clothes. For a child who had few toys, this was truly a magnificent present. My Christmas gift from *"Papa Noël"* (Santa) that year had been two oversized pencils, one blue and one red—not exactly a child's dream. I had so longed for a doll! And here was one from America, bigger and more beautiful than any I could possibly imagine.

My aunt left with promises that we would meet in America before long. In the meantime, life went on in Paris. The most difficult times for me turned out to be the summers, when the schools were closed. My parents seemed to have a preoccupation with fresh air, and, as far as they were concerned, there was no fresh air in postwar Paris. They insisted every summer that I be shipped somewhere out in the country for my own good, while they remained in the city working.

The separation, particularly from my mother, was hard to endure. I desperately loved her and felt that I could not live without her. She hurt me deeply by sending me away to stay with strangers. As usual, my protestations were ignored. The summer after my sixth birthday was the worst. I was placed with an elderly couple who earned extra money by boarding children during their vacations from school. Two other little girls, who happened to be first cousins, were also spending the summer there. These two were a team that teased me mercilessly. I was the youngest and an outsider. I barely spoke French and felt painfully lonely and homesick.

Once, when I peed in bed—an unusual occurrence for me—the couple punished me by locking me in a closet. There I sat in total darkness for what seemed to be hours. The *cabinet noir* (black closet) method of punishment was a favorite of theirs. This was not a disciplinary tactic with which I was familiar. A *gifle* (slap in the face), another common French punishment, would have been preferable. I was used to physical punishment, since my father had no compunctions against a smack on the bottom once in a while, and at school corporal punishment seemed to be an integral part of the curriculum.

After that unhappy summer, my parents' zeal for fresh air continued, but mercifully they found another, more nurturing place to send me in subsequent years. Merine, a woman in her seventies who lived in the country on the outskirts of Paris, became my surrogate grandmother. She was childless, had never married, and she adored me. She also had a real toilet in her house, the kind you sit on. And a real bathtub in the bathroom. It was a life of luxury. In time, I began to look forward to spending summers with Merine.

In all fairness to my parents, their preoccupation with fresh air may have resulted from the fact that at some point in our early Paris years I developed tuberculosis. My memory of the illness is foggy. I remember only that my mother and I lived on a farm for several months while I was convalescing. I enjoyed having Mother all to myself, and I loved the farm animals, particularly the chickens that ran around the yard. Mother doted on me. I liked the attention, except when it came to her milk mania. She got it into her head that milk was the source of life, and I wasn't going to get better unless she drowned me in the stuff. Every night, we had a battle with the same outcome: I was forced to drink large quantities of hot milk that tasted worse than medicine.

When we returned to the city, and I went back to school, I underwent a mysterious treatment. It consisted of a weekly visit to a clinic where I would be isolated in a dark room with other children, all undressed down to our panties and outfitted with goggles to protect our eyes. For a short period of time, we would be exposed to some kind of ultraviolet lamp. At first, the experience was frightening, but, since it was a regular occurrence, I became used to it.

In later years, when I asked my mother for details about this illness, she responded with the usual fogging defense she used when asked about something she didn't like to talk about. "Oh, I don't know if it was really TB," she said. "You had some kind of lung problem; I don't remember what it was." I suspect that my mother felt some shame about her child having been exposed to a disease associated with poverty and unclean living conditions. Her defense against clarity was meant to protect; instead, it confused me. Only recently it became clear to me that the disease that struck me in my childhood was indeed tuberculosis. In a newspaper article, I read about the revival of an old treatment for TB, namely the one I had undergone in Paris in the late 1940s.

Whether it was the medicine, the radiation, or the milk, something worked, and I was given a clean bill of health. Shortly after my bout with tuberculosis, we moved to another part of Paris. Perhaps the disease was an impetus for my parents to seek better living conditions. Our new apartment building at 34 Rue de la Chine was less picturesque, but also less run-down.

There was hot running water in every apartment, and only three families shared a bathroom, with one toilet to a floor in this three-story building. The bathroom in the hall had the same configuration as the one on Rue de la Huchette, a hole in the ground with footholds on either side. This time, however, the room was cleaned regularly, and the most offensive odor was usually the smell of disinfectant. I found a way to make my visits to the bathroom more tolerable by conjuring up an imaginary friend who lived there. Françoise was a French girl my own age with interests identical to my own. She kept me company whenever I went to the bathroom. As a matter of fact, we developed such a good relationship that when I received a special gift, I brought it into the bathroom to show it to her. I also had an imaginary horse that I kept tied to the banister downstairs, next to a dark area behind the stairs. Whenever I went to the store, I would climb on my horse and gallop there. I must have been a wondrous sight galloping down the street, mumbling to myself. But I was not self-conscious in those days. With my imaginary friends, I had found a creative solution to my loneliness.

Another way for me to cope with my solitude was reading. My vivid imagination found a home in the world of books. A particular favorite of mine was a series written by the Comtesse de Ségur about a mischievous little girl named Sophie. The best of the series was *Les Malheurs de Sophie* (The misfortunes of Sophie). Sophie, the heroine, was my shadow self who did all of the things I lacked the guts to do. I, a well-behaved, self-controlled child, was cautious; my namesake was a risk taker who kept getting into trouble. She meant well but somehow found herself in one mess after another; still, she always managed to get herself out. I got a vicarious thrill from her endless adventures.

In later years, my heroine was Joan of Arc, another fearless French female distinguished by her courage. Born into a world of catastrophic events, Joan, a peasant girl, had defied all conventions of medieval society. Dressed as a male, she led the French army into battle. Perhaps her disguise resonated with my own hidden identity. After I saw the American film shown in France with Ingrid Bergman in the role of St. Joan, I pasted a newspaper photo of her over my bed and prayed to it every night, as one would to a picture of the Virgin Mary.

Whatever the fascination, it was gratifying to have a heroine to worship. But imaginary friends and literary heroines had their limitations. I set out to find the real thing and found it in Denise Léger, a slight, soft-spoken fair-haired girl in my third-grade class. What drew me to her was a recognition that she, too, was a bit shy and lonely; she looked as though she could use a best friend. One day, she asked to borrow a pencil from me. I said, "Sure. You can keep it, if you'll be my friend." She accepted my offer.

Denise came to have the special status of a "best friend," but I made other friends as well. I was learning the pleasure of belonging to a peer group. Yet, although I felt appreciated and affirmed by my peers, a part of me always felt on the outside. I knew that I was different, that my unusual experiences had set me apart.

This feeling was highlighted around the time when my friends, all Catholic, began to have their First Communion. That religious ceremony was a special event in their lives. They planned it for months; they got to wear beautiful white dresses and celebrate with family and friends. I could not understand why I, too, could not have a communion. My parents said, "We are Jews, and we don't celebrate such an event." I think that this was the first time that I encountered the concept of my Jewishness. There had never been any religion other than Catholicism in my life. My mother had taken me to Mass in Zimna Woda. I had worn a medal of Mary and baby Jesus around my neck for years. Why were they now saying that we were Jewish? It was very confusing; I didn't like it. I decided that, when I grew up, I would convert to Catholicism. I announced it to friends and neighbors; they approved. My parents remained silent on the subject.

In most ways, however, we fit into life in postwar Paris pretty well. There was a lot of poverty, and everyone seemed to be struggling to make a living. Since beef prices were high, horse meat was a common substitute. *Chevaline,* a type of butcher shop devoted exclusively to horse meat, was a fixture in the neighborhood. With a horse's head prominently displayed in the front of the store, it was easy to locate. Rabbit, a delicacy in other parts of the world, was also relatively inexpensive. Cheap wine was readily available to all—even children would drink it with a meal. A wine store was across the street from our house, and I would sometimes go in with an empty bottle that the owner would fill from a huge barrel.

Directly across the street from our house was a lamppost. Each night, a man would climb up on a ladder he set up against the post and light the lamp. Life went on with a regularity that was comforting and safe. My parents, too, seemed more at peace than I had ever seen them before. From time to time, my father would wake up screaming during the night and my mother complained of stomach problems, but they didn't dwell on the past. They were concentrating their full energies on adapting to their new world.

I loved going to school, where I felt appreciated. Being a good student became a part of my identity. Each year, I was the recipient of special prizes that gave me a wonderful sense of self-esteem. The French elementary school system was a very hierarchical one. At the end of the school year, each child would be rank ordered with regard to her academic achievement. The top three students would receive prizes. I could always count on being one of those, usually the first. Another highly competitive process was a popularity vote. Every student picked a favorite classmate in a secret ballot. The votes were then tallied and the one with the most votes received the *Prix de Camaraderie* (prize of friendship). The prizes were usually wonderful books; I collected quite a few.

Is it any wonder that when the long-awaited visa to America finally came through in September of 1951, I received the news with mixed emotions? I knew that this was the event that my parents had anxiously awaited for many years. They had always considered Paris a mere stopping point along the way out of Europe. Father had also applied for a landing permit to Australia which was granted just around the time that we received the visa to the United States. Clearly the latter was their first choice.

Everyone was impressed to hear that we were moving to America. But the loss of the home I had grown to love was great. The thought of separating from Denise hurt unbearably. We vowed to write to each other and did for a while.

The journey across the Atlantic was exciting. We booked passage on a luxury liner, the *New Amsterdam*. Luxury is indeed the right word. We traveled third class, yet I couldn't imagine anything more luxurious. I, who had never eaten in a restaurant, found the dining room particularly memorable. I could not figure out the appropriate utensil to use. Each place setting had about four different sets of forks, knives, and spoons. The mood of my parents was jubilant. No one minded the seasickness that was a part of the experience.

I spent many solitary hours on deck, my face pressed against the railing, looking out at the horizon, fascinated by the shades of blue, green, and gray stretching out endlessly as far as my eyes could see. The waves crashing against the sides of the ship, their white peaks appearing and disappearing in regular rhythm, lulled me into a trance-like state. I found myself transported back to the world I had just left behind. Faces of friends, snippets of conversation, and images of Paris visited me.

Sometimes it felt disconcerting to be suspended in time and place, adrift between an old life already fading and a new one still unknown. I anchored myself by making a new friend on board. François, a boy my age, like me, had been transplanted into this unreal, in-between place. With him as my companion, I found the courage to explore the massive ocean liner. We became partners in mischief when we snuck into first class to see how the other world lived.

After several days' journey—I think it was about a week—we finally arrived in New York. I was awakened and brought up on deck to get a look at the Statue of Liberty. The excitement was palpable.

When we got to our destination, everybody disembarked at the pier in New York—everybody but us. One by one, the passengers had been called. François and his parents were among the large group that exited the ship. But our names were not on the right list. For some unknown reason, we were being detained. My parents became frantic with worry. Were we going to be sent back to France? I knew something terrible was unfolding.

The list we were on was the one that was destined for Ellis Island. By 1951, Ellis Island was no longer an automatic stopping point for immigrants entering the United States. It was now designated as the place for questionable immigrants whose fate was to be decided by a judge after a hearing. I learned that our predicament was due to the fact that Uncle Sam, my aunt's second husband who didn't want to sponsor us, had denounced my father to the authorities claiming that he was a communist. The charge had to be investigated.

We were detained on Ellis Island for three weeks. It was a terrible ordeal for us all. My parents were distraught. They had that look of despair that I had not seen in several years. At night, we were separated from my father, who slept in a large hall with other men. I was with my mother and many other women and children. The place was drab and dark; the huge halls echoed with sounds of silence. A high wall around the island with barbed wire fenced us in. We could see the skyline of New York; it seemed close but completely out of reach. I went to school during the day, it was my only respite from the gloom. The teacher gave us some paper dolls to cut out, but I would not be consoled.

We appeared before the judge separately. I think my father was first. I don't remember if I went in alone or with my mother. I don't remember the questions, only the anxiety. We must have given the right answers, because, at the end of three long weeks, we finally made it to the promised land. The words inscribed on the Statue of Liberty seemed written expressly for us: "Give me your tired, your poor, your huddled masses yearning to breathe free." At last America welcomed us.

Chapter 8

Lost and Found in America

In 1957, the very same year that we became citizens of the United States, Father purchased a cemetery plot. It was clear that we had reached our final destination. The refugee journey was over. Psychologically, it would take a long time to feel at home in this land, but there was no turning back.

My parents had learned English in their youth, but I did not know a word of this strange and difficult language. I practiced my new name. It looked the same as the French version, but the accent was in a different place. Now I was Sophie with the emphasis on the "o." It took some getting used to.

When we first arrived in New York, we rented a small apartment in Brooklyn in the vicinity of Coney Island. Ironically, the place we ended up in turned out to be a Jewish ghetto of sorts. A fancy one, to be sure, but a restricted place nevertheless. In order to enter Sea Gate, the small resort community on the edge of Coney Island, you had to pass inspection at the gate. A guard checked his list to be sure that you were either a resident or an expected visitor. When we arrived in September, Sea Gate was fairly empty; the summer crowd had probably just left. By the time they returned the next spring, we were gone. Sea Gate was peaceful and beautiful, a totally new world for me. The fresh sea air was intoxicating. The wide expanse of water and sand was calming. I walked on the deserted beach for hours. I discovered treasures: seashells, bits of driftwood, even a wounded seagull that I tried to nurse back to health. The beauty around me was breathtaking. But somehow, it made me acutely aware of my loneliness.

Shortly after we settled into our three-room apartment on the first floor of a private house right off of the beach, I was enrolled in the local elementary school located in Coney Island, about a twenty-five minute walk past the gate. The son of our landlord was a fifth-grade teacher at the school, and he happened to speak French fluently. A lucky coincidence! It was therefore decided that I would go into his class rather than entering the sixth grade, where I really belonged. Mr. Mullet was a sensitive man who made an effort to facilitate my transition. Often, he drove me to school in the mornings and allowed me to study English during class time.

My struggle with the language those first few weeks of school led to some memorable experiences, humorous in retrospect, but not so funny at the time. Once, with Mr. Mullet out of the room, I desperately tried to communicate to my peers that I had to go to the bathroom and didn't know where it was. The children gathered around me, realizing that I wanted something but could not express it. Someone handed me a piece of chalk and pointed to the blackboard. The idea was good, but I was not about to draw a picture of a toilet in front of those boys. I was humiliated and very uncomfortable until Mr. Mullet returned.

When asked about my father's place of birth for school records, I tried to translate the name of the town where he was born. Tluste means *greasy* in English. So my school records listed Greece as my father's birthplace.

Another predicament I found myself in because of my inability to communicate took place probably in the second or third week of school and was more serious in its consequences. We had established a routine in which my father picked me up every day after school. After a couple of weeks, he became resentful of this chore and proceeded to needle me, "You should be able to find your way home by now. What's wrong with you? It's not complicated." It seemed pretty complicated to me—all those streets and turns. I did not trust my sense of direction; perhaps all that moving around in my formative years had a negative effect on my sense of spatial orientation. After all, by the time we moved to Sea Gate, I had lived in eight different apartments, not counting the hotels in Paris and our brief stay at Ellis Island. Still, I was ashamed of my fear of getting lost; my father's taunting made me want to prove that I could do it. So, one morning, I announced that I was ready to make it home by myself.

Big mistake! I was lost in Coney Island for hours. After walking in circles for awhile, I began to cry. I couldn't approach anyone. I didn't speak English; I didn't know my address. How could anyone help me? A little girl around my age walked up to me and began asking questions. I answered her in French and continued to cry. She took me by the hand and brought me to her house. An elderly lady, probably her grandmother, tried to help. They called a policeman. All three went through my school bag to see if there were any clues. Miracle of miracles, they discovered an address. It seems that, that very morning, my parents had filled out some application for school. There it was, neatly printed—my home address!

The policeman brought me home. As we neared the gate, I saw my father approaching; he looked frantic with worry. Now that I felt safe, I could enjoy the drama. Secretly, I was glad that my father was worried. Serves him right for taunting me, I thought. If he was contrite for pushing me prematurely into independence, he never showed it; he was not a man to apologize. He remained critical and impatient with me; our relationship only deteriorated through the years.

Once again, I found comfort in school. I learned English quickly; luckily, languages came easily to me. Soon, I was able to follow the lessons along with the class and felt a little less isolated. The children were friendly and fascinated by the fact that I came from Paris. As far as the rest of my background was concerned, it seemed too complicated to divulge. Besides, I took my cue from my mother. Once, when someone reacted to her accent and asked her, "Where do you come from?" I heard her answer without hesitation, "Paris." I got the message that hailing from Paris was a source of status, while being a refugee from Eastern Europe was something to keep under wraps.

The atmosphere at school was very different from what I had been used to. For the first time, I was attending coed classes. In Paris, boys and girls occupied different buildings of the same school, and there was a wall dividing them in the school yard. In this new place, the atmosphere was less formal. The children did not sit at attention; they did not get slapped for bad behavior; and they got milk and cookies at least once a day. Sometimes, things happened that were a great mystery to me. For instance, one day the teacher said a couple of words, and suddenly the children jumped under their desks. What a strange sight! It took several of those drills before I understood that my classmates were practicing for a bomb attack. That was the early 1950s, when the threat of a nuclear attack was a potential reality.

For many months, I suffered from a nagging feeling of loneliness. Without being able to put a name to the experience, I was mourning the loss of my life in Paris. Only gradually did the feeling subside.

The children in my class were very friendly and warm to me. At one point, they elected me president of the class. I think it amused them to have a president who barely spoke English. Since one of the responsibilities of the role was to keep the class quiet when the teacher left the room, the word "shadap" (my version of "shut up") was one of the first English expressions I learned.

Although I got along with everyone, I felt a particular affinity for those children who were unpopular and did not fit in well. My radar for loneliness was probably finally tuned. Consistently in my life, I have been sensitive to the suffering of others and have taken particular satisfaction from helping those unable to fend for themselves.

An incident from the Sea Gate days stands out in my mind. In the school yard, I came to the aid of a girl, an overweight child, who was trapped by a group of boys making fun of her. With my limited vocabulary and swinging my school bag menacingly, I managed to distract them so that she could escape to safety. No doubt my sensitivity to those falling prey to bullies was close to home. But, at the time, the connection to my own persecuted childhood eluded me.

Spring came to Sea Gate and with it another move for us. It had been understood when we rented our apartment that the bargain rate we paid was for the winter months when the place was not likely to be occupied. As a desirable summer rental, it was well beyond our means, so we had to vacate.

Meanwhile, Aunt Henrietta, who lived in the South Bronx, had been searching for a permanent place for us to live, preferably close to her. So when an apartment became available directly next door, we all rejoiced, except for Uncle Sam. Having failed to keep us out of the country, he found himself unable to stem the inevitable tide of our entry into his life. His resistance met with my aunt's greater determination to become more deeply involved with us. The conflict between them escalated.

Even though I knew that my Uncle Sam was responsible for the Ellis Island fiasco, I was fond of him, in spite of myself. He was a colorful character. Uncle Sam was an ugly man, with hanging jowls, a big belly, and a cigar hanging perpetually from the corner of his mouth. He was always somewhat disheveled and unkempt and smelled of stale cigar smoke, but he had a twinkle in his eye and seemed to be fond of me.

He was unconventional and mischievous. His first gift to me was a gun—a very realistic, sleek, black metal gun. It looked like the real thing. I think it scared my parents. I loved it.

Sometimes when I visited him, Uncle Sam would entertain me and get me to be a coconspirator in his mischievous deeds. One day, very early on a Sunday morning, he was still in bed when I came in. Aunt Henrietta was in the kitchen making breakfast. He whispered to me with a bad-boy grin, "Let's wake up Laura." Laura was my aunt's best friend who lived in Brooklyn. She was obese and moved around with difficulty. So Uncle Sam dialed her number, let it ring and ring, and when a breathless voice at the other end answered, he quickly hung up. That was his idea of fun.

I laughed but felt embarrassed for him. I knew that he was being mean and immature. Still, he fascinated me. He was a departure from all the serious adults who surrounded me. But Uncle Sam's presence in my life was destined to be short lived. The last time I saw him was when the police came to take him away. By that time, he and my aunt had separated, and he was violating an order of protection. When he tried to force his way into the apartment, she called the police.

Once we were settled into our new home on Trinity Avenue in the South Bronx, it was time to begin another new school. This was to be my fourth elementary school in six years. Change was not difficult for me, but the overnight transition from the fifth to the sixth grade was not easy. I arrived in the sixth grade in April; by June, I was expected to graduate with my class. I was still trying to master the English language, but now I had to catch up with other subjects as well. Everyone expected me to manage, so I did. Being good at adapting to what was expected of me became my specialty.

I am still in contact with some of the children from my sixth-grade class. Recently, at one of our reunions, Ray, a middle-aged retired policeman, told me that he remembers a French song I taught the class. My classmates assumed that I was French and called me Frenchy. No one suspected that I was a Holocaust survivor from Eastern Europe. That was fine with me; I saw no need to tell the whole complicated story. I assumed that no one was really interested in it anyway. Without recognizing it as such, I was still in hiding; there I would remain for many years.

A wall of silence was erected around the subject of the Holocaust after the war—a wall that would remain in place for several decades.

Some have referred to it as "a conspiracy of silence." Survivors wanted to forget, and the world wanted to forget as well. The emphasis was on looking to the future and putting the past behind. The philosophy of "let sleeping dogs lie" prevailed. Holocaust survivors were "protected" by society from facing their traumatic past. A friend who lives in Sweden, originally from Galicia, provides a poignant example of this protective attitude. Irena had survived the war hidden in a convent. Her mother perished, and she was eventually reunited with her father in Lwów. At school, whenever the subject of the war would come up, Irena was sent out of the classroom so that she would not revisit her wartime ordeal.

My parents, like many other survivors, believed that only those who had lived through the Holocaust could possibly understand what they had experienced. On the outside, stories of survival were met with disbelief or pity. My parents did not want to be perceived as victims. Victims evoke mixed feelings in others; besides compassion, a sense of contempt for weakness often surfaces. Vulnerability makes people anxious; it's like a contagious disease, like seeing your own fragility reflected in the eyes of others.

A kind of split had developed in our lives between the world outside and the world inside the home. To the world outside, we were hardworking immigrants struggling to adjust to life in America and succeeding pretty well. On the inside, we were members of a secret club—a society of those who had suffered and who knew firsthand the evil that humanity was capable of. Americans, by contrast, were seen as superficial and naive; they had no clue about the real nature of humanity.

Although I was on the inside, I was excluded from the club. Membership was restricted to those who had suffered; I did not qualify because, as my parents maintained, I was too young to have been aware of events going on around me. In their attempt to shield me, they decided that it was best to keep me uninformed. Whenever I asked my mother a question about the war years, she began to cry and effectively ended any possibility of a conversation about the past. My father was impossible to talk to. He did not engage in conversation; he lectured me. His slow speech was labored and unfocused, and there was always the sense that at any moment the smoldering rage inside him could erupt. I did not feel safe talking to him about any subject, let alone the Holocaust.

My mother was a social being and never lacked for acquaintances or friends. Her closest relationships, however, were with survivors and refugees like us. In France, we occasionally visited with survivor families. In America, the community was much larger, and we met socially on a regular basis. A few of the couples had known each other before the war, while others were introduced by mutual friends. Each survivor had a unique tragic story, but all had one thing in common: they were part of the secret society that had suffered and managed to survive.

During those evenings when the families socialized, we children were relegated to a separate room. The grown-ups talked of many subjects, but somehow they always ended up talking about their traumatic experiences. If we entered the room at that point, they looked uncomfortable and became quiet. It was clear that their stories were not intended for our ears.

My parents had their community of survivors. As for me, I did not feel a part of that group, even among the children of my parents' friends. Instead, my community became the neighborhood children. The American kids made it easier for me to follow my parents' injunction to forget the past. My history was irrelevant with that group. I could start from scratch, create a new identity. I organized the Polly Pigtail Club. Polly was a children's magazine heroine who was the central character of a group of girls. Later, when boys captured my interest, the Polly Pigtail Club gave way to hanging out on the stoop and watching the boys play stickball on the street. On the weekends, we partied and danced to the sounds of the new rock-and-roll rhythms exploding into 1950s society. The boys, with their sleek greased hair carefully shaped into DAs (ducks' asses), and the girls, with their wide crinoline skirts decorated with poodles, were my peers. It was good to be accepted into a peer group.

My parents' penchant for fresh air continued in America. Every summer I was enrolled in camp. With her customary ingenuity, my mother found charity-run camps so that no cost was involved. The problem was that each camp had a two-week limit, so I sometimes attended several different camps over a single summer. That was never seen as a problem for a child who was used to "parachuting" in and out of new situations.

One summer I found myself in a camp run by Hehalutz Hatzair, a Zionist organization. Apparently, my parents were not fussy about ideology. The fact that no one in my family had any interest in Zionism was no deterrent. My resolution to convert to Catholicism had been abandoned shortly after we arrived in America when I discovered that it was the Jewish children who seemed to share my values and with whom I felt most comfortable. But I was still a long way from identifying myself as a Jew, and Zionism was a totally alien concept to me.

At camp Ein Harod, my fellow campers idealized Israel, and many planned to emigrate there in the future. As for me, I was interested only in Israeli music, dancing, and the boys. When camp was over, I continued to attend weekly meetings in Manhattan until my parents heard rumors that the organization had communist affiliations and promptly took me out.

At this point, school was the most stabilizing force in my life. Once again, it was a powerful source of self-esteem for me. By junior high school, I had mastered English pretty well, and, before long, I was getting recognition for my academic work. For some reason, which still is a puzzle to me, I developed a special aptitude for spelling and became the eighth-grade spelling bee champion. But my favorite subject was always art. Drawing came naturally to me. My parents valued and encouraged it from the time I was small. Through all of our travels, my mother managed to save my childhood scribbles, some dating back to the Chorzów days. My father had enjoyed drawing in his youth and eventually returned to it.

Although they encouraged my interest in art, my parents had no idea about ways to nurture or develop it. Guidance in that direction came from unexpected sources. I worked as a baby-sitter for a little boy whose mother was a teacher at the High School of Music and Art, a public school in New York where talented children could pursue a secondary education with a major in either art or music. She encouraged me to apply.

My art teacher was also immensely supportive and spent many extra hours after school helping me to develop a portfolio and to prepare me for the entrance examination required for the High School of Music and Art. My parents were surprised that this teacher, an African American (or Negro, as people of color were called in those days), would devote herself to helping a child from an alien culture. Until they came to the United States, my parents had met very few people of different races and did not expect the generosity or dedication that they encountered in that woman. They were very grateful to her, and, when I was accepted, they bought her a beautiful leather-bound book as a gift. My parents often embarrassed me with their penurious ways, but that time they did the right thing, and I was proud of them.

I would soon have another reason to be proud of my father, a rare experience for me. Most students entered the High School of Music and Art in the ninth grade, although some began in tenth. I was scheduled to enter in the ninth, after completing only two years of my three-year junior high school. When I informed the school that I was leaving at the end of the eighth grade, I encountered unexpected resistance from the administration. Perhaps they did not want to lose one of their best students, a member of the honor society, or maybe it was just bureaucratic irrationality. Whatever the reason, my father, irate about the school's position, went to the principal to fight my cause. Soon it was all arranged, and I was ready to begin high school. It felt good to know that I could count on my father to fight for me; I appreciated the fact that he was not cowed by authority.

With my entrance into Music and Art, I was ready to embark on a new journey. It was a time of great change for me. Unlike earlier years, when changes were precipitated by the cataclysmic events in the outside world, these changes were inspired by adolescence and were primarily internal.

During my high school years, I became a citizen of the United States, an identity that felt quite natural to me by that time. In the process of becoming citizens we had the opportunity to formally change our last name from Reichman to Richman, a name that sounded less German and more American. In our eagerness to assimilate, we had used our new name from the moment we arrived in the United States, but now it became official. Also, by the order of the Court, Mother became Dorothy instead of Dorota. I remained Sophie until adulthood when I decided to change the last letter of my name from an e to an a. Sophia sounded more like my original name, Zofia. The immigrant's struggle with names and identity notwithstanding, I felt like a regular American girl. I spoke English without an accent, at least as far as most people could tell. Occasionally, someone with a particularly sensitive ear would ask where I was from, but, for the most part, I no longer needed to have an explanation for a cumbersome past.

Chapter 9

Struggles and Triumphs
of Adolescence

I entered the High School of Music and Art in the fall of 1954. It was a stimulating, creative environment, unlike any I had been exposed to previously. The school was a true melting pot of different cultures and social classes. Children who hailed from ethnic ghettos studied side by side with those who came from privileged upper middle-class families. Our talent was a great equalizer, at least in principle. Personally, I was intimidated by the presence of my articulate and sophisticated peers who seemed so sure of themselves.

Surrounded by those bright, talented youngsters, I became more inhibited and self-conscious and tended to fade into the background. In art classes, I continued to excel; in academic subjects, I withdrew and did a lot of daydreaming. When my father met with my geography teacher on parent-teacher conference night, he was asked if I was embarrassed to speak in class because of an accent. "Does she have an accent?" Mr. Marienhoff asked. "What do you mean, asking me if she has an accent? You should know," my father answered.

As much as I tried to blend in, to avoid being noticed, I felt that I stood out and seemed different from my peers. One of the things that contributed to this feeling was the fact that I could not afford the material things that others took for granted. Although both of my parents were employed, they saved all of their earnings; we lived as if we were destitute. When I needed to purchase art materials for my classes, my parents said that we could not afford them and insisted that I go to the administration and request financial aid. The school provided me with oil paints and other art supplies. I hated being a charity case.

My clothes were hand-me-downs from Mariella, the daughter of my parents' friends from Europe, who was a few years older than me. Her father, a dentist, had come to America before the war and had made good, so Mariella had an abundance of clothes and was always happy to make room in her closets for more. As for me, I wanted to pick my own new outfits, like the ones I eyed in neighborhood shop windows. The only time I had anything new to wear was when my mother sewed it for me. Her sewing talent was questionable. She had not been able to earn a living as a dressmaker and was now working in a factory sewing brassieres. Whenever she attempted to make a dress for me, something always managed to go wrong. The seams would come apart or the fabric would be reversed, like the time she cut a magnificent piece of velvet, rich in color and beautiful in design, on the wrong side so that the back and front of the dress did not match when she sewed them together.

Miss Ridgaway, my homeroom teacher, an elderly spinster who looked as if she came from another era, once called me to her desk. "Sophie, I hope you don't take this the wrong way, dear," she whispered hesitantly. "I was cleaning out my closet and found some outfits that I thought you might be able to use. I don't want to offend you . . ." Her voice trailed off. She pointed to a little wicker basket filled with clothes under her desk. I had never seen Miss Ridgaway look so uncomfortable. I assured her that I was grateful. And indeed I was. But my appreciation for her generous gesture was mixed with a sense of embarrassment; at that moment, I realized that I must be wearing my poverty on my sleeve, so to speak. As it turned out, her clothes were finely tailored and attractive. She was an art teacher and had a sense of style. The fact that I was fourteen and wearing the clothes of a sixty-plus-year-old seemed not to concern anyone—after all, beggars can't be choosers. Thereafter, from time to time, Miss Ridgaway would call my attention inconspicuously to a little basket of clothes under her desk that she had put aside there for me.

After my second year in Music and Art, my parents announced that we were changing apartments once again. They had saved enough money to leave the South Bronx and move to a better middle-class neighborhood. Since our arrival in America, five years earlier, we had already lived in Brooklyn and the Bronx. Now we were moving to Queens. All of my protests and cries about losing my friends were ignored. At least it was agreed that I would not have to transfer to a new high school. With four subway train connections, I could travel from Jackson Heights, Queens, into Harlem in Manhattan, where Music and Art was located.

Our apartment in Jackson Heights was larger and brighter than previous ones but still only had one bedroom like the others we had lived in since coming to America. For reasons I never quite understood, my parents arranged to sleep in the living room while I was given the bedroom. It had been the same arrangement in the Bronx. Giving up their bedroom for me is a gesture I would not have expected from my parents. They did not believe in pampering me and went out of their way to make sure that I was not "spoiled like other only children," a sentiment they frequently expressed. When once, in a fit of anger, I announced, "I'm going to my room!" My father countered with, "You have no room in this house; it's my room. I pay the rent here."

Perhaps there were reasons why they were avoiding privacy. Their relationship was strained. They argued frequently and bitterly. I did not see much love between them. My father was always angry about one thing or another; he constantly blamed and criticized. My mother complained and retaliated in her passive-aggressive style. She played the victim but somehow usually managed to get her way. In childhood, I perceived her as the more passive of the two and believed that my father was in charge. In adolescence, I began to realize that she was really the one in control.

Money was always a major issue for them. My mother was concerned with it; my father was obsessed with it. For him, money was not to be spent but to be saved. The more money in the bank, the more secure he felt. He was not only stingy with others; he denied himself material things as well.

In America, he worked as an accountant, a suitable profession for a man preoccupied with keeping track of money. Eventually, he got a job working for the city government and was in charge of reviewing claims for reimbursement by physicians. It was an ideal job for a man who was suspicious of professionals overcharging for their services, and one who was bitter about his own missed opportunity to become a physician.

My father's preoccupation with money took on ridiculous proportions. For instance, there was the incident of the moldy hot dogs. He had purchased a package of frankfurters, and, after a time, they took on a slimy, greenish tint. It was clear they had spoiled. He refused to throw them out and insisted that my mother prepare them for him for lunch. She worried that they would make him ill, but her objections were to no avail until she offered to buy the hot dogs from him. So he sold them to her. She promptly threw them in the garbage; everyone was happy.

One of the consequences of this great concern over money was that I lived with a sense of being a burden to my parents. In adulthood, when I had a pet cat, my father figured out how much money the cat was costing me per year. This unsolicited information made me wonder if he had calculated how much of an expense I had been to him over the years. Perhaps that was one of the reasons that my parents never agreed to let me have a pet other than a bird or a turtle. How much can a bird eat, after all?

Accounting was a way of life in our household. On my mother's birthday, my father would give her ten dollars as a gift. Then, on his birthday, seven months later, she would give him the ten dollars back. This went on for years. Once, he broke the pattern and brought her flowers. That day she received eight dollars as a birthday gift, after he deducted the cost of the flowers.

I have often wondered what kind of people my parents would have been had they not been victims of the Holocaust. Were those eccentricities a result of the trauma that they had lived through? Was my father's hoarding behavior directly related to having spent sixteen months at Janowska, starving, and without any possessions to call his own? Was their relationship affected by the fact that my father owed his life to my mother? Did that make him resentful rather than grateful? Such questions have no answers. For me, there was never a "before the war" since I was born into it. I would never know what kind of people my parents had been and how much the war had influenced their personalities.

It was clear that they were suffering. Sometimes, I would come in to the house in the evening to a darkened room, with only a single light from a green shade casting an eerie shadow on the wall. My father would be sitting alone, silent, staring out into space, lost in some world of horror and death.

Then, there were the nightmares. Screams in the middle of the night that awakened me and reminded me that the hell he had escaped from was only as distant as the next dream.

My mother handled her pain in a different way. It found expression through her body in the form of ulcers and various intestinal ailments. She suffered from insomnia; she worried all the time, expecting disaster at every turn.

When giving testimony about her Holocaust experiences, my mother was asked, "Do you think about these things very often?" She answered:

> Yes . . . yes, and I try to push it in the back of my head. But my husband couldn't get over it. All day he was sitting in his room looking on this book [the book he wrote about the concentration camp] and thinking and thinking about so many friends. He couldn't get over it. Well, I guess I have a different disposition because I try to push this back, but it comes back all the time.

My mother's attempt to push her past to "the back of her head" was matched by my own tendency to stay away from anything having to do with the Holocaust. I avoided books, films, and discussions on the subject. There were, however, a few exceptions to the psychological ban on dealing with my history. At some point in high school, I read *The Diary of Anne Frank* and was moved immensely by her story. My reaction certainly was not unique; Anne's diary has had that effect on countless individuals, but I realized that it resonated with something deep in my own soul. She was "a hidden child," a term I had not yet been introduced to, but a concept that I could identify with, in a powerful way.

Another unusual experience was watching the film *Stalag 17* with my parents. We rarely went to the movies together, and a war film was not my choice, but for some reason I agreed to go. The film was about a group of American prisoners of war in a Nazi concentration camp. It was both tragic and humorous and presented the subject in a way that was bearable for the three of us. This was the first time that I had an encounter with what life was like in a concentration camp; it allowed me to touch my father's experience in a distant, safe way.

But the forces of repression were strong, and those isolated events did not herald a change in my way of coping with the trauma of the past. My goal was to escape from the oppressive home atmosphere into a world where the biggest concerns were school grades and dates for the prom.

For my friends and me, the focus was on the present and the future. The past seemed irrelevant. Only once, and only with one friend, did the subject of the Holocaust come up. Heidi, a fellow student at Music and Art, also lived in my Jackson Heights neighborhood, and we traveled to school together. She was a recent immigrant from Germany and spoke with a heavy accent. She was friendly, but we were not close; I sensed a certain distance from her. One day, we got into a discussion about the war; to my utter amazement, Heidi announced that she was sorry that Hitler had lost the war, because, she said, "He was good for Germany." I was shocked. I tried to enlighten her, but I knew that no matter what I said, Heidi's views on Hitler were not about to change. What surprises me most today, as I think about that encounter, is that, in spite of Heidi's pro-Nazi sentiments, our friendship continued through high school and beyond—a fact that probably says more about my tendency toward denial than about my tolerance for differences.

Anita, another friend from Jackson Heights who traveled to Music and Art with us, was also of German descent, but her values and beliefs were totally different from Heidi's. Anita was one of my closest friends and remained so for many years.

During my adolescence, friendships provided the greatest source of satisfaction in my life. Deep, intimate relationships with girlfriends made up for the difficult times at home. Boys seemed to be another species, not people you could share intimate secrets with. Still, I daydreamed about them and had many crushes. In fact, I made it a point to develop a love interest in every class, since it made going to school much more fun. But none of my love objects were ever privy to my feelings, unless my blushing and stammering gave me away. Then, when I turned seventeen, I fell in love.

I met Robbie at a dance and was surprised to find that someone so charming and self-assured could be as interested in me as I was in him. He projected the image of a young man who knew exactly where he was going and that anyone who accompanied him through life was fortunate indeed. We were both impressed with his intellect. What some may have seen as pretentious, I saw as brilliant. He carried a book of Plato's *Dialogues* in his back pocket and decided to educate me in the world of philosophy. I was a very willing and eager student. When he introduced me to the world of sexuality, I was again eager to learn. This was the 1950s, a time when "going all the way" was not something that "good girls" like me did. Petting, however, was an acceptable alternative.

At seventeen, Robbie turned out to be as inexperienced sexually as I was, despite the sophisticated image he liked to project. That was fine with me; I preferred to discover the mysteries of sexuality together. Prom night, parked somewhere in Poughkeepsie in the back of a Buick, I discovered that my ideas about male anatomy derived from naked statues were inaccurate. What I felt in my hand that night had no resemblance to the little sculptured penises I was familiar with from my trips to the Greek section of the Metropolitan Museum of Art.

Robbie introduced me to many new and exciting ideas and activities. He took me to a seance somewhere in Brooklyn; he introduced me to hypnosis; and, for a nickel, he thrilled me with romantic rides on the Staten Island ferry. I was desperately and completely in love.

When our parents realized that we were becoming seriously involved, they attempted to break us up. A refugee from Eastern Europe was not what Robbie's parents had in mind for a daughter-in-law; they were upper middle-class Jews who had better prospects planned for their only son. My own parents subscribed to the same philosophy of "stick to your own kind." For some time, they had been urging me to become involved with the son of survivor friends, whose advances I had rejected.

The fact that we were both planning to go to college in different places was even more of a problem than our parents' objections. Robbie was heading to an engineering school in upstate New York, and I was about to begin City College in Manhattan.

I, who was so accustomed to separations by now, felt this one very deeply. Yet, in my heart, I knew that this relationship would not end this way. I was developing a sense of my own power. Life had taught me that things did not come easily and that, if I wanted something, it was up to me to make it happen. I was not easily defeated by obstacles.

As I developed a greater sense of autonomy and personal power, my conflicts with my father escalated. My relationship with him seemed to have been problematic from the start. Perhaps on some deep level, he was still the wolf behind the attic door who intruded into my close relationship with my mother.

Father had always seemed partial to my little sister Jasia. His tears, the only ones I ever witnessed, spoke of his heartbreak when she died.

Maybe she had seemed more like his own child, she who physically resembled him and had never been separated from him as I had been.

The powerful bond that I had with my mother and my mistrust of him may have deterred Father from trying to get close to me. I was my mother's child, and she probably liked it that way, maybe even encouraged it without awareness.

I imagine that it would have taken considerable effort on his part to develop a better relationship with me. But he was suffering the aftereffects of the trauma he had lived through and apparently was unable to transcend it sufficiently to reach out to his child. Perhaps he tried. I remember taking long walks with him in Paris. Also, I have a fond memory of a time on Trinity Avenue when he broke up a fistfight between a boy and me, and then chased the boy down the street. It felt good to be protected by a father.

The academic sphere was the one area where he tried to be involved with me. But instead of becoming closer, we clashed there as well. I experienced him as overinvolved in my academic performance and resented the help he insisted on giving. Once, I was preparing for an algebra exam; he insisted on drilling me despite my protest. When I brought home a failing grade, he beat me. The next day, I went to the guidance counselor and appealed for him to intervene. Today, my father would probably be brought up on child abuse charges. Back in 1956, the counselor called my father in to school for a "talk." On the day of their meeting, I returned home from school to a chill in the air. My mother spoke. "How can you say such things about your father at school? Don't you know that he only wants the best for you?" My father stopped speaking to me for months after that. The silent treatment was a frequent occurrence at our house; it did not unduly disturb me. I was relieved that he no longer meddled in my schoolwork. When I got a grade of 94 on my next algebra test, I felt vindicated.

My father never spoke to me about his experiences in the camp. I had some recognition that his rage was a by-product of those experiences—of years of having to submit to inhuman treatment without fighting back. But when that rage was directed at me, the understanding did not help. Sometimes I felt that he was reliving the nightmares of Janowska; only now he was the persecutor and I, the victim.

One Saturday night, on a date with Robbie, I stayed out later than I had promised. I returned to find that I was unable to enter the house. My parents had decided to lock me out as a punishment. I tried my key; it turned in the lock, but I could not get the door open. Then, I realized that they had piled furniture up against the door to bar my entry. No amount of ringing the doorbell or pleading from the outside had any effect. Robbie and I looked at each other with consternation. What did they expect of me? Did they want me to spend the night with my boyfriend?

Just because they were irrational, I was not about to do anything that I would regret. I decided to go to a friend's house. It was still relatively early in the evening and Anita was out with her boyfriend, but Mrs. Bohnenberger, her mother, welcomed me and made up an extra bed. Then, she called my parents and reproached them. "How can you let a teenager roam the streets at night? No matter what she did, it's not right to lock her out. Don't you realize it's dangerous?" I suspect that Mrs. Bohnenberger's sensible words were cutting and shame inducing for my parents. She, a German immigrant, seemed more concerned with the welfare of their child than they themselves appeared to be.

The more assertive and rebellious I became, the more controlling and enraged was my father's response. His potential for violence scared me but never enough to deter me from doing what I believed was right. In fact, I seemed to derive strength from those confrontations. I was developing a sense that I knew best what was right for me. Somewhere along the way, I had shed my compliance. Directly or indirectly, I found a way to assert my own needs in the face of his attempts to control me. For instance, when he forbid me to use the telephone in his absence and placed a lock on it to prevent me from using it, I learned from a friend how to remove the lock, make my telephone calls, and replace it before his return. My sense of myself as a competent person in charge of my life was growing. At seventeen, I vowed to myself that I would never take abuse quietly.

The last time my father threatened me with physical violence stands out vividly. He had literally backed me into a corner of a walk-in closet in our apartment. His face distorted with rage, he lifted his arm to strike me. I reached for an ice skate hanging on the hook of the closet door and held the blade to his face. "If you hit me again, I won't hesitate to use it," I said calmly, while shaking inside. He backed off and never struck me again.

Years later, in analysis, I talked about my rebellious adolescence. I felt somewhat guilty about my behavior and the stress that I had put my parents through during those years. I expected that the analyst would conclude that I had been a disturbed adolescent. To my surprise, he commented that the rebellion was a healthy sign. It was part of a necessary struggle to become my own person in an environment that was potentially destructive to my autonomy.

Recently, I came across an autobiographical statement written in October 1958, at the start of my freshman year in college. It provides a window into my thinking and feelings at the age of seventeen. The following are excerpts that illustrate how I conceptualized my past and coped with it at that point in my life.

> I was born in the midst of the war, in Poland. Although it was no trivial matter anywhere in the world, the war turned out to be more of a nightmare in my native land than in other European nations.
> I am not seeking pity or expressing self-pity when I make this statement, for I have no right to complain about my early years. Through the sacrifices of my mother, I became a chubby, almost well-fed baby, with practically no imprint of the chaos around me. . . .

This passage highlights my tendency to minimize the effects of the "nightmare" on my life. It reflects how I internalized my parents' beliefs that, since I was so young, I was not affected by the trauma. I believed that because of my mother's sacrifices, I had no right to complain or feel sorry for myself.

> I never had difficulty making friends. The latter is a great asset because I have traveled so much and have had to meet new people constantly. Perhaps my ability to get along stems from my continual moving . . .
> During the first two or three years in America, I experienced a feeling of "homesickness" for what I had termed my "homeland," but there was another feeling strongly predominant, one of the glory in being the center of attraction. My new friends would call me "Frenchy" and make me talk in French while they would listen with their mouths open and admiration in their eyes.
> Now, I am accustomed to the American way of life and have transformed so completely that few people can guess my past life from talking to me. . . .

In these passages I recognize the connections between my history of displacement and the way that I function in the world, but I seem compelled to give it a positive spin and deny the reality of the tragedy. It's almost as though I perceive my experiences as an asset to my development. The loss that is expressed as "homesickness" is immediately followed by thoughts of being special and appreciated. I certainly became adept at turning lemons into lemonade!

After writing about my history, I described my personality and my concerns. It is interesting to me that much of what I struggled with at the time of writing continued to be themes throughout my life.

> I don't believe I understand myself well enough to analyze my character. I know I am sensitive; it takes little to bring tears into my eyes, whether they are tears of joy or of pain.
>
> I don't like living under assumptions. I want the truth laid out before me so that there will be no misunderstandings among my friends and me. I tell the truth and expect frankness in return.
>
> To my misfortune, "daydreaming" takes up most of my time. I suppose a psychiatrist would analyze me as a person escaping reality and yet consciously I love life and have no reason to escape into a dream world. . . .
>
> Another problem (which probably stems from my lack of self-confidence) is my inability to express myself verbally. When I am with friends, I forget that I have a speaking problem, and words come naturally. But when I join a group discussion, I become more conscious of the way I speak than of the things I say and as a result I grasp for words, blush, get confused, and usually sit down in exasperation. Although I feel my point is as important as that of my neighbor, I am afraid to participate. My problem seems trivial but it is of constant worry and adds to my lack of confidence.

Apparently, when I wrote those words, I did not realize that living under "assumptions" is another version of living in hiding and that my longing for the truth is a desire to be out in the open. Similarly, I did not make the connection between my difficulty in expressing myself verbally and the early injunction against speaking the truth. It would take many years of analysis before that recognition.

Chapter 10

The College Years:
New Avenues and Dead Ends

My high school years had come to an end. There was no doubt that college was the next step, but my choices were limited to schools close to home with no tuition required. Cooper Union, a professional art school in New York City, was the first choice for many Music and Art graduates. Anita and I took our entrance examinations together. She passed; I failed. I was greatly disappointed. Only years later, after Anita had joined the ranks of disillusioned artists struggling to make a living at boring commercial art jobs and I had found great satisfaction in my own profession, did I realize how fortunate I was to have been rejected from Cooper Union. It is one of the ironies of life that sometimes our failure to get what we want turns out to be a blessing.

My second choice school was the City College of New York (CCNY). In the 1950s, and for many years prior to that, CCNY was considered to be one of the best schools in the United States. Known as the Harvard of the poor, it was a place where a young adult with good high school grades could get an excellent free education. In those days, if you didn't make City College, you had to consider a private university, such as New York University, where the academic standards were lower and the tuition was high. Fortunately, I was accepted to CCNY.

My father urged me to go to school part-time in the evenings, so that I could get a full-time day job and contribute to the rent at home. Unlike many parents who wish to give their children what they themselves lacked when they were growing up, my father subscribed to the principle that what was good enough for him should be good enough for his child. Since he had not been able to depend on his own parents for financial support for his schooling, why should I?

It was my conviction that my father's desire for me to work came from his philosophy rather than from our financial situation. By the late 1950s, my parents had come into some money. The indemnification law of 1953 had made restitution funds available to compensate victims of Nazi persecution. By 1958, when I was applying to college, my parents had both received substantial sums of money as well as lifetime pensions from the German government.

I resisted my father's urging to seek a full-time job and attend night school. My mother backed me, and I registered as a full-time student. Next came the issue of a major. From childhood years on, my standard answer to the question, "What do you want to be when you grow up?" was "A writer and an illustrator." My first attempt at being an author was at the age of ten. Before leaving France, I began writing a story about a little girl who had been separated from her real parents and was living with a couple who had adopted her; possibly that was a thinly veiled expression of the wish to have a different set of parents. I don't know how much promise I showed as a writer, but I do know that I found immense pleasure in writing and drawing pictures to go with the text. We left France before the story was completed, and, once in America, I concentrated on writing in English. Changing language midstream felt too complicated a task, so the project was abandoned.

Several years later, I wrote another story about a child who had lost his parents. Titled "The Boy with No Name," it was about a young boy whose parents had perished in the war. Apart from the fact that this was the only reference to the war and its aftermath in my writings, the most interesting aspect of this short story was that it was written under a pseudonym—Dorothy S. White. In this fascinating combination, I took my mother's first name, Dorothy, and her maiden name, Weiss, translated into English. In the middle, I inserted my own initial, S.

Why did I not claim the authorship? Did I need to disguise it— first, by making the hero a boy, then, by using a pseudonym? Did the story and its title express my sense of confusion about my own identity? Was I so merged with my mother that I attributed my ideas to her? Or was the use of her name a way to give myself permission to write about an unspeakable subject?

By the time I entered college, I was no longer thinking about writing as a career. I had other interests, including philosophy and art, and

I didn't feel pressured to make a choice at that early stage of my academic life. My parents, forever practical, had some ideas of their own about a suitable profession for me. They encouraged me to consider teaching French, since I spoke the language fluently and it seemed reasonable to make a career of it. When I showed no interest, they suggested other possibilities in the field of commercial art, such as fashion design or textile design. But I had neither interest nor aptitude in those areas. I decided to continue studying fine arts and wait for inspiration in one direction or another. It came unexpectedly in the second half of my freshman year.

One of the most interesting classes that I signed up for introduced me to the concept of art as a technique in the treatment of emotionally disturbed individuals. There I learned about art therapy, a form of psychotherapy particularly useful with people who have difficulty expressing their psychic pain verbally. In the course, we were introduced to the work of Margaret Naumburg, a pioneer in the field of art therapy and author of several books on the subject.

The concept of using art for self-expression and therapy was a novel one for me. I had been drawing and painting with great satisfaction for many years but had not thought of art as a means to express my inner world. I created pretty pictures, realistic replicas of what I saw in the world around me. Whether I was painting a portrait, a still life or a landscape, my goal was to render as realistic and accurate an image of my subject as possible. When it came to creating something from my imagination, I found myself at a loss for ideas and lacking in talent. For me, painting was never an opportunity to express spontaneous feelings. In retrospect, I believe that the same inhibitions that kept me from expressing myself verbally were blocking my ability to make full use of the self-expressive potential of art. Perhaps it was not safe to give my imagination free rein.

My father's relationship to art was similar. He had always loved to paint, and when he retired, he became a prolific artist. Every wall in his apartment was covered with his artwork. His painting style was primitive; the subject was usually landscapes. They were representational creations in bright colors based on what he saw around him. Only one painting stood in contrast to the others in the mood that it communicated, a self-portrait revealing a tortured anguished face; that painting alone seemed to capture his tormented inner world.

Despite a lack of great artistic talent, my father derived immense pride and pleasure from the activity and its final product. The energy and enthusiasm with which he immersed himself in the process were a stark contrast to the invisible shroud of death he usually seemed wrapped in. He came back to life through his creative activity.

Fascinated by the therapeutic potential of artistic expression, I set out to learn more about art therapy as a discipline. After reading Margaret Naumburg's books, I decided to contact her. She lived in New York, and, when I spoke with her on the telephone, she was responsive and warm; we arranged for a meeting at her home.

That grande dame had a striking appearance. The fact that she was on the other side of middle age did not stop her from dressing dramatically in bright patterns and intense colors. She sat across from me on the couch in her parlor and seemed to revel in my admiration of her work. As we talked, I began to have an uneasy feeling that she was interested in having me as a patient and was subtly trying to seduce me to enter treatment with her. That was not on my agenda; I just wanted to study the technique, not experience it firsthand.

In response to my questions about the study of art therapy, she explained that no training programs were available but that she herself taught several courses on the graduate level at New York University. She recommended that I major in psychology and take those courses after graduation. I agreed, thanked her for her time, and we parted. I followed the plan; I declared a psychology major, and four years later, I would study with Miss Naumburg in graduate school.

Now that my career goals were clear, I turned my attention to my social life. It was okay, but I missed Robbie. We had split up during the summer before beginning college, and I felt an empty space where he had been in my life. I dated but without heart; other boys just did not measure up. Before long, we both responded to the powerful desire to reconcile and resumed our relationship—this time, long distance and in secret because of our parents' disapproval. We devised an elaborate scheme to exchange mail. I would write to him directly at his dorm at Rensselaer Polytechnic Institute (RPI), while he would address his letters to Carl, a friend of mine at CCNY, who would then deliver them to me. The arrangement worked pretty well, but letters only stirred greater longing. I made the decision that somehow, some way, I would join him in Troy, New York.

At eighteen, I had a sense of personal power that surprises me today. Perhaps it was the grandiosity of adolescence that made me feel invincible to the restrictive forces around me and gave me the feeling that I could direct my own life. Obstacles in my path were merely a challenge to overcome. And there were certainly many obstacles to joining Robbie in upstate New York.

Getting my parents to finance college was out of the question. So, I transferred to night school, found a full-time job, and saved my money assiduously. Also, I applied for a student loan. Reluctantly, my mother agreed to co-sign for me. That took care of college tuition for at least one year. Of course, I would work part-time at school, as I had been doing since I began college.

The next order of business was to arrange for a transfer. RPI was an engineering school, predominantly male in its student body, but some female students were accepted. A counselor at the school told me that I would have to take science courses to qualify for acceptance. No problem; I was ready to sign up for anything as long as I could be near Robbie.

I enrolled in a physics course; after five exams, I realized that, no matter how much I studied, my zero average was not going to get any higher. I was grateful when the professor allowed me to drop the course without a failing grade on my record.

Without science, RPI was no longer an option. I came up with a viable alternative. In the same town there was a "sister school" for women—Russell Sage College—located in a perfect spot for someone interested in an RPI male. So, I sent in my application and, in my second year of college, was accepted as a transfer student.

My bewildered parents could not understand my determination to go to school in Troy when I could have a free education at City College, but at least they did not stand in the way of my transfer.

In January 1960, the middle of my sophomore year, I arrived at Russell Sage full of anticipation and ready to resume my relationship with Robbie. Unfortunately, by that time, Robbie had lost interest in me and had taken up with another girl. As if that wasn't bad enough, she lived in my dorm. What utter humiliation, to have engineered such a complicated move only to end up having to watch the boy I loved kissing another girl at the dormitory door on Saturday nights!

The event that led to my discovery of Robbie's infidelity eludes me today. I suppose that some scenes are better left unremembered. The image that stays with me is a day of mourning down by the riverside where I sat for hours, crying and writing bad poetry about unfaithful lovers. It must have been cathartic; I remember returning to the dormitory with a resolution to put the pain behind me.

My capacity to deal with psychic pain developed early in life and served me well at times such as these. Ever since I can remember, I lived with a sense that no one could seriously hurt me because my inner self, my core, was never truly touched by others, no matter how intimate the relationship. When occasionally someone did reach me, as Robbie had, I found another means of protection. After the initial shock, a blanket of numbness would descend on me, and I would no longer feel the pain of loss.

Previous experience had taught me that male attention would take some of the sting out of Robbie's rejection and help me to move on. Meeting boys was not difficult in a college town where the male-to-female ratio was overwhelmingly in my favor.

Robbie had introduced me to some of his college friends a few months before my transfer to Russell Sage. By the time I arrived in Troy, I had a small circle of male friends. After Robbie and I broke up, I maintained some of those relationships. It pleased me to think that the guys whose opinion Robbie valued were interested in me. His best friend Fernando* became my special friend as well. Fernando was an exchange student from Brazil who had come to America to study engineering. Fernando was a nobleman, a count, who hailed from a family that wielded a great deal of power and influence in several cities in Brazil. He was the youngest of three children. A popular magazine had featured a story about his two older sisters who were members of high society in Rio de Janeiro. Meanwhile, Fernando's parents were worried about their young son, who seemed dangerously close to becoming a playboy and an alcoholic. I have a clear memory of Fernando in his navy blue paisley bathrobe answering the doorbell one Sunday morning with a martini in his hand. Fernando was charming and more sophisticated than any twenty-year-old I ever met. Later that year, he was involved in a car accident—driving while intoxicated. His parents shipped him back home, and I lost a friend.

I didn't have many to spare. At Russell Sage, I felt like an alien. The place was more like a finishing school than an institution of higher learning. Most of the girls were biding their time until Mr.

---

*Name changed.

Right appeared. Dressed in their pleated preppy skirts and circle pins (those were very popular that year) they were ready for him. Except for the fact that I found myself at Russell Sage because of a guy, I had little in common with my fellow students. If I attempted an intellectual conversation, it was usually met with a glazed stare and a rapid change of subject. In that sea of future Stepford wives, meaningful friendships were hard to find. Eventually, I did discover some kindred spirits among those who were considered misfits like myself.

From the very beginning, I seemed to be out of step with everyone else. When I first arrived, I came to the dining room in a dressy outfit and small heels, only to find my peers casually dressed. By the weekend, I got the hang of it and dressed more casually—only to discover that Sunday was dress-up day at Russell Sage.

The "dramatic look" that appealed to me in those days—eyes heavily rimmed with black eyebrow pencil, pale lips, and long dangling earrings—was common in New York City among certain artistic types but rare at Russell Sage. I was once called down to my dorm mother's room and admonished for looking like a beatnik. Imagine that prune-like lady with ice-blue eyes and hair to match accusing me of looking strange! But in 1960, white hair with a bluish tint was the height of fashion for a dorm mother while dark eye shadow without lipstick was the sign of rebellion in a student.

There were all kinds of rules, some written, some understood. One hot day in late spring, I wore a pair of shorts. As I stepped outside of the dorm and headed for the library, one of my dormmates suddenly swooped down on me covering me with a trench coat. From her window, she had seen me crossing the street and realized that I was headed for serious trouble in my shorts. "Russell Sage girls never wear shorts on the street," it said in the rules of conduct handbook, which I hadn't read.

The physical surroundings were also different from what I was accustomed to. There was not much of a campus in this run-down city of Troy, but the school buildings and dormitories had an old-world charm about them. Our dorm was a Victorian mansion, beautifully decorated with antique furniture. We met the boys who came to call in the parlor or sitting room. Weekly convocations were held in a chapel. It was a piece of Americana that was foreign to me, a world that I did not feel myself a part of but could appreciate nevertheless. I felt enriched by the experience.

Still, when the year came to an end, I had had enough of Russell Sage. If I chose to remain another year until graduation, I would have to apply for additional financial aid and go further into debt. By now it was clear that Robbie was a lost cause. The new fellow in my life, Charly, was returning to New York City for graduate school. Besides, I was missing the stimulating, intellectual atmosphere of City College. All things considered, it felt like the time to return home.

By my senior year, I was back at CCNY and living at home once again. Readjustment was not difficult. In fact, I appreciated the college much more the second time around and felt that I truly belonged in that liberal, intellectual community. Psychology courses had been among the most interesting subjects at Russell Sage, but course offerings were limited. At CCNY, there were more options and better teachers.

My mother seemed pleased to have me at home. As for my father, he was preoccupied with his own studies. He had enrolled at Baruch, the business branch of City College, where he was taking evening courses toward a bachelor of business administration (BBA). I find it remarkable to think that a man who had been through so much, at the age of sixty, was able to mobilize himself to undertake a rigorous course of study with youngsters about a third his age. I don't believe that the degree was necessary for him to practice his occupation. He was a college graduate and had the papers to prove it. But he wished to have a degree from the United States. Some of the credits he had accumulated in Europe were transferred toward the BBA but not many; he had years of part-time study ahead.

He immersed himself in his work with great dedication. He had always enjoyed learning and developing his mind. In Europe, even after earning a college degree, he had continued to take courses at an institute of higher learning until the advent of war. Now he was in his element again, doing what he loved best. Furthermore, his student status gave him an acceptable excuse to distance himself from my mother and me and allowed him to gracefully withdraw from social contacts. Whenever my mother urged him to socialize, he would silence her with, "I have to study. You can go by yourself." She respected his educational aspirations and left him alone.

Whatever the motivation, his achievement cannot be minimized. This man, whose emotional life was so constricted, was able to continue exercising his mind. In that respect, he was more fortunate than many survivors whose lives were forever limited by the traumatic experiences they endured during the war years.

My mother's work history was more typical. Professionally speaking, she seemed to work her way down in the world. In her youth, she had shown great promise. She was the only daughter in her family of origin to have graduated from college. Yet she never made use of her teaching degree. She went from one work situation to another, each requiring less intellect and less skill, until she ended up in a sweatshop doing piecework for a living.

Shortly after we arrived in America, my mother convinced my father to go into business. Her own father had run a successful dry-cleaning establishment, so she encouraged my father to do the same. They took whatever savings they had accumulated up to that point and purchased a cleaning store in the South Bronx. Both of them worked very hard. I remember seeing him bent over the huge pressing machine, sweat pouring down his brow, while she worked the cash register and did tailoring and alterations. But their hard work did not pay off. The dry-cleaning store down the street was franchised and could charge much lower rates. The one across the street had been there longer and had its established clientele. With such stiff competition, it was no wonder that the business operated at a loss and had to be abandoned after a couple of years.

After that failed business venture, my father was able to obtain a secure position working for the city government. As for my mother, she found work in an undergarment factory where she sat at a sewing machine all day long, side by side with other immigrant women, most of them uneducated. It was hard and boring work, but she never complained. She did not value her intellect and had no aspirations for herself. Her fulfillment came from other sources. Her social skills were highly developed, and it was there, in the world of interpersonal relationships, that she found her greatest satisfaction.

My mother always seemed somewhat awed by my own love of learning and dedication to study. "Why do you have to sit for so many hours with your books?" she would ask me in a tone that conveyed a mixture of admiration and pity. "Don't feel sorry for me; I love it," I would answer. "You take after your father," was her conclusion. In that context, though in no other, I was proud to be identified with him.

College years were drawing to a close for me. With a psychology major, graduate school was assumed. No jobs were available in the field of psychology without graduate work. Once again, I did not ponder over choices. City College had an excellent program in psychology on the master's level, so that was where I headed. One step at a time—it was not important to think about the finish line as long as I enjoyed the journey.

Graduation itself was anticlimactic. It never occurred to me to mark that rite of passage with a college ring, a yearbook, or a celebration. I never considered attending the graduation ceremony. My mind was already on the future.

My father raised the issue of rent again. I knew that this time there would be no reprieve; I would have to attend graduate school on a part-time basis and get a full-time job to pay my way. That made the decision to move out easy. If I had to pay rent, I might as well live on my own. My mother was distressed. "It's a shame for a child to move out before she's married," she said. "It's not done; what will people say?"

Eventually, she tearfully acknowledged that she understood how difficult it was to live with my father, and that in my place she probably would do the same. I got her empathy but not her financial support. The next task ahead was to find a job.

In the early 1960s, a shortage of elementary school teachers existed in New York City public schools. As a result, an opportunity was available for graduates from allied disciplines, such as psychology, to enter the profession with a provisional license. I took the licensing exam with the understanding that I would make up several education courses over the following year. In the fall of 1962, upon graduation, I became a kindergarten teacher.

One of my closest friends from high school, Helen, was planning to move to Manhattan and was looking for a roommate. Everything was falling into place.

Selina Weiss, born Lubliner, my mother's mother, who died in 1939 just before the start of World War II. Her name, written across the photograph, is not the one she was known by. Everyone called her Zofia (Zosia); I was named after her.

Simon Weiss, my maternal grandfather, owned his own business in Lwów, Poland. He, like all of my grandparents, died before I was born.

My paternal grandparents, Moses and Sara Reichman, who lived in the *shtetl* of Tluste in prewar Poland. Moses was a barber and a *felczer* (physician without a medical degree), and Sara was a midwife. My grandmother's maiden name was Fuchsberg, and she originally came from Sambor, another town in Galicia.

Rembrandt" LWÓW PASAŽ HAUSMANNA

My mother, Dorota (Donia) Weiss as a little girl in Lwów in the early 1900s.

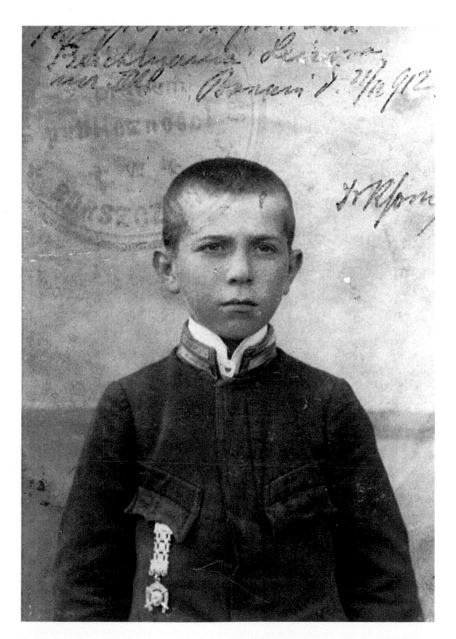

My father, Leon Reichman, as a young boy in December 1912, a couple of weeks before his twelfth birthday.

My mother's oldest sister Salomea (Lucia) with her young son Misio. Aunt Lucia was killed by a bomb fragment in her apartment in Lwów during the German attack on Poland in September 1939. Misio escaped Nazi-occupied Poland by joining the Russian army; and in 1965 he emigrated to America with his family.

My mother's sister Jadwiga (Jadzia) Weiss who was later murdered by the Nazis along with her five-year-old daughter Bianka after they were discovered in hiding.

Marceli (Chesko) Weiss, my mother's youngest brother, on the street in Lwów. Uncle Chesko, his wife Julia, and their three little boys were murdered during the German occupation, probably in Belzec death camp.

Zygmunt Reichman, my father's oldest brother, and his family in Tluste. My father is the young man standing in the back row, far right. Zygmunt and his entire family perished in the Holocaust.

My father's brother Jack Reichman with his wife Sara (Sadie) in the 1920s soon after they came to America. Jack died in New York in 1945 from a brain aneurysm.

My father's sister Henryka Reichman in the 1920s before she left Poland for America.

My parents not long after their marriage in the late 1930s.

This photograph of my mother, which bears the signature Oleszkiewicz, Maria, was part of her false identity papers. The real Maria Oleszkiewicz was a Catholic Pole who died before the war. With the help of a priest, Donia obtained Maria's birth and baptismal certificate and took on her identity from April 1942 until liberation in July 1944.

Copy of document used by my mother to establish her false identity during the war years.

I am about one year old in this photograph taken shortly before we went into hiding. The teddy belonged to the photographer.

In Zimna Woda, a small village near Lwów, in the summer of 1942. A playful moment with the only people who knew our true identity. The three women posing for the camera are, from left to right, my mother, Ewa Donikowska, and Marysia Huppert (the daughter of mother's friend, Jerzy, who found her this hiding place). The man looking on is Tadeusz Witwitcki. The baby in front is me.

In Zimna Woda in the fall of 1942, I am sitting in my mother's lap. The two women in the picture on either side of my mother are Ewa Donikowska and her mother. The men are unknown to me. Of this group, only Ewa knew our true identity.

The religious medal I wore around my neck to pass as a Catholic during my hiding years.

Me as a five-year-old in Chorzów, Poland, in 1946. My hair has been carefully curled for the occasion of the photograph.

A school photograph of me in Paris, France, in 1948.

My fifth grade class, Paris, 1951. Our teacher (standing) Madame La Brude was nicknamed, "Madame la brute" because of her brutal discipline. My best friend, Denise Léger, is the third child in the first row left (checkered smock, arms folded), and I am sitting behind her (button-down sweater, black collar). Not long after this photo was taken, we emigrated to America.

Identity card/passport issued in France for our emigration to the United States in 1951. My mother and I shared the same document.

My graduation picture from the High School of Music and Art in New York in 1958.

Mother and her only surviving brother Marian (Manek) Bialowski when he came from Poland to visit her in America in 1971.

Spyros and I posing like an old-fashioned couple for our wedding picture in 1976.

Irrepressible Lina at age four.

Spyros and I in the late 1980s. Spyros's mustache is his trademark.

Our family recovering on the Island of Ereikousa on the Ionian Sea in Greece, the summer of 1995. Our dear friend Sam Tsemberis took the photo.

Photograph of the painting I did in 1995 titled *Hidden Traumas: Zosia and Lina*. It appeared in *When Memory Speaks: The Holocaust in Art* by N. Toll (Praeger, 1998).

Chapter 11

Illusions of Freedom

The 1960s had begun: a time of upheaval for the nation, a time of questioning and reevaluating everything that was inherited from the past. Young Americans, raised on the belief that they were entitled to make their own decisions, rejected the values of previous generations and challenged the basic premises of the past. Social and political movements sprang up on various fronts. The African-American struggle for social justice gave birth to the civil rights movement; the women's liberation movement challenged sexism in our society; and opposition to the war in Vietnam gave rise to the antiwar movement. Protests often erupted in violence on college campuses and in the streets.

There were profound changes in morals as well. Young people rebelled against what they viewed as a repressed conformist society by advocating a sexual revolution and turning to recreational drugs, such as marijuana and LSD.

The 1960s was a turbulent decade, but it was also a time of idealism and exhilaration. Personal freedoms were dramatically expanded. It was the age of "The New Frontier" and of dreams and hopes for a "Great Society."

For me, it was a new beginning. For the first time in my life, I was truly on my own, making my own decisions and not feeling accountable to anyone but myself. I didn't question the past; I simply didn't think about it. Now that I was no longer living in my parents' house, I didn't need to be confronted with any reminders of my early history.

The Holocaust was so far behind that it didn't seem a part of my world. If the subject of my childhood came up in conversation, I answered questions with facts. "Where were you born?" "In Poland." "When did you come to America?" "In 1951." "Do you have any siblings?" "No, I'm an only child." I never elaborated or volunteered information. If someone pressed, I told the story of my life without emotion, in a matter-of-fact, robot-like way. It was as though I was describing someone else's life. Even my own voice sounded strange to me. The message to the listener was, "Don't ask." Few people did in those days. World War II was a closed subject. The nation was soon preoccupied with the new war in Vietnam.

I was not interested in politics, only in my narrow, circumscribed world of work, school, and friends. Teaching kindergarten was fun and challenging, especially since I had never been formally prepared for the profession. I was fortunate to find myself working side by side with a talented, experienced teacher. The kindergarten classes in the public school in the South Bronx where I was assigned were divided into two sessions, one in the morning and one in the afternoon. Loretta, my fellow teacher, taught the morning class while I assisted; then, we reversed the order in the afternoon. There were about fifty children in each class, one hundred between us—a daunting number, but with Loretta's great skill, quite manageable.

Loretta and I appeared to have little in common. She was an African-American woman a few years older than I who lived in Harlem. Her goal in life was to meet a doctor and to marry as soon as possible. When we first met, she seemed somewhat cool toward me, her manner brusque and matter of fact. Soon, however, she let me see her warm, generous side, and we became good friends.

Teaching was gratifying, but I knew that it was merely an interim job for me—a way to make money to support myself while I studied psychology. I had not forgotten my commitment to Miss Naumburg. As soon as I entered the graduate program at CCNY, I obtained permission to take some art therapy classes with her at NYU.

The classes were interesting, but I soon realized that during my college years I had moved beyond what Miss Naumburg had to offer. As an adjunct technique, art therapy was valuable, but as a discipline, it was limited. In contrast, the field of psychology was boundless and fascinating. I was grateful to Miss Naumburg for having steered me toward psychology. Now I knew I had found my life's vocation.

Many professional choices are available in the field of mental health. What appealed most to me was the idea of helping people to understand themselves and to lead their lives in a meaningful and fulfilling way. I thought about becoming a psychoanalyst. Helen, my roommate, laughed at me. "A psychoanalyst? Are you crazy? Don't you realize how many years of school it takes to become a psychoanalyst?" Helen's words didn't discourage me. I knew that if I wanted to be an analyst, I would make it happen no matter how many years it took. Unlike Helen, who dropped out of graduate school that year, I did not view academic life as a sacrifice of immediate gratification for future gain. I was never big on sacrificing the present for the future. My philosophy, born out of the ashes of the Holocaust, was present oriented. Having grown up in an atmosphere of constant danger, I was aware of the fragility of life and the uncertainty of the future. To me, life was precious and had to be lived to its fullest.

Although I did not concern myself with ultimate goals, I did keep them in mind. A focus on the present with an eye to the future best describes the philosophy I developed by my early twenties. I decided that once I completed a master's degree, I would then consider what to do from that point on. The present was a good place to be. Work and graduate school were stimulating, and my social life was never dull. It was a time of exploration and experimentation.

One day, Loretta invited me to a dance in Harlem. As it turned out, I was the only white person in the room. There, I met Donny, a charming, aspiring actor, who later told me that, at our first meeting in that dimly lit dance hall, he assumed that I was a light-skinned black. It was amusing to me that I, a very fair Caucasian, could be taken for a Negro. The idea of "passing" seemed to hold a special fascination for me; I experienced a slight thrill at the thought that someone could mistake my identity. At the time, I did not connect the fact that my strong reaction probably had its roots in my childhood experience of having successfully passed as a non-Jew.

Donny and I dated for awhile. He introduced me to the world of Harlem and the world of drugs; I smoked my first marijuana cigarette with him. He never pressured me but seemed eager to acquaint me with a world that was new for me. For my part, I was able to contribute to his growth as well. He was struggling with college, a world I felt confident in. I helped him with his term papers. Each of us appreciated what the other could offer. We were both enriched by our encounter. I must confess that I also enjoyed the fact that we made heads turn when we walked down the street together. Back in the early 1960s, it was unusual to see racially mixed couples. I knew that if my parents ever learned of our relationship, they would disapprove. That thought actually gave me a degree of satisfaction. Although I believed myself to be free from their influence, my rebellious attitude suggests that I was still tied to them.

Donny was one of a number of young men I dated at that point in my life. I enjoyed meeting people from cultures different from my own. I was eager to experience as much of the world as possible.

Consciously, I was exhilarated by my freedom. On another level, I was probably anxious about being completely on my own with no one to answer to and no one to set limits. For someone like me, who had grown up in a restrictive, controlling environment, freedom was a mixed blessing. Without awareness, I took steps to end my state of freedom prematurely. Fourteen months after moving out of my parents' home, not yet twenty-three years of age, I got married.

My mother's attitude probably influenced me more than I realized at the time. Referring to my decision to marry, she once said, "In your condition, you had to get married." No, I was not desperate or pregnant, but, according to Mother, an unmarried girl living away from her parents' home was in a vulnerable position and needed to find a husband as soon as possible.

I met Mark* in my first year of graduate school. He was a muscular, nice-looking young man with angular features and lively hazel eyes that reminded me of my father's eyes when the sunlight shone on them. With his dark complexion and very curly jet black hair, he looked more like a light-skinned black man than a Jew. He had taken on the role of class clown in our physiological psychology class. His loose associations and playful manner kept everyone laughing. "Do fish ever get thirsty? Do they drink the water?" he once asked the professor. I was drawn to his spontaneity and lack of inhibition; it was a striking contrast to my own reserve.

Before the end of the semester, we had begun to date, and six months later we were married. The fact that I lost my virginity with Mark three months before our wedding probably had something to do with my decision to marry him. Though it was the early 1960s, 1950s morality still reigned supreme. "Nice girls" like me did not shed their virginity easily. I had managed to hold on to it through the years of sexual awakening and exploration. But now that I had finally gone "all the way," I needed to legitimize it with marriage.

We married in November 1963. It was an impulsive decision. Mark's parents were simple, uneducated people who owned a small

---

*Name changed.

clothing store in the Bronx. They were pleased that their twenty-five-year-old son was getting married. They were Jews without much of a Jewish identity, but somehow we ended up with a religious ceremony held in a rabbi's chambers. It was a small wedding with only the immediate family members attending; my father was conspicuously absent. He complained that we had not given him sufficient time to request a day off from work. Furthermore, he would have preferred a secular ceremony since he did not approve of religious weddings, and finally, he was not impressed with my choice of mate.

I took the afternoon off from teaching and got in trouble for it. Mrs. Kennedy, the principal of the school, admonished me for being irresponsible. I felt her reaction was unreasonable, since I had made sure that the afternoon class was covered. Several weeks later, one of the teachers assigned to the other kindergarten class came running into my room shouting, "Kennedy's been shot!" For a brief moment, I felt a hint of satisfaction; justice was served. However, the victim turned out to be John F. Kennedy, not my admonishing principal.

The shadow of the great tragedy fell on our wedding celebration. My mother, having planned a party in our honor at her house, had invited some of her friends. Unfortunately, the day turned out to be the very same Sunday set aside for the nation to mourn Kennedy's passing.

Not an auspicious beginning for our marriage, perhaps it was prophetic of events to come. It did not take long for me to realize that Mark and I were a bad fit. At the age of twenty-two, I did not know myself well enough to make a good match. Marrying young was like playing Russian roulette, a dangerous gamble. One had to be lucky to make a wise choice without the benefit of experience and self-knowledge that usually comes with time.

Early marriages were common in those days. In my circle of friends, many were either engaged or in the process of finding a mate right after college graduation. Loretta had approached marriage with the same no-nonsense style with which she approached teaching. She was very clear about goals and objectives and had no difficulty implementing her strategy. During the year that we taught together, she met her doctor and married him in June at the close of the school term. After a splendid wedding reception at the Tavern on the Green in New York City, the couple headed south where a new job awaited the young doctor. Loretta and I lost track of each other; I never learned if she was one of the lucky ones at marriage roulette.

As for me, I was definitely not lucky. What I initially admired in Mark, namely his spontaneity, I came to perceive as impulsivity and immaturity. I had realized that Mark was a troubled soul even before we married. He told me that he suffered from chronic depression as a teenager. The knowledge of his troubled history did not deter me from marrying him. On the contrary, I was drawn to him even more, for it stirred my rescue fantasies and evoked the grandiose feeling that my love could save him from his suffering. Having lived with survivors, I was intimate with psychic pain. I derived a sense of importance and self-esteem from being able to help and heal.

Mark's depression, however, was perplexing. His suffering was well masked. In social situations, he was the life of the party, an entertainer who could make a room full of people laugh with abandon. He performed in comedy clubs, at first as an amateur, later for pay at resort hotels in the Catskills. He added magic to his comedy routine and regaled audiences with clever tricks and sleight of hand. He was never at a loss for words—the larger the audience, the better his spirits. At home, however, he was morose and silent much of the time.

The pleasure Mark derived from his avocation was in stark contrast to the discontent he felt in his daily work. Like me, he earned his living teaching elementary school, but, unlike me, he lacked the long-term goals to give him direction. He soon dropped out of graduate school and seemed resentful and envious of my own professional commitment.

The depth of Mark's hateful feelings toward me were expressed one day in a way that shocked and frightened me. He was in the habit of using marijuana to deal with his troubled feelings. After my brief experimentation with "grass," as we called it then, I did not feel the desire to smoke, and I rarely joined him. On that particular occasion, I watched him smoke several joints. Suddenly, he slipped into a strange agitation. "Sophia, I'm scared," he said. "Take the knives away so I can't hurt you." I was confused and hesitated. "Get the knives out of the drawer! Get rid of them!" he shouted at me. "Let's get out of here," I said, trembling. "Let's leave until it wears off." We walked the streets in our neighborhood until he felt that he was back in control. After that bad trip, he stayed away from drugs, but the incident left its mark on me. I never felt quite safe with him again.

Our relationship was deteriorating. I felt lonely and isolated. I turned to friends for emotional support. Anita, my high school friend, was having marital problems of her own, and we found comfort in each other's company. My roommate, Helen, who had moved out when Mark moved into the apartment, was supportive as well. But the person I found most empathic was my mother. It had been many years since I felt that I needed her, and she seemed to thrive on that situation. Now we had something in common—a bad marriage. Although I'm certain that she could never acknowledge the truth of it to herself, I believe that she derived some satisfaction from my miserable marital condition. It brought us together; we could commiserate about our disappointment in men.

On the surface, my mother was pleasant to Mark, but her hostility was evident. One day at a gathering at her house, she stared at his new fashionable footwear and loudly exclaimed, "Mark, what a beautiful pair of shoes you have on!" Then in Polish, under her breath, she added, *Ohydny buciki*—hideous shoes. Her friends laughed. Mark, of course, did not get the joke. So I translated, while my mother cringed. My relationship with Mother was close, but we clashed regularly on the issue of her deceptive ways. She seemed to get pleasure from creating illusions and nourishing secrets, while I hated anything that hinted of dishonesty. Since my adolescence, I had committed myself to exposing her lies, half-truths, and manipulations.

When it came to the issue of honesty, my parents were direct opposites. My father told the unembellished truth at every opportunity, regardless of how insensitive or brutal it might sound. He seemed to lack social grace and often alienated people. Personally, I found his honesty refreshing and preferred it to my mother's dissembling; at least I could trust his words and not have to read between the lines. On reflection, I wonder if his directness was less a matter of lacking the social skills to get along in the world and more an expression of his impatience with the niceties of social intercourse.

My father did not like his son-in-law and made no pretense about it. I did not expect otherwise. He never had approved of any of the young men that I had dated and let me know that, as far as he was concerned, Mark was the worst of the lot.

Father resented the fact that soon after our marriage we purchased a Volkswagen, a German car, and he refused to ride in it under any circumstances. Fifty years later, the connection between the Volkswagen and the Nazi war effort has come to light. We now know that Jews provided slave labor for the automobile factories of the Third Reich. In fact, it is said that the "people's car" was conceived by Hitler who reportedly helped with the original design. Today, I understand my father's feelings; at that time, I was oblivious to such matters and perceived it as another eccentricity.

I regret that I did not appreciate some of my father's finer qualities. He was a man of strong convictions and ideals. He once proudly showed me that he was a card-carrying member of the NAACP (National Association for the Advancement of Colored People) and a member of Amnesty International, an organization that fights political oppression the world over. The fact that Leon Richman, the most stingy individual I have ever known, was willing to pay dues to any organization spoke to the level of his commitment to such worthy causes. It surprised me and made me realize that there was much about him that I did not understand.

There were precious few traits that I valued in my father. The one characteristic that I truly admired in him was his love of learning and his commitment to complete his education. In 1964, he graduated from CCNY at age sixty-three with a bachelor of business administration, just one year before I received my master's degree from the same institution.

After completing my degree, I was finally ready to enter the mental health field. A wonderful opportunity came up. Hunter College was looking for a testing assistant, someone to provide psychological testing and counseling to students. It was a faculty position. When I was offered the job, Mark became upset. "It's only part-time; we can't afford it," he declared. "It's twenty hours a week, and it will give me time to work toward a PhD," I responded. "But you can make more money in teaching," he argued. "I know," I said, "but this is an investment toward the future." He wouldn't budge.

This concern about money was reminiscent of my father's preoccupation. I was beginning to fear that I had unwittingly chosen a man who had a lot more in common with my father than I cared to realize. I had been so determined to make a different choice for myself and yet had somehow found a man who shared my father's worst characteristics and had none of his redeeming qualities. The irony of that situation was hard to bear.

I did not feel that Mark had my best interests at heart. Deep down, I believed that his objections were not really about money but about a concern that I would outdistance him professionally and ultimately leave him behind.

I took the position at Hunter College in spite of Mark's objections. He found ways to get back at me. One day, when he picked me up after work and we headed down the long staircase leading to the first floor, he suddenly climbed on the banister and slid down like a mischievous nine-year-old. I was mortified. I looked around furtively. What if someone saw him? Another faculty member or one of my clients? How would I introduce him? "This is my husband Mark, the overgrown child who slides down the banister yelling 'WHEEE.'" I had enough trouble feeling like a mature faculty member myself. At twenty-five, I looked about fifteen years of age; people were constantly mistaking me for a student. The previous week, an elevator operator at Hunter College had ordered me out of the faculty elevator, saying, "This is only for faculty members. You have to use the stairs." I had to show him my faculty ID card to prove my status.

As time went on, Mark's passive-aggressive behavior became less passive and more aggressive. His anger was expressed in fits of rage during which he destroyed things that I cherished. The abuse escalated gradually; ultimately, it became physical. The first time he slapped me, I packed a suitcase and left the apartment in tears. I headed to my parents' house in Jackson Heights. The first words my mother uttered when she opened the door were, "Did any of the neighbors see you come in?" She was obviously embarrassed that her daughter's marriage was not going well. With her attitude, I realized that I wouldn't get the support I needed to separate from Mark; I soon returned to our apartment.

One slap led to another and another. The abuse became more frequent and seemed more out of control. After each incident, Mark was contrite and apologized profusely. He promised it would never happen again and declared his love for me. I no longer believed the empty words, but I felt too weak to leave the marriage. It was then that I decided to seek psychotherapy.

Chapter 12

Gathering Strength

I entered the world of psychotherapy with some caution. By the time I reached my twenties, I did not automatically imbue authority figures with wisdom. One of my favorite childhood stories was "The Emperor's New Clothes," in which a child exposes the fact that the emperor is really naked, and the clothes that everyone marvels at are merely figments of a collective imagination. Survivors as a group are wary of those in authority and skeptical about what they offer. I had learned from my parents to treat those in positions of authority with respect without necessarily believing that they deserved it. My experience with my own parents, the original authorities in my life, reinforced the idea that those in power do not necessarily know what is best.

With this attitude, I set out to find a therapist who was worthy of respect. Upon the recommendation of one of my friends, I enrolled in a summer course offered by a psychoanalytic institute on the use of projective drawings in understanding personality. The professor, Dr. Hammer, had edited a wonderful book on the subject, and I was impressed. When I learned that he was my friend's therapist, he seemed like a perfect choice for me.

So began my first therapy experience. Dr. Hammer seemed different in the consulting room than in the classroom. He was more formal and removed, behind his big desk. After our initial session, he asked me to lie down on the couch and report whatever came to mind. He was silent most of the time; once in a while he uttered a pronouncement, which took on great importance, since he spoke so rarely. After forty-five minutes, he made a sound with the drawer of the desk, sliding it back and forth. This signaled the end of the session. Like a trained seal, I got up and left.

I had no clue how this technique would help me with my unhappy marriage. After several months, I quit. Then, I tried again. This time, I approached another friend who said that her former therapist, Dr. Bunsen,* had helped her. He was "especially good with mothers," Annie said, meaning that he had helped her to separate from her own controlling mother. "The only problem," she said, "is that he holds on to patients." Apparently, he had made it difficult for her to leave when she felt ready to. But, for me, at the beginning of therapy, issues of termination were irrelevant. The fact that Dr. Bunsen was affiliated with a low-cost referral service was a definite plus since my earnings of eighty dollars a week limited my possibilities for psychotherapy.

I began working with Dr. Bunsen, a tall, stooped man with a serious demeanor and an uncanny resemblance to the portrait of Sigmund Freud that hung on his wall. The office, located on the Upper West Side of Manhattan, was a dark place on the ground floor and seemed removed from the realities of everyday life. The smell of stale cigarette smoke permeated the air. Dr. Bunsen sat in an easy chair behind a couch, smoking one cigarette after another. He said little, and his face was emotionless. He seemed distant and humorless. Rumor had it that he had once trained to be a rabbi and had opted to become an analyst instead. The rumor turned out to be false, but, in truth, Dr. Bunsen approached analysis as if it were a religion. He was orthodox in his theoretical orientation and faithfully followed the tenets of psychoanalysis as laid down by Freud at the turn of the century.

Once again, unwittingly, I had found my way to a Freudian analyst. In those days, the mid-1960s, many New York psychologists and psychiatrists undertook psychoanalytic training at institutes that were traditional in orientation. There, they were taught psychoanalysis, a specific kind of psychotherapy developed by Freud based on the notion that unconscious mental processes determine much of human behavior. The technique designed to bring to light these unconscious mental processes required the analyst to listen quietly to the free associations of the patient lying on a couch. The patient reported whatever came to mind; the analyst made occasional interpretations and maintained a stance of objectivity and neutrality. The attainment of insight was the therapeutic goal of this endeavor. The analyst subscribed to a specific theory of development and psychopathology and interpreted all associations within that framework. Insight usually meant that the patient would come to understand the nature of the internal conflicts and, as a result, would no longer suffer from neurotic

---

*Name changed.

symptoms. It was not until many years later, when I myself studied the discipline, that I realized that this was only one kind of psychoanalysis—a traditional classical approach that, in my opinion, is limited and limiting.

As defined by the classical orientation, psychoanalysis is a long-term process requiring regular sessions four or five times per week. However, since few patients had the means to take on such a rigorous treatment, most New York analysts also practiced a modified, less intense version called psychoanalytic psychotherapy. In this adaptation, the basic psychoanalytic principles underlying the theory remained, but the frequency of visits was adjusted. I agreed to twice weekly individual sessions and, eventually, to group therapy as well.

In reality, I had little idea about what I was getting into. For instance, I did not know that Freudian analysts discourage patients from making any major changes in their lives while they are in analysis. Since the therapeutic goal is the attainment of insight, the patient is encouraged to talk and analyze rather than to take action. Had I known that, I doubt if I would have signed on. After all, with time, Mark was becoming more violent, and my agenda in therapy was to get out, as soon as possible—both out of the marriage and out of that costly treatment. With my part-time income, even a low-cost treatment was expensive.

Dr. Bunsen was more interested in my past than in the here and now of my life. He encouraged me to talk about my relationship with my parents. I was happy to oblige. It was gratifying to have someone bear witness to the frustrations of my childhood and adolescence. I valued the opportunity to talk about myself to someone who seemed truly interested. When it came to his interpretations, I sometimes had the distinct impression that he was trying to fit me into some preconceived notions. For example, he was hard pressed to apply the ubiquitous Oedipal complex, the hallmark of Freudian theory, to my life. The notion that the child is sexually attracted to the parent of the opposite sex and competes with the same sex parent did not fit the experience of my father as the intruder in my life and my mother as my love object. Determined to somehow fit me into the Procrustean bed of his theory, Dr. Bunsen decided that I must have a "reversed Oedipal complex": that I was attracted to my mother and experienced my father as a rival for her affection. Although such an idea may have satisfied his need to make sense of my life, it did little to add to my own self-understanding.

Given the prominent place that psychoanalysis ascribes to early childhood events in determining adult personality, it was striking that in my analysis we rarely touched on the subject of the Holocaust and its impact on my life. I did not intentionally hide my history; I merely mentioned the facts without getting into the feelings. Beyond the description of the events, there seemed to be nothing else to say. At the time, I was totally unaware of the profound and lasting effect of those events, and apparently Dr. Bunsen did not recognize it as a relevant factor in my life either. In that respect, he was no different from most mental health professionals of his day. In general, most clinicians were ignorant of the fact that the impact of the Holocaust on survivors and their children was profound and far-reaching. They failed to recognize that many of the symptoms that presented in therapy actually were related to wartime experiences and their aftermath. Sometimes, the connections were subtle and indirect. It would have taken a special sensitivity to the issues to realize the relationship between the past trauma and the present problems.

Mental health professionals were not immune from the conspiracy of silence that followed the war years. The denial of the significance of the Holocaust was a way to protect against the powerful feelings that lie beneath the surface. Without awareness, therapists colluded with their patients to avoid that painful subject. The fact that so many New York analysts, like Dr. Bunsen, were Jews with roots in Eastern Europe whose distant relatives had perished in the Holocaust, may also have influenced their reactions to those who survived and could bring the horrors directly into the consulting room.

A veil of numbness had surrounded me for years. I had no idea that underneath my composed exterior were powerful emotions waiting to erupt with the proper stimulus. In the second or third year of my analysis with Dr. Bunsen, I joined his therapy group. It met once weekly in his office. One of the members of this group was the son of a survivor. One day, he talked about his father's concentration camp experience. Suddenly, without warning, I began to sob loudly and uncontrollably. The cry came from deep within. I had never cried for my own father yet here I was sobbing for someone else's parent. The outburst felt strange to me. I could make no sense of it nor use it as a means to enter a world that 1 had buried away. I merely noted it as a sign that there must be unresolved feelings lurking behind my smooth facade. Although the experience remained isolated and undigested, it heralded an important change. The icy numbness was beginning to thaw. From that time on, every once in a while and with increasing frequency, my emotions would erupt without warning. A word or image relating to the Holocaust could trigger tears that appeared disconnected from conscious thought.

The analysis continued for years. It seemed endless. Meanwhile, life went on. I continued living in my unhappy marriage with occasional outbursts and crises when Mark would go on a rampage, after which I would search for apartments to rent. The few times that I did attempt to end my marriage, I received no encouragement from Dr. Bunsen. On this issue, he seemed neutral. His interpretations were meant to enlighten me, not empower me. At the beginning of my analysis, I had found an apartment in Queens and was prepared to sign the lease. Nervous about making an independent decision of this magnitude, I asked my mother to meet me there on my lunch hour so that she could check the place out. When I brought up the subject in my next session, Dr. Bunsen pointed out that I was overinvolved with my mother and that my need for her approval was neurotic. Although his observation was undoubtedly correct, it reinforced the feeling that I was not ready to take such a major action on my own and discouraged me from moving. I gave up the apartment and remained with my husband.

Periodically, I made other feeble attempts to leave Mark. The truth is that I could barely support myself with my part-time job and had no other means of financial support. Back then, spouse abuse did not get the press it receives today. It was not recognized as a prevalent social evil, and few supports existed for battered women. In my characteristic defense style, I minimized the seriousness of the situation. It was not a beating, I said to myself, only a slap, a push, or a punch—nothing to be alarmed about. Besides, neither my parents nor my analyst seemed concerned about my situation.

Therapy, which I originally pursued to find the strength to leave my marriage, was, paradoxically, making it easier for me to stay in it, for it provided me with an outlet for my feelings of despair. Moreover, the fact that other sources of satisfaction existed in my life also helped to make it more tolerable. My work at Hunter College was gratifying, particularly as I began to take on more responsibility. Students were seeking me out for personal counseling, and my supervisor was encouraging me to work with them. At first, I was uneasy with the idea that I, with troubles of my own, was called upon to help others with their problems in living. But my supervisor's faith in me, combined with the positive feedback I was receiving from my clients, gave me the confidence I needed to counsel others. In my work setting, I was able to feel competent and valued.

By 1966, I was enrolled in a PhD program in psychology at New York University and enjoyed the classwork and the community of fellow doctoral students. I spent many hours in the library where I found refuge from my unhappy home life. My academic world, unlike my volatile marriage, was predictable and within my control.

My mother and I were gradually drifting apart. I no longer confided in her, since I now had someone else to tell my troubles to. My analytic work was helping me to distance myself from her and see her in a more objective way. She was disappointed with the growing distance between us, but life brought her consolation. It came with the arrival of her beloved nephew, Misio, the son of her eldest sister who had left Lwów with the Soviet army in 1941 at the start of the German occupation. He survived in Russia and, unlike most of my relatives, he had the opportunity to actively fight against the Nazis. After the war, he returned to Lwów and settled there with his Russian bride, Olga. By the time he returned to Lwów, we had already left for Chorzów in Poland. It was my mother's fervent hope that, someday, we would all be reunited in America. That hope was realized during the 1960s when Misio, his wife, and their two adolescent sons arrived.

I was excited to meet my cousin Misio and his family. Unlike most people who have a sense of themselves as members of an extended family from the beginning of their lives, I lacked that experience and longed for it. In my childhood years, the only family I knew were my parents. The three of us were an isolated unit in a world devoid of blood relations. Then, very gradually, relatives began to surface from distant parts of the world. First, I met my Aunt Henrietta when she came to visit us in Paris; then, when we arrived in America, we were greeted by my two cousins, Eugene and Abe, and their families. These were the sons of my father's brother, Jack, who had emigrated to the United States in the 1920s.

For reasons unknown to me, Father quarreled with his nephews and, before long, they disappeared from our lives. For many years, the only relative who was part of our small family circle was Henrietta, my father's sister. Now, with Misio's arrival, there was once again an opportunity for the extended family experience that had been missing in my life. My mother was ecstatic with joy. She doted on her nephew as if he were her long-lost son. My father was not especially impressed with him. He hated his conservative politics but tolerated him for my mother's sake.

Surprisingly, my cousin and I did not seem to have much to talk about. The subject of the Holocaust was avoided for the most part. No one seemed interested in the past. Misio, who now called himself Martin, and his family were determined to get Americanized as fast as possible. After having lived under communist rule for so many years, they embraced capitalism without reservation and set out to fulfill their American dream.

The 1960s were drawing to a close. The atmosphere was charged. Everyone around me seemed to be protesting. The reaction against the war in Vietnam was gaining momentum, particularly in colleges around the country. It was an interesting, stimulating time to be working in a university setting. As a faculty member, however, I found myself in the odd position of representing the establishment when, in fact, my sentiments were with the students and their struggles. A number of the males coming into the counseling center where I worked were attending college primarily to obtain a student deferment from the draft. Other young men were fleeing to Canada for the same reason. Mark himself had narrowly escaped induction into the army. Because of his psychiatric history, he was classified as "Four F" and exempted from service.

The entire society was in a state of unrest. Various disenfranchised groups were fighting for power: blacks, women, students. The times were exciting, but I also found them somewhat frightening. I had a strong reaction to angry confrontations between people on opposite sides of the issues, particularly when they took place at mass rallies. At the time, I made no conscious connection to the violence of my childhood, yet I knew that my feelings of anxiety were unusually strong—so strong that I walked out of meetings when I sensed the explosive tensions in the air.

In 1968, as the SDS (Students for a Democratic Society) were blowing up buildings to make their point, I took a full-time position as a counselor at New York University. I have a vivid memory of standing in the street in Washington Square in front of the Counseling Center as a group of police in helmets, armed with clubs, menacingly marched toward a mob of students who were shouting curses at them and carrying a banner protesting the war in Vietnam. As the two groups approached each other, I was flooded with emotion. Tears came to my eyes and my heart pounded. I wanted to run away, but I felt rooted to the spot, unable to move.

Finding employment at New York University, where I was working toward my PhD, was a fortuitous move. Not only was it a full-time position with an adequate salary and benefits, but, more important, it entitled me to tuition remission, which meant that I could obtain an expensive graduate education for free. At last, I was in a position where I could support myself adequately and seriously consider a divorce.

The pressure to leave Mark was mounting. Even my body began to protest. I awoke one morning with a spasm in my neck so severe that I could not turn my head in any direction. My therapist said, "You're holding your anger in your body like a cornered animal that arches its back when it's attacked." His comment made sense; anger in my marriage had to be contained. Confrontations with Mark were like forays into a minefield, a mere step away from a deadly explosion.

The insight, however, did not cure the pain in the neck. Eventually, I went to see an orthopedist who was not impressed with psychological theories about psychosomatic symptoms and found a physical basis for my problem. "It's a worn disk," he declared pointing to the X ray. He recommended a neck brace and heavy dosages of Valium. Then, he told me that I reminded him of Barbara Harris, the actress in *A Thousand Clowns,* and that, incidentally, she was one of his favorite actresses. It seemed an odd thing to say. Later that week, a mysterious package arrived at the Counseling Center from Saks Fifth Avenue addressed to me. Inside was a bottle of expensive perfume, body lotion, and dusting powder, and a card from the good doctor with best wishes for a speedy recovery. It finally dawned on me that the middle-aged married man was making a pass. I received it with a mixture of feelings. I was surprised, flattered, and disturbed, all at the same time.

When I talked about my discomfort with the orthopedist's advances, Dr. Bunsen said, "You can't handle the attention of a mature man." Is he encouraging me to have an affair? I wondered. I had no intention of complicating my life with an affair. But, in truth, it was nice to know that someone found me attractive. It reassured me that the breakup of my marriage did not have to mean a lonely existence.

Whether it was the Valium, the neck brace, or the orthopedist's attention that made the difference, the pain in my neck eventually subsided. Perhaps it was because I finally left Mark, the real pain in my life.

After the many aborted attempts to separate, it was difficult to identify the actual moment when I knew that there was no turning back. I was ready. In late December 1969, before the beginning of the new decade, I found an apartment in Washington Square Village, the New York University housing complex. I paid my first month's rent, and left Mark within the week. Nervous about his reaction, I moved in with my cousin Martin and his wife Olga until the end of the month, when my new lease went into effect. Then, on a cold January morning, while Mark was at work, I packed up my half of our belongings—one of our two cats, one night table, one chest of drawers, and a single bed. As I left, I glanced at the double headboard with a twin bed on one side and an empty space on the other, a lasting image of a ruptured relationship. As I sat in the front seat of the moving van, sandwiched between two brawny moving men, one of them said to me, "So, you're leaving your husband, eh? You'll be back." "No," I said. "I don't think so."

Chapter 13

On My Own Again

Mark stood by the large plate glass window in my new apartment overlooking the well-manicured garden in Washington Square Village. Night had settled on the city, and the lights glowed in the tall buildings surrounding us. "What if I were to jump?" he asked without emotion. His question hung in the air. I thought to myself: Is he serious? Is he threatening me? Would he really jump from my thirteenth-floor window? I had no idea how to respond. Should I laugh, call his bluff, or reassure him that I still cared about him and didn't want him to hurt himself? When I didn't react to his satisfaction, he tried another approach: "My therapist says I'm suffering from clinical depression. If he hospitalizes me would you visit me?" He glanced at me to see my reaction. I tried to hide my emotions. "Yes," I answered matter-of-factly.

Mark certainly knew how to create a drama. I steeled myself against being drawn into it. I truly felt sad that he was having such a rough time with our separation, but I was not willing to feel guilty or give up my hard-won freedom. It was difficult to believe that I had spent six years of my life with this man who seemed a stranger at that moment as he stood in my studio apartment threatening to jump out of the window and trying desperately to exert an impact, to elicit a bit of sympathy from me. In the beginning of our relationship, there had been an implicit understanding that I would rescue him from his depression. Now, I was breaking the silent pact; I was saving myself instead. After many tears and four years of psychotherapy, I was no longer remotely interested in playing that role.

For the first time in my life, I was living on my own, with no roommate, no boyfriend, no husband, or parents. Whatever apprehensions I might have had initially about living alone, I found myself enjoying my freedom. I felt safe in my apartment. Washington Square Village was like a college dormitory with private apartments. Surrounded by university staff and faculty, I felt a part of a community. My office was around the corner, and classes were all within walking distance.

I began to date a college professor in the English department who also lived in the housing complex. I went out with other interesting men that I met in the course of my daily life. I was in no hurry to start a serious relationship; I had a lot of catching up to do. The 1960s had ushered in a sexual revolution that I had not been a part of, but now I was a single woman entering a new decade.

The course work toward my PhD was almost completed by that time, and I had begun working on a dissertation while still living with Mark. Now that I was on my own with less distractions, I was able to concentrate on finishing the work. Always practical, I had chosen a topic that seemed relatively simple to develop. I had no grand ideas about making major contributions to the field. A minor contribution was good enough for me.

In the department of educational psychology where I was enrolled, the subject of individual differences in cognitive styles was particularly popular. It was the topic of a number of doctoral dissertations coming out of that department in the late 1960s. I realized that I could easily build on the work of my predecessors and add to the fund of knowledge in the area.

My particular interest was in a specific dimension of cognitive style, namely, "conceptual tempo." That construct, as defined by the famous psychologist Jerome Kagan, referred to a tendency toward fast or slow decision times on cognitive tasks. Kagan had identified two distinct styles of functioning—one he called "reflective," the other, "impulsive." In numerous experiments conducted with school-age children, he was able to demonstrate that the tendency to be reflective or impulsive was stable over time and affected the quality of performance on a variety of intellectual tasks. Kagan theorized that anxiety over task competence is a basic factor in conceptual tempo differences. For the impulsive, the source of anxiety derives from the expectation that he or she will be judged incompetent if responding too slowly. For the reflective, the concern is about making mistakes. The greater the fear of making a mistake, the more reflective and cautious the performance.

Although most researchers agreed that functioning at either extreme of the conceptual tempo was a sign of rigidity and therefore not desirable, Kagan's work highlighted the advantages of a reflective style over an impulsive one. Reflectives are better problem solvers and perform more accurately on complex tasks.

I found this research interesting and realized that it had personal significance for me. I had always thought of my tempo as notably slower than that of the average person. In a culture that equates speed of thinking with intelligence, my tempo was no source of pride. Furthermore, I had often felt somewhat handicapped in academic settings when taking standardized tests under timed conditions.

The notion advanced by Kagan, that a slow tempo is actually a function of a reflective personality and cognitive style and that it is to be encouraged, was a novel and reassuring idea. What I had experienced as inhibition, he cast in a positive light and labeled reflectiveness. I was eager to explore the topic further. I decided to extend his work to a college population and to test my idea that timed conditions of testing actually discriminated against those with reflective styles of functioning.

Since part of my work as a counselor of students involved teaching freshman seminar classes, I had access to a pool of willing subjects for my experiment. I developed a straightforward study, not especially glamorous but scientifically sound and relatively simple to conduct. The goal was to determine the effects of individual differences in conceptual tempo on abstract reasoning performance under varying conditions. The results supported my expectation that the imposition of a time limit on the abstract reasoning task was more detrimental to the scores of reflective than to those of impulsive students.

At the time that I conceived and developed this dissertation topic, I was not aware of its deeper psychological significance for me. Although I realized that my style was reflective and cautious, I did not fully appreciate its connections to my hidden childhood until recently. Now I realize that my conceptual style probably had its genesis in the hiding experience and was born of self-preservation. Thus I learned early in my life that mistakes were to be avoided at all costs. I was carefully taught to watch, to take in, to weigh potential consequences, to hold back my responses. Impulsivity under such circumstances could mean death; on some level I understood the danger, even as a toddler.

The experience of writing a dissertation was the most interesting and gratifying part of the entire doctoral process. I had a good relationship with my carefully chosen doctoral committee. The chairman, Dr. Ralph Goldner, had a paternal attitude toward me. He was as eager to see me graduate as I was. Only once did he and I strongly differ.

In order to keep the study simple, I had limited my sample to female students. When I wrote up my results, I used the female pronoun when referring to my subjects. "You can't use the female pronoun when you're writing a scientific paper," he said. "You must use the universal masculine gender," he insisted. "Do you mean that I have to write 'he' when I mean 'she?'" I asked incredulously. "Yes; that's the correct form." I protested, but he stood firm. I was not about to get into a power struggle with someone who had all the power. So, dutifully, I changed every feminine pronoun to a masculine one. I am certain that a few short years later Dr. Goldner could not have insisted on this antiquated style and gotten away with it, for our society was becoming sensitive to signs of male chauvinism wherever they were found.

I handed in the completed dissertation by the beginning of the summer of 1970 and scheduled my oral defense for the fall. The Counseling Center was closed for vacation. The summer stretched out before me. It was the first summer of my liberation. Mark had always been reluctant to travel. Now that there was no one to hold me back, I decided to spend the summer in Europe. It was an exciting time, and I felt so free that it made me uneasy. Would all this success and happiness come to an end? I worried that the plane would crash on my way to Europe and I would never obtain my PhD.

Apprehensive about traveling on my own, I planned the trip with a friend, a hippy type with long straggly hair who always looked as if he needed a bath. Before long, we realized that we were incompatible traveling companions and parted ways in Paris.

When I reflect on my visit to Paris, the first since I had left for America in 1951, it surprises me that I had no desire to see the places where I had lived as a child or connect with the people I had known during the five years I had lived there. Apparently, the past had no conscious interest for me then. I was eager to explore new avenues and to have adventures. I had no set plan of travel and allowed chance meetings and spontaneous impulses to set my course. My reflective style notwithstanding, I was letting impulse guide me.

Despite my parents' warnings to stay away from German soil, I ended up spending more time in Germany that summer than anywhere else. After leaving Paris, I decided to take a side trip to visit Martin's son Serge, who was stationed at an army base near Stuttgart. My parents were distressed, but I was immune to their reaction. As I was growing up, in my family, the word "German" was synonymous with evil. With my limited knowledge of my parents' experiences, the intensity of their feelings seemed to be an overreaction. From my vantage point, the idea that one would boycott Germany and German made things made no sense. Perhaps if they had been more forthcoming about their personal traumas during the Holocaust, I might have understood their reaction and been more empathic to their feelings.

I left my cousin Serge in Stuttgart and headed for Venice, a place I had always wanted to see. On the night train, I shared a compartment with a young woman and her brother. We took an instant liking to each other and before long were engaged in conversation. I learned that Christina was an American stationed at an army base in Germany, not far from the one I had just left. She worked for the USO and had a lot of time off for traveling. She was taking a brief vacation and spending it with her younger brother visiting from the United States. By the time we arrived in Venice, we were friends, and Christina invited me to return to Germany to spend a few days with them at the army base and then to travel together in Germany and Austria. It was a generous and intriguing offer, and I took her up on it.

With Christina as my guide, I explored Southern Germany and was charmed by the beauty of Bavaria. After an excursion to Salzburg, a picture-postcard town in Austria, Christina offered to introduce me to Berlin, both East and West. We crossed over at Checkpoint Charlie and entered the strange world of East Berlin. It was colorless and dismal, as if time had stood still since World War II. It was a striking contrast to the thriving, cosmopolitan metropolis of West Berlin on the other side of the wall.

At the end of August, I returned to the United States with rich memories and a marvelous sense of freedom. I had successfully met the challenge of traveling on my own and had made lasting friendships along the way. Now, I was looking forward to completing the final step toward my degree.

The news on the home front, however, was disconcerting. I learned that one of the three members of my committee, who had traveled to Europe over the summer, had been arrested on a drug charge. He and his young wife, also a faculty member at NYU, were now languishing in a German jail with no release in sight. I had chosen Dr. John Regan,* a young hip member of the NYU faculty, to serve on my committee because he was smart and knowledgeable about my topic but primarily because he was easygoing and pleasant and would not make trouble at my orals—important considerations for a doctoral student eager to complete her degree. What next? I wondered nervously, visions of the complicated process being stalled just at the finish line. But Dr. Goldner was reassuring. "Don't worry" he said. "John signed off on the project; we can manage without him." I was certainly happy that I had not tangled with Dr. Goldner on the matter of male pronouns.

Germany seemed to be the place on my mind that year. Soon after my return to the United States, I learned that my parents were preparing to go to Saarbrücken, a city in Germany. The circumstances of their visit, however, were totally different from mine or from Dr. Regan's. My father had received a summons from the German government to testify as a witness at the trial of Fritz Gebauer, the notorious Nazi commandant of Janowska. My mother was granted permission to accompany him, and, in November, they embarked on a journey to the one place on earth where they had vowed never to set foot. My mother had returned to Poland by herself in 1961 to reconnect with the few remaining family members still living there. My father had refused to go; Europe held too many bitter memories for him. This journey, however, was different: he was performing a duty for those who had not lived to see justice done.

My father described the trial in his unpublished manuscript.

> When I entered the grand jury location I recognized the accused Gebauer. He was sitting between two lawyers. In the back was the rest of the grand jury, twenty-four gentlemen together with the prosecutor and his staff, about forty people.
>
> I was asked by the head of the jury in what language did I wish to testify. I chose the German language. I had to describe the behavior of the former commandant of the death camp.
>
> Gebauer was already jailed for almost eight years according to the information I got from the German Consulate in Manhattan where I was asked to testify what I knew about the former commandant of the extermination camp in Lwów.

---

*Name changed.

I was asked by the grand jury to mail in my script to the court to be examined. When I stated that the script was coded and that only I myself could read and understand it, the answer was: "Send it in, we will be able to decipher it." I agreed.

My wife got permission to assist at the trial. Also present was the Jewish congregation of Saarbrücken. Two other witnesses were also summoned to testify, but they were not allowed to be at my hearing. At the end of the depositions I had to swear.

Back in New York, I made a copy of my notes and mailed the copy, asking to be informed of the verdict. After a couple of weeks, I got an answer: "The verdict will be published in the local papers." To find out what the verdict was I wrote a letter to the congregation. The answer was: "Sentenced to life."

My parents did not speak of the trial or any of its details with me. I knew, however, that the experience was profoundly meaningful for them. Almost thirty years had passed since my father had encountered Gebauer, one of the monsters responsible for the tortures and deaths of so many at Janowska; the crimes he had witnessed there were forever etched in his memory. I suspect that he chose to testify in German to ensure that Gebauer would understand every word and nuance of his testimony.

On that momentous occasion, Leon Richman had an opportunity to point his finger at his tormentor and see justice carried out. I can only imagine how satisfying and healing this experience must have been for him. I regret that he never discussed his feelings about this experience with me.

Even if my father had attempted to share his experience with me, I probably would not have understood it. I knew too little about Janowska back then. My father had not yet translated or published the book describing life in the concentration camp, and all that I knew about his imprisonment came from the fragments that I overheard at social gatherings with survivor friends. Besides, I was preoccupied with my own life.

Shortly after my return from Europe I became involved in a relationship that was all consuming. I had met Karl,* the object of my affection, through my friend Doris, a member of my psychotherapy group who had been a Catholic nun for most of her adult life. Now at the age of sixty or so, Doris, who had lost her faith along the way, had

---

*Name changed.

made the difficult decision of leaving the convent. She had moved to New York, begun psychotherapy with Dr. Bunsen, and had taken the position of administrator in the Association of Pastoral Counselors. Her job brought her in contact with many young men and women from various religious denominations who were training to be counselors and psychotherapists. One of those young men was Karl.

Karl, who hailed from the Midwest, had been a Roman Catholic priest for a number of years and was beginning to reconsider his life choice. At the age of thirty-nine, he had decided to enter analytic training at the Institute of Religion and Psychiatry, a program preparing priests, ministers, and rabbis to work with clients. For Karl, the institute was an acceptable way out of the priesthood. When I met him in 1970, he had just begun his first year at the institute and was still functioning as a parish priest.

When I first saw Karl, I thought he was the most handsome man I had ever seen outside of the movies. He was tall, well-built, and, with his sculptured features, resembled a young Clint Eastwood. He had an aura of gentleness about him that I found immensely appealing. Years of seclusion in the priesthood had made him shy and slightly uncomfortable in the presence of others, particularly women, but that seemed to add to his charm. When at a loss for words, he resorted to an irresistible radiant smile. He was such a young thirty-nine, both in looks and manner, that it was difficult to remember that he was ten years my senior.

On the surface, we came from totally different worlds; deep inside, on a primitive level, I was no stranger to his religion. In my early years, Catholicism had been an important part of my life; in fact, it had been instrumental in saving it. Faithfully and regularly, my mother had brought me to church in Zimna Woda during those years in hiding. There, she relaxed and enjoyed "the show" as she later referred to it. It was one of the precious few places where she could feel safe. I became as familiar with the sounds and scents of the Catholic Church as with the air I breathed. Perhaps those early traces and the positive feelings associated with the Church made me more open to the possibility of an intimate involvement with someone whose entire life was shaped by Catholicism.

Another noteworthy fact about Karl was his German background. Although it was never an issue between us, I was always aware of it. Was it merely a coincidence that my two most intimate relationships, at that point in time, were with German-Americans? Or was it a way to prove to myself and to my parents that not all Germans should be condemned; that some like Anita, my best friend, and Karl, my boyfriend, were fine individuals.

If my parents did not approve of this match, they kept it to themselves. I knew that they were recovering from their disappointment with my separation. Mark's photograph remained prominently displayed in their front room for a long time, until I finally asked them to remove it. I assumed that my mother wanted to keep up appearances and never told any of her friends about the separation.

Upon my return from Europe, I was in a wonderful psychological place. I felt independent, strong, and free. Mark had stabilized and had settled into his own life. He had consulted a lawyer to formalize our separation and had decided to pursue an annulment of our marriage rather than a divorce. An annulment required some maneuvering since, by that time, we had been married for seven years, but as far as I was concerned, whatever means he chose to end the marriage was fine with me. I just wanted out, the sooner the better.

I began dating Karl casually, but the intensity of his feelings for me were contagious. He threw himself into our relationship with the passion of a first love. In retrospect, I suppose that he relied on this passion to help him separate from the Church, no easy struggle for someone whose entire life had revolved around religion. At thirty-nine, he was still a virgin. I was flattered to be the first woman to play a romantic role in his life. Caught up in the intensity of his feelings for me, I responded in kind. The feelings of love that had been numbed for so long were unleashed. I felt alive.

In October, I passed my oral examination and earned the long-awaited doctorate. In November, the annulment of my marriage became a reality. I was about to turn thirty and I could not envision being in a better place at that stage of my life.

That winter, I broke my ankle on a skiing trip. Daily life became much more complicated. On crutches, even making myself a cup of coffee was an impossible task. Karl offered to give up his own apartment and move into my studio. Living together seemed uncomplicated.

At that point, Karl was still functioning as a priest, although he had petitioned the Vatican for dispensation of his vows, thereby initiating the process of leaving the priesthood. On Sunday mornings, we headed together to the parish where he had been temporarily assigned. On the way, in the car, I often helped him to write the sermon that he planned to deliver that morning. There was something humorous about a godless Jew like me writing Roman Catholic sermons. The idea made me smile but also made me feel somewhat uncomfortable; I was an impostor, deceiving innocent people. When we arrived at the church, I would hang back a few yards to make certain that no one would suspect the nature of our relationship. On the church steps, when parishioners greeted Karl reverently and kissed his hand, my discomfort made me look away. When it came time to take Communion, I watched the others approach the altar. Sometimes I was tempted to go up myself to know what the experience was like, but it felt sacrilegious so I didn't.

Looking back, I realize that, through this strange charade, Karl and I were participating in a reenactment of my early life. We were both in hiding and playing a role, but this time life and death were not at stake for me. Although I was in analysis with Dr. Bunsen at the time, I don't think I had any awareness of the significance of those events and their relationship to my past. Dr. Bunsen was too busy searching for Oedipus to help me recognize and understand the meaning of my choices and my behavior in the context of my Holocaust experience.

Karl himself knew little if anything about my life during the war, since I rarely talked about it. He did meet my Uncle Manek, however, when he came to the United States in 1971 to visit my mother. That was the first time that I too met my Uncle Manek, the only sibling of my mother's who survived the war. The relationship between my mother and her brother appeared somewhat strained. No doubt the ghosts of their murdered siblings cast a shadow in the room. Although Manek was the sibling closest in age to my mother, they had never been emotionally close. He was somewhat of an enigma to her. During his stay, she was bewildered by the extent of his devotion to his adopted religion. As soon as he arrived, he located the neighborhood Catholic church and nothing would dissuade him from his daily visits there.

To me, Uncle Manek at age seventy-one seemed to be a kindly old man with a warm smile and few words. I wondered how he experienced the fact that I was living with a Roman Catholic priest. The subject was not broached. We seemed to have little of substance to discuss. It was the first and last time that I would ever see him. He died in Poland two years later.

Now that my degree was completed, I began to think about the next step professionally. In order to identify myself as a psychologist, I needed to become licensed, so I prepared to take my licensing examination in the fall. My work at the Counseling Center continued to be satisfying, but I realized that I needed more training to be a competent therapist. Besides, I found counseling as a specialty to be relatively superficial. I was drawn to psychoanalysis, and I applied to the New York University Postdoctoral Program for psychoanalytic training. It was the natural choice for me over other institutes for it had an excellent reputation, and, as an NYU faculty member, I was entitled to total tuition remission—an offer one could hardly refuse with the high cost of analytic training.

My professional life in place, Karl and I headed to Europe in the summer. My visit there the previous year had been so wonderful that I wanted to repeat it and share it with Karl. I was beginning to have a sense that his feelings for me were undergoing a change. He seemed more distant. It was subtle; he denied it, but my sensitive antennae were picking up static. I hoped that traveling together would bridge the growing distance.

By the time we returned to the United States, the static had turned to cacophony. Traveling together had created more tension and widened the gap between us. Karl became immersed in his analytic training. In addition to the course work and his own analysis, he was seeing patients at the institute clinic under supervision. We rarely discussed his cases because of ethical considerations of confidentiality, but there was one patient, a young social worker, who seemed to preoccupy him. He was going through some crisis in his work with her, and I developed an uneasy sense that he was overinvolved and having difficulty managing his emotions. Around the time that I experienced the change in Karl, I had a dream.

Walking down a country path, I come across a large tree with strawberries growing on its branches. I reach for the most beautiful one and pick it off the tree. As I am about to eat it, I suddenly realize that only its front is beautiful; the other side, the one that had been hidden from view, is totally rotten.

My associations to this dream led me to realize the extent of my growing disillusionment with this relationship. Karl had seemed perfect when I met him, a beautiful man, like an exquisite strawberry, one of my favorite fruits. Now, just a year later, I was looking at the other side of him and found it rotting.

My dream expressed what my unconscious already knew. We broke up soon after. Almost immediately after moving out of my apartment, Karl became romantically involved with Susan,* his patient. It was of little consolation to know that my instincts had been right when I suspected that his involvement with her had crossed the boundaries of a therapeutic relationship. I heard from mutual friends that he terminated working with her and, within weeks, was dating her. Eventually they married. Both continued to practice psychotherapy.

Apparently Karl felt no more bound by the ethics of his profession than by those of the Catholic Church. I realized that the same sense of specialness that had led him to the priesthood, now appeared in a different cloak.

During our final meeting, which took place shortly after our separation, he had the audacity to suggest that we resume dating while he maintained his relationship with Susan. He was surprised that I would have no part of this arrangement. I guess he thought that he could have it all; the man's narcissism was boundless.

It took me a long time to recover from the pain of that betrayal. My usual defenses were no longer as effective as they had been earlier in my life. Perhaps years of therapy had diminished my capacity to cut off my feelings. The month that we broke up, I sat for my licensing examination and had such difficulty concentrating that I worried that I would not pass. Fortunately, I managed to get through it successfully and within the year became a full-fledged psychologist.

That fall of 1971, I began my analytic training and started a small private practice. As before, my work was my salvation. In that arena, I could count on feeling effective and valued. If only my personal life was as satisfying as my professional one! I had to acknowledge to myself that, when it came to serious relationships with men, my judgment left something to be desired. I consoled myself with the thought that at least my relationships were improving; Karl was a better choice than Mark had been. True he had been unfaithful and lacked integrity, but at least he was not physically abusive. Also, more important, this time I had not overstayed. But as my thirtieth year drew to a close, it was clear that I was still a long way from where I ultimately hoped to be in my personal life.

---

*Name changed.

Chapter 14

Healing Relationships

My first year in analytic training was an eye-opener. It was now more than five years since I had first walked into Dr. Bunsen's office on the Upper West Side. For many years, I had assumed that Dr. Bunsen's therapeutic approach was typical and standard. I used him as a model in my own work with college students who came to the NYU Center for personal counseling. I would often think: What would Dr. Bunsen say now? How would he interpret what this person is saying? I found myself emulating his style, even though it didn't feel natural or comfortable. For instance, when I was asked a question, I answered with another question in his tone of voice: "Why do you ask?" I figured that was the way a good therapist handled questions.

Now, as I was exposed to the ideas of other professionals in the field, I was beginning to realize that Dr. Bunsen's responses were only one of many ways of working with people. As I came to understand the nature of Freudian theory, I could see how Dr. Bunsen was influenced by it, but I also noted that others with the same theoretical orientation were less rigid. Not all Freudians were as limited as Dr. Bunsen. My supervisors, my teachers, and other students in the program all offered different approaches to working with people and new ways of understanding psychodynamics and psychopathology.

One of the most important concepts that I learned from my supervisors and my readings was that the relationship with the therapist is a crucial element in psychotherapy. "It is the relationship that heals"— this maxim refers to the fact that the main ingredient determining the success of psychotherapy is the interpersonal relationship that the patient has with the therapist, rather than the therapist's theory. Through the creation of a safe environment, the therapist makes it possible for the patient to engage in deep self-exploration. When a person feels understood and cared about, he or she is able to grow and develop in ways that had been blocked or short-circuited.

These ideas made sense to me. What I valued most in my work with Dr. Bunsen was the opportunity to speak about things that I normally did not share with anyone. Having him interested in what I had to say was gratifying. Unfortunately, I did not always feel understood or appreciated by him. I had been aware for a long time that many of Dr. Bunsen's interpretations fell short of their mark. Furthermore, at times I experienced his detachment and aloofness as a painful rejection.

A particular incident comes to mind. We had a session late in the day one New Year's Eve. As he walked me to the door, I wished him a Happy New Year and, without thinking, tried to give him a hug. He recoiled, as if I had stepped on his toe. I felt ridiculous and apologized. Such moments of spontaneity were rare for me; his response heightened my self-consciousness and reinforced my inhibition.

In his aloofness and formality, Dr. Bunsen was very much like my father. The irony is that my perception of Dr. Bunsen could be interpreted as a classic example of transference. Transference, the concept that the patient displaces his or her feelings from past relationships onto the therapist, is one of the cornerstones of psychoanalysis. So, when I commented to Dr. Bunsen that he reminded me of my father, he was delighted that the analysis was progressing as expected. The reality—that Dr. Bunsen actually had a number of characteristics in common with my father—was never acknowledged. Incidentally, it did not elude me that, to my knowledge, the only professional paper that Dr. Bunsen ever presented was on the subject of money and psychoanalysis.

By the summer of 1972, I had completed a full year of postdoctoral studies and I was well on the way to developing a psychotherapy practice. Patient referrals were coming in regularly from colleagues in the NYU Postdoctoral Program. Furthermore, I had joined a group practice with some graduates from the American Foundation of Religion and Psychiatry that provided support and referrals as well. From time to time, I ran into Karl, who was also involved with the group practice. By then, I had recovered from the pain of our breakup, although the bitterness remained long after the sorrow was gone.

At this point in my life, I had few concerns about my career; it was progressing well. My personal life, however, was another matter.

Now that I was over thirty, the prospect of parenthood was no longer as distant and abstract as it had seemed in my twenties. If I wanted a family of my own, and I did, the time to find a mate was fast approaching. I had been dating regularly but without much enthusiasm. Dr. Bunsen was critical of the men I was dating. One day he said to me, "How is it that none of the men you date make more than fifteen thousand dollars a year?" I was insulted by his remark. First, it was not true; most of the men in my life were professionals with adequate incomes. Second, in my value system, the measure of a man was not in his income. I had never been materialistic nor considered wealth a priority in my life. I was used to taking care of myself; I did not need financial support from a male. Dr. Bunsen's comment highlighted the differences in our values and set the stage for the beginning of the end of our relationship.

One warm day in late July, shortly before Dr. Bunsen's annual August vacation, I left my therapy session and headed for the coffee shop around the corner. That was my usual routine. The neighborhood coffee shop named the American Restaurant by its proud Greek immigrant owners was a perfect place to have lunch and digest my therapy sessions. The place was always busy with bilingual waiters scurrying about. The clatter of dishes and the din of conversation provided a neutral backdrop for my thoughts. I was a regular. Twice a week, at the same time of day, I would head for a table in the back. I knew all of the waiters on that shift. That day, however, there was a new face among them—a beautiful, expressive face with a ready smile. He followed me to the back of the restaurant with a voluminous Greek menu under his arm, all the while grinning at me. I smiled back politely but with reservation. I was not especially interested in making conversation, and I didn't want to encourage his attentions. This was my special time for reflection. The rest of my busy schedule did not afford me the luxury of time for reverie.

I did not need the menu to know what I wanted. I ordered a cold shrimp plate. He took my order then returned, as if he had forgotten to tell me something. "You like shrimp?" he asked. "Yes," I answered, somewhat annoyed by the intrusion. He was oblivious. "Have you ever had a Greek dish called Shrimp Tourkolimano? It's made with whole shrimp, feta cheese, capers, and tomatoes. It's magnificent. You would probably love it."

Why is he telling me this? I wondered. "No, I never have," I answered. "Sounds good."

"The best place in New York to get Shrimp Tourkolimano is in a great new Greek restaurant called Adonis. They have Greek dancing there, too."

"How do you spell that?" I asked, writing it down in my notebook.

He went off to wait on other tables and returned. "I can take you to Adonis if you like."

Oh, now I understood—he was trying to pick me up! He probably doesn't realize I'm much older than he is, I thought. I ignored his offer and smiled uncomfortably.

"My name is Spyros," he continued undiscouraged. "What's yours?"

"Sophia."

"Oh, you have a Greek name," he lit up.

"I know it's Greek, but not in my case." We exchanged a few more words, as he kept returning to my table between serving other customers.

Then, before I left, he attempted to put a pencil and a pad in my hand. "Why don't you write your phone number on here? I'll call you and take you to Adonis."

I declined to take the pencil. "No. Thank you, I'm not interested," I said as gently as possible, not wanting to hurt his feelings.

"Okay. Maybe you'll change your mind. I'll give you my phone number." He scribbled a number down and placed it next to my empty plate. He certainly was persistent.

There was an immensely attractive quality to this young man with the dark curly hair and eyes the color of coal. His handsome physique and chiseled features were reminiscent of Michelangelo's *David,* but this was no marble statue. He exuded life and sexuality.

His eagerness to impress me made me smile. In our brief conversation, he managed to let me know that he was taking the Evelyn Woods rapid-reading course. I guess the metamessage was, "I'm not just a waiter. I'm interested in bettering myself." I was almost tempted to take him up on his offer, but I reminded myself that I did not need another romantic fling. A waiter in his twenties was hardly material for a serious relationship. At thirty-one, there was not much time for me to waste. Dr. Bunsen had recently commented that if I continued on my course of casual dating, I would end up a lonely old woman living with a bunch of cats. I did not want to validate his dire prediction.

Two weeks later, I was shopping in Gimbels department store. I entered the empty elevator; there, following directly behind me, was Spyros, the young Greek waiter. Grinning, he said, "This time I'm not going to let you get away!"

Our chance meeting that day in August 1972 seemed fated. I decided to give fate a chance. With Dr. Bunsen on vacation, I could postpone dealing with difficult questions such as: Why, if I wanted a serious relationship, was I wasting my time with a young man who had just turned twenty-one?

By the time Dr. Bunsen returned from vacation, I realized that Spyros was special and that I didn't want to stop seeing him, at least for the time being. As long as I was focused on the present rather than on the future, I was happy to be with Spyros. When we were apart and I thought about him, I found myself smiling. He was different from the men I had known in many respects. He seemed comfortable with himself and unusually self-assured for someone so young. When he walked me home from Gimbels on that fateful day, and I told him about myself—my former marriage, my profession, and my postdoctoral studies—he said, "Are you trying to discourage me?" I appreciated his candor. Older, more sophisticated men had sometimes been intimidated by my background but not Spyros. His maturity was probably largely due to the fact that he had been working for many years and had assumed adult responsibilities early in his life. In fact, it seemed that he had gone directly from childhood to adulthood, bypassing adolescence.

Most appealing about him was his zest for life and his boundless energy. He never did anything halfheartedly. Previously, I had been attracted to the walking wounded: men who suffered from depression and seemed weighted down by their problems. Spyros approached life with enthusiasm and a great appetite; he devoured life. He was emotional and made no excuses for it. He did not feel that he had to hide his feelings or apologize for them.

His feelings for me were intense, and he was clear and direct about them—no game playing. I had been burned; I was cautious; but, before long, I was swept away once again. Perhaps there was some safety in knowing that the relationship was not going to go too far. At twenty-one, Spyros had no intention of becoming involved in a long-term relationship. I set aside practical considerations and allowed myself to experience the moment fully.

The first time we made love, a dozen long-stemmed red roses arrived the next day with a note, "Gimbels has twelve elevators!"—that was a reminder of our fateful meeting. Later that summer, when I attended a professional conference in Hawaii, he called me long distance from New York to tell me how much he missed me. His generous spirit was evident in his actions. His attitude about money was the antithesis of my father's—money was to be enjoyed, not squirreled away for future calamities.

His life force found its expression in music. He loved Greek folk music with a passion and was eager to introduce me to it. One of his earliest gifts to me was an album titled *The Ballad of Mauthausen* featuring the work of composer Mikis Theodorakis, a famous contemporary Greek composer, who had written a series of songs dedicated to the memory of Greek Jews who had died in the Mauthausen concentration camp during World War II. Spyros was one of the very few people in my life who seemed interested in my Holocaust background and was not dissuaded from asking questions when he received vague responses to his queries. When he met my parents for the first time, he raised the subject with them as well. My mother's tears brought a speedy end to his questions. I suspect, however, that she respected his interest.

Both of Spyros's parents, who emigrated from the tiny island of Ereikousa on the northeast coast of Corfu in Greece, had experienced the Nazi occupation firsthand. His mother's family had hidden Jews and saved them from deportation to the concentration camps. Spyros had grown up hearing countless tales about sadistic German soldiers terrorizing the inhabitants of Ereikousa during the occupation.

I met his parents and his two younger siblings. His parents spoke no English, despite the fact that they had lived in America since 1950. They presented an interesting contrast to my own parents, who made learning English their priority. Our two families illustrated the basic difference between immigrants and refugees in their attitudes toward their countries of origin. For my parents, refugees from hell, there was no return to the land of their birth; they were exiles who had nothing to return to. In contrast, Spyros's parents, proud Greek immigrants, regarded Greece as their homeland and therefore never truly assimilated to this country. They had one foot in America and the other in Greece. Almost every summer they made their pilgrimage there. All three of their children, born in America, were expected to marry Greeks—not just any Greeks, but those whose roots were in Ereikousa. All of Spyros's cousins had had arranged marriages.

For obvious reasons, I was quite a threat to his family. I was the first non-Greek woman ever to cross the threshold of their apartment in Chelsea, one of the original Greek neighborhoods in New York. Spyros had dated women outside of his community, but he had never before brought any of them home. The first time I met Angelina Orfanos, his mother, she grasped my hand tightly and held it as she cried, uttering a lament in Greek. Later, Spyros translated the words that she had repeated over and over again like a dirge: "Spyros, what have you done to me?"

Our unconventional relationship was difficult to understand for many in our circle of family and friends. We were two people from very different worlds and at different stages in our lives—an odd couple. If we merely had been having an affair, it might have been more acceptable; but, after a few months, it became apparent to those close to us that we were becoming seriously involved with each other.

Of all those who disapproved, none was more vocal than Dr. Bunsen. I wasn't expecting a blessing, but I was not anticipating a condemnation either. After all, it was my life. I had hired him to help me understand myself better, not to tell me how to live. When he labeled my relationship with Spyros "a neurotic choice," I felt that we had come to an impasse.

At that point, I was in the second year of my psychoanalytic training program and meeting regularly with a supervisor whom I respected. I decided to consult with him about my personal dilemma. I told him that I was having doubts about my analysis, that I felt that my analyst was judgmental, and that I suspected that his values were getting in the way of his objectivity. After hearing the details, his words to me were: "Sophia, trust your feelings."

When I confronted Dr. Bunsen with my intention to leave therapy, he warned me that I was about to make a mistake that I would regret. He told me that Annie, the patient who had originally referred him to me, had ended up breaking down after leaving therapy prematurely against his advice. If this gratuitous information was meant to dissuade me from leaving him, it did not work. In fact, that breach of confidentiality served only to reinforce my conviction that I was doing the right thing. That was my last session with Dr. Bunsen. I have never regretted leaving; I only regretted staying for as long as I did. Six years in a bad marriage and six years in a bad analysis.

My relationship with Spyros grew deeper as time went on. It was surprising how well we got along. Although we came from such different worlds, our interests and fundamental values were similar. I came to feel that, on a basic level, I had more in common with him than with any of my previous partners.

At first, I felt uncomfortable about the difference in our ages. The thought that by the time I turned forty he would still be twenty-nine was distressing, but somehow the age difference seemed to become less significant with the passage of time. Our relationship was good for us both. I felt loved and treated with respect and appreciation. He seemed to bring out the best in me. With him, I felt funny, smart, and attractive. My influence on him was positive as well. I valued and understood him in a way that had been missing in his life. He had always shown great intellectual promise, but his provincial parents, frightened of losing him to the American world, had held him close to home. For example, when in the summer of his junior year in high school he was offered a full scholarship to Yale, his parents had refused to allow him to go.

For him, I represented the world that his parents had tried to shield him from, the world he wanted to be a part of. Now began a new phase in his life. He returned to college—he had been dropped from engineering school three years before we met and had been self-educating. He decided on a psychology major and became a full-time student while continuing to work as a waiter. He seemed to work day and night and managed to do it all well. His enthusiasm about learning was exciting to witness. Sometimes, on his way home from class, he would call to share an idea or thought stimulated by what he had just heard; he could barely contain his excitement.

Spyros's maturity and intellect impressed his teachers. He managed to develop personal relationships with many of them. We socialized with them and with people of different generations and backgrounds. We both had the capacity to connect with many different types of people. He was as much at home with a dishwasher as with a professor, and as comfortable with young children as with their grandparents.

Our only problem was the ticking of my biological clock. It was getting louder, but Spyros was turning a deaf ear to it. Still in his twenties, he had plenty of time ahead. He assured me that he was committed to me, but commitment for him meant love, not marriage and babies. Periodically, I would decide that the sensible thing to do was to go out with other men. We would separate painfully, but the magnetism between us always seemed to draw us back together.

Within three years of entering college, Spyros graduated with honors. He took a teaching position in a Greek elementary school and began graduate studies at NYU. He seemed to be following in my footsteps.

As Spyros's intellect was developing at amazing speed, I too was moving forward professionally. I left the NYU Counseling Center for a higher-paying position as a psychologist in a community mental health clinic affiliated with a major mental hospital. This was a half-time position that enabled me to concentrate on my developing private practice and gave me a chance to work with an entirely different population. Then another opportunity came up with the Catholic Diocese of Brooklyn, where I worked as a psychologist with school-age children in parochial schools. Once again, I found myself in the Catholic world. "Not a coincidence," declared my supervisor, who knew my personal background.

My years in the NYU Postdoctoral Program came to an end in 1975, when I received my certificate in psychoanalysis. I was approaching thirty-five years of age, I had been in school most of my life, and I felt that my education was now complete. My professional life had a momentum of its own. Now, it was time to address my personal life more directly; I could no longer ignore the internal conflict between my love for Spyros and my desire for marriage and motherhood. They seemed to be mutually exclusive. I turned to therapy once again. Despite my previous disappointing experience, I trusted the process and believed that with the right therapist I could resolve my dilemma.

Therapy the second time around was a very different experience from my first encounter with it. My perspective from both sides of the couch was helpful in making a wiser choice of therapist. I selected Dr. Sabert Basescu (Sabe), a man who had been my teacher and later one of my supervisors. I was well acquainted with his view of the world, and I felt that we approached life from similar perspectives. I knew that he would not impose his own values on me or try to fit me into preset categories; in short, I trusted him.

In him, I found the father I had always wished for—the sensitive, wise man who could guide me. When I look back over my choice of therapists and supervisors, it is interesting to note that they were all male. Since I have known at least as many competent females in the field, I must conclude that my choices were guided by a desire for a positive father figure. Sabe fulfilled that need. He accepted me without judgment. He was not invested in my making certain choices over others—whether I stayed with Spyros or not was my business. His job was to help me understand the meaning of that relationship in my life. He was neutral but never detached. I felt that he cared about me and had my best interests at heart. Sometimes we disagreed, but we always had mutual respect for each other's viewpoint. It was a healing relationship.

Gradually, I found the strength to put my desire for a full life ahead of my love for Spyros. It was not an instance of a decision of the mind over a decision of the heart. Rather, it was an internal shift. My feelings were beginning to change; for the first time in the four years that I had been with Spyros, I found myself attracted to other men. To my knowledge, my behavior toward Spyros did not change, but he must have picked up a subtle difference in my feelings and sensed the possibility that he could lose me. At the eleventh hour, just as I was about to become involved with another man, Spyros asked me to marry him.

A Greek drama ensued. For his family, it was a Greek tragedy. A manipulative Jewish divorcée, practically old enough to be his mother, had ensnared their firstborn son. My father-in-law boycotted our wedding ceremony, and my mother-in-law wore black. Only a few of Spyros's 300 relatives came. His mother had told them all that she was not going to attend, and they took their cue from her. Then, at the last moment, she appeared in her funeral dress and cried bitterly throughout the ceremony.

After the champagne and wedding cake, and after most of the guests had gone home, my mother-in-law took Spyros and me aside. Addressing me, she asked him to translate. "There has been much resentment between us. I did not want you for a daughter-in-law, but I know that you love my son and we both want the same thing: his happiness. I hope that from this day on, we can put the past behind us and get along." I was impressed with the way she confronted the situation. She was a simple woman with a second-grade education; she never learned to read and write, even in her native language, but she was bright enough to realize that, unless she made amends, she risked losing her son.

This marriage was definitely not a match made in heaven. My parents were not happy with it either. Father did not think much of Greeks—he often grumbled about how he had once been cheated by a Greek taxi driver. I enjoyed reminding him that when we first came to America, I listed Greece as his birthplace by translating the name of the Polish *shtetl* where he was born, Tluste, as "Greasy." For Mother, the fact that as a result of this marriage she would have another chance at becoming a grandmother made up for the fact that this was not a son-in-law she could brag about to her friends.

For the most part, my parents' objections centered on the wedding plans rather than on the marriage itself. We had chosen to be married at our home on Thanksgiving Day and asked our dear friend Beth, a psychoanalyst who also happened to be a Protestant minister, to perform the ceremony. My father, who would have preferred a civil ceremony, threatened not to come to the wedding, and my mother got into a major power struggle with my husband-to-be.

Mother was probably embarrassed about the whole wedding affair, and she did not want to have any of her friends know about it. For all I know, she may not have even told them that I was no longer married to Mark. Her friends had married off their daughters to more acceptable men—Jewish businessmen or doctors, men with money or status. These girls had had proper wedding ceremonies followed by fancy receptions in large halls. As far as Dorothy was concerned, this wedding of ours promised to be a strange affair, something to downplay or keep quiet about.

At the last minute, Mother realized that there was a major obstacle to keeping this event under wraps. Ela, our cleaning lady, had been hired for the day to help with serving and cleanup. Ela was part of a network of Polish women who immigrated to the United States and found work in the homes of refugees. There seemed to be an endless stream of these Polish cleaning ladies. As soon as one returned to Poland, she recommended a friend to take her place. Ela worked for us as well as for many of my mother's friends. To her great dismay,

Mother realized that unless Ela was kept from the premises, her friends would soon hear the details of our wedding.

There was a showdown. Mother announced, "If Ela comes, I'm not coming." Spyros said, "We can't tell Ela not to come at the last minute; she's counting on the work. She could have found another job for Thanksgiving." Mother was unsympathetic. I refused to be manipulated. I said to my parents, "I hope that you both come; your presence is important to us. But if you don't come, we'll manage without you."

Spyros proposed a solution. "Dorothy," he said, "if you pay Ela for the day, and do the serving and cleanup yourself, we'll send her home as soon as she arrives." Spyros knew that he was not letting Mother off easy; she hated paying for services that were not received. But, apparently, she hated even more the idea of Ela describing the wedding to Mrs. Bonom, her friend and rival. On our wedding day, Ela arrived bright and early, carrying a lovely bunch of daisies. Mother paid her and summarily sent her on her way. In a brilliant stroke, Spyros had found a way to satisfy everybody and send an important message to his mother-in-law: he was not a man to be controlled or manipulated. Dorothy had met her match.

Chapter 15

The Life Thread

On our wedding day, Spyros, without prompting, made a promise to my mother. "I'm going to make Sophia happy," he declared. I expect that, at the time, she was somewhat skeptical, but, over the years, she had to admit that Spyros meant what he had said.

Her son-in-law was a challenge to Dorothy. He did not look especially good on paper, so to speak. He was not someone she would ever have chosen for her daughter, but she recognized that he was an admirable young man. He was strong and assertive, yet he could be sensitive and affectionate. She could see how much I loved him and what a devoted husband he was.

It was hard not to like him. With his good looks and charming personality, Spyros drew people to him like a magnet. There was a heroic quality about him. Raised on Greek mythology, he had internalized some of the ideals of the heroes and gods of his ancestors. He seemed to be good at everything. He ran marathons; he was knowledgeable about an endless variety of things; he read voraciously. Dorothy could discuss music and politics with him. They had interests in common, and, in many ways, they were very much alike. They shared a zest for life, a highly developed social intelligence, and an inclination to act on the world. Both had forceful personalities.

Because of those similarities, sometimes they clashed. In the early stages of our relationship, their encounters with each other were guarded, but, in time, they grew to love each other deeply.

My father, on the other hand, remained distant and formal with his son-in-law. A few months before our wedding, he had published his book on Janowska. He gave Spyros a copy with an inscription addressed to "Mr. Orfanos," a strange way to address a young man whom he had known for four years and who was about to become his son-in-law. Although my father never openly voiced any criticisms about Spyros, neither did he say anything positive about him; he merely tolerated him—that was the most that one could expect from that cold, remote father of mine.

The publication of Leon's book was a significant event in his life as well as my own. He had waited for more than thirty years to translate the manuscript written in Polish during his years of hiding in the attic in Zimna Woda. Now, at the age of seventy-four, he was finally ready to share it with the world.

Unable to find a publisher, he decided to go with a vanity press and paid several thousand dollars to have the manuscript translated and published. Spending the money was exceedingly difficult for him, but he rationalized it with the fantasy that he would recoup the entire sum from book sales. He proceeded to sell copies to all his friends and acquaintances.

He was immensely proud of that accomplishment, but, at the same time, he experienced a great deal of anxiety. I suspect that he was troubled by paranoid thoughts about the possibility of retribution from Nazi sympathizers. Perhaps that was why he declined to have his photograph displayed on the book jacket. As the book went to press, he became ill and was hospitalized. I don't remember the specifics of the illness, but I strongly suspected that it was precipitated by the emotional turmoil of emerging from hiding.

When I visited him in the hospital, he talked about the book party that he expected me to give in his honor when he got well. I never did. It was difficult for me to be generous with my withholding father. He gave me one copy of his book as a gift but a short time later asked me to give it back because he had a customer who wanted to buy it. He promised to replace it when he received more copies from the publisher but somehow never got around to it. He was willing, however, to sell me copies so that I could give them out to my friends. For these he charged me full price and told me that since I did not have to pay him the New York City sales tax, I was getting a break! Later, I discovered that, as his daughter, I was entitled to a discount from the publisher, so I purchased copies directly from Vantage Press at half the price that he was charging me.

When he died six years later in 1982, I found that he had left me hundreds of unsold copies of the book. It was the only thing that he left explicitly for me in his will.

The publication of the book marked a significant phase in my life; it was a turning point. I believe that, symbolically, it gave me permission to deal with the Holocaust and undertake the long journey back into my own personal history. Up until that time, I did not have a clear idea of what my father had endured at Janowska. Reading the details was painful and difficult; it took a long time to finish the book. At around that same period, I found myself reading other accounts of the Holocaust. Books and films on the subject began appearing regularly. Society finally seemed to be awakening to the subject. Professionals were starting to look at the impact of the Holocaust on the second generation, the children of survivors. A journalist, Helen Epstein, the daughter of survivors herself, wrote a book titled *Children of the Holocaust* based on conversations with children of survivors. My mother bought me a copy. I recognized myself and my family in the pages of Epstein's book. That was merely the beginning. It would take many more years before I would come out of hiding.

I was too busy moving forward to look back. I gave my analyst a copy of my father's book, but, instead of using it as an opportunity to enter the secret place where my Holocaust memories were buried, I treated it as a kind of good-bye gift. I had reached my goals in analysis, and I prepared to terminate. It would take another seventeen years before I would return to analysis with Sabe to address that part of my past.

The desire to marry had been inextricably bound with my wish to have children. At the age of thirty-five, with another birthday just around the corner, I did not have much time to delay childbirth. Spyros and I agreed that after the wedding we would throw away the diaphragm. Of course, we expected that nine months later, we would be parents.

Month after month, the prospect of parenthood seemed to be fading. After more than a year of trying to get pregnant, we consulted the medical establishment. It was a painful shock to discover that we were among those growing numbers who suffered infertility.

Following years of treatment and disappointments, I became pregnant only to experience a miscarriage during the first trimester. Until it happened to me, I had never stopped to think about the traumatic impact of a miscarriage or of infertility in general. It had never occurred to me before that, for many couples who were unable to give birth to a baby of their own, an adoption was a last alternative and was

preceded by many years of pain and loss. The only positive development from these tragic life experiences was my heightened sensitivity to the pain of others in similar situations.

Finally, in the fall of 1979, I became pregnant once again. It turned
out to be a difficult and risky pregnancy. In the fifth month, shortly after the amniocentesis procedure and before we learned that we were
going to have a girl, I went into premature labor and had to be hospitalized to prevent her untimely birth. The labor contractions were
stopped by the medication that I was given, and I was sent home with
instructions to be as inactive as possible for the remainder of the pregnancy. Fortunately, at the time, my office was in my home, so I was
able to continue working without leaving my easy chair. When
Spyros returned from a full day's work, he had to attend to household
chores: shopping, cooking, laundry, all of the things that we had
shared prior to my confinement. He never complained; in fact, he insisted that this was a wonderful opportunity for him to share in the
pregnancy and to feel indispensable.

My husband was thrilled with the idea of becoming a father. He
was determined that the baby would love music. He held earphones to
my swollen belly and played classical and Greek folk music for our
daughter-to-be. The advantage of knowing the gender of the baby
ahead of time was that we could give her a name and relate to her,
even before her birth.

I suggested the name Lina, a version of Angelina, my mother-in-
law's name. In the Greek-Orthodox family, children are often named
after living relatives. In contrast, it is in the Jewish tradition to give
children the names of those who have passed away. Since both of my
parents were alive, I did not consider passing on their names. I did,
however, choose Joanna for a middle name, the name of my little sister who had died shortly after the war.

Two years later, we made a strange discovery. My mother found a
photograph of her own mother with a signature in the corner. The
name Selina was clearly written on my grandmother's photograph.
Then my mother remembered that, although my grandmother had always been called Zofia, her real name was, in fact, Selina. Was it a coincidence that I had chosen the name Lina? Was it unconscious
knowledge? Had I somehow known my grandmother's real name?
Had I seen the photograph and registered the name without remembering it? Whatever forces were operating, Lina represented the un-

ion of our two families: she carried both my grandmother's name and Spyros's mother's name.

Sensitive to the interaction of mind and body, I tried to remain calm during that precarious pregnancy. For the most part, I was successful; then, as my due date approached, I received a couple of unnerving telephone calls from Mark and his new wife, a pediatrician whom he had married a few years after we separated. Since our parting ten years earlier, I received only one communication from him prior to those telephone calls. About five years earlier, I had received a bizarre and disturbing note from him. It included a receipt from the ASPCA, the animal shelter in New York, indicating the date and time of the death of our cat, Midget. That was the cat that I had left in his care when I moved out. The note said, "I thought you would like to know that Midget is no more. She was too much trouble to take care of and I didn't know what else to do with her . . . " Midget had been my birthday gift to Mark a couple of years before our separation. Since she was young and apparently healthy at the time of death, I could only assume that her murder was a symbolic gesture meant to convey the death of our relationship. I never responded to the note. If I ever had any doubts about how disturbed my ex-husband was, this communication certainly confirmed them. I was relieved that he was no longer a part of my life.

When I received his telephone call, I felt uneasy but tried not to show it. My response reminded me of the times when we were together and I cautiously avoided confrontations because of my fear of his irrationality and his potential for violence. I was polite on the telephone, and we chatted for awhile; I could not figure out the reason for his call.

Then, a few weeks later, I received another call. This time, it was from his wife. We had never met. She sounded distraught. "We're separating," she said. "I'm leaving him; I want him to get out of my apartment, but he won't go." She continued, "He's destroying everything in the place, and I'm afraid of him. Was he violent when he was with you? Was he drinking then?" "No," I replied, "he was not an alcoholic; but yes, he was violent." She asked me, "How did you handle it?" "Very carefully," I said. She told me that he had recorded my last conversation with him and played it back for her. "Why?" I wondered. She had no answer. I wished her luck and said, "There is life after Mark." I never heard from either one of them again.

Lina clung to life through the entire pregnancy. By May, the eighth month, I was given permission to leave my easy chair. We enrolled in a Lamaze class with Elisabeth Bing, one of the pioneers of natural childbirth. At the time, I had no inkling that Ms. Bing had fled Nazi Germany as a young girl. The movement she led after she settled in America has virtually transformed the obstetrical profession. We are fortunate that she escaped. How many others who could have contributed their talent to our world perished?

Spyros and I were beginning to relax and believe that we were really going to become parents at last. But our worries were not yet over. Two weeks after my due date, on Friday, June 13, 1980, I went into labor.

After eighteen hours of labor, a sudden crisis developed. The fetal monitor attached to my abdomen signaled that the baby was in distress. I was rushed into the delivery room. Several physicians swooped down on me and placed an oxygen mask on my face; I heard someone over the loudspeaker frantically paging Dr. Abelow, my obstetrician, who was on another floor attending to other patients. I heard one of the doctors say that if Dr. Abelow didn't come immediately, they would have to perform an emergency cesarean section without him. I felt a wave of panic washing over me, then I lost consciousness.

When I awoke in the recovery room, Dr. Abelow and Spyros were looking down at me, smiling. "Happy Flag Day!" said my doctor. "You have a perfect baby girl." I kissed his hand in gratitude. Spyros beamed, "She's a ten and she's beautiful!"—referring to the APGAR scale and to the Bo Derek film *10*. "Who does she look like?" I asked. "Your father," he answered. Oh no, I thought, that was the last person in the world I wanted her to resemble.

Spyros was exuberant. He kept running from the recovery room to the nursery to look at his daughter, then back to the recovery room to me. He had witnessed Lina's birth despite the fact that he had been asked to leave the room as soon as it was evident that an emergency C-section would have to be performed. "They told me to leave, but I figured that they were too preoccupied to insist, so I stood on the side quietly and watched the whole time." Spyros was not about to miss the birth of his daughter, the most important event in his life. Later, he would joke to friends, "I know Sophia inside out," a grim reference to having seen my insides on the operating table as the doctor cut into my abdomen to pull Lina out.

On the door of my hospital room, in the spot reserved for my name, Spyros wrote in: Lina's Mother. It was the first time that I faced my new identity. When they finally brought Lina into my room, after what seemed like an eternity, I looked at her apprehensively, half expecting to see a mini version of Leon. What I saw was an adorable little face, pale and sweet, with a tiny nose and a bald head adorned with a long blond cowlick on top and a skimpy fringe of hair in the back of her neck, resembling a friar's coif. She did look a bit like my father, I had to admit.

My baby's undeniable resemblance to my father finally put to rest a vague suspicion of mine—that Leon Richman was not really my biological father. My doubts probably derived from a deep-seated wish to disassociate myself from the man who had hurt me by his apparent rejection. Given my mother's duplicitous nature, such an idea did not seem terribly farfetched. I even confronted her on the subject one day, when I felt particularly brave. Despite her assurance that he was indeed my birth father, I was not fully convinced until the day that I saw Lina in the hospital room.

Although my child resembled my father, she also reminded me of my baby sister Jasia. As I held Lina in my arms, the memory of my frail little sister came back to me vividly. It was a wondrous thing to realize that the life thread had not been severed, that it continued in the next generation.

Lina's birth was a momentous event in our families. She was the first grandchild on both sides and was cherished by all. Even my father managed to smile at her. "She's an exceptional baby," he said. Finally, my father appreciated someone in my life. When she was born, he visited me in the hospital and awkwardly handed me a check for five hundred dollars, saying, "Now that I have seen your baby, I would like to give you this check."

It is said that children of Holocaust survivors are "memorial candles" to those who did not survive. They are invested with the memories and hopes of their parents who unconsciously transmit their own traumas to them. With Lina's birth, the shadow of Jasia's death hung over me. I had not thought much about my little sister in the intervening years; now, I could not get her out of my mind. Acutely aware that Jasia had died at fourteen months, I anxiously counted the months until Lina had passed that marker. When Lina entered her fifteenth month, I breathed a sigh of relief.

There were no logical reasons for my fears; Lina was a healthy and strong baby. She was unusually alert. At the hospital, the nurses had nicknamed her Bright Eyes because of her alert look. She was very responsive and seemed neurologically advanced. She was early at everything—an early walker, an early talker—a delightful baby.

We felt that we had hit the jackpot. After years of infertility and despair, we had our miracle baby. What's more, this baby was easy to love. At two weeks of age, she slept through the night and only occasionally had to be awakened so that I could relieve my engorged breasts like a cow ready to be milked. Actually, the breast-feeding experience was immensely gratifying for both of us. Lina was a hearty feeder who could be heard sucking from across the room.

When it came to motherhood, everything seemed almost effortless. Even our child care arrangements fell smoothly into place. I continued my private practice on a part-time basis, so that I could breast-feed and spend time with Lina. My mother-in-law, who lived across town, was thrilled to take care of her grandchild during the three days that I worked in my home office. My own mother, who adored being a grandmother, was a bit jealous of Angelina's time with Lina, but, because of her own advancing age and the geographical distance between us, she was able to visit and baby-sit only irregularly.

In May 1982, just before Lina's second birthday, Leon Richman died of a heart attack. The attack that killed him had been preceded by a milder one a few months earlier so that, in effect, I had a chance to prepare myself for his death. I realized that this was a final opportunity to make contact with him, to say the words that had been left unspoken. At the same time, I knew that whatever had divided us all these years was insurmountable. We had nothing to say to each other.

At the funeral, I read a short passage from the book that he had written. It referred to a conversation that he had with an inmate at Janowska, a tailor struggling with a moral dilemma.

> . . . a tailor told his story: "I had nobody but my little girl. I had a good *Ausweis* (identity paper). But when they took away my only daughter, I wouldn't leave her. They herded us into a school, together with thousands of others assigned to deportation. Then they forcibly took my daughter away from me and threw me into this camp. And here I am. Do you think I did the right thing? People say I didn't, because I couldn't save the child anyway and so my sacrifice is to no avail. But I think," the tailor

went on, "that I'd never find peace in life if I hadn't gone with the child."

"People are wrong," I told him. "You have done the right thing." (p. 218)

For me, that passage illustrated the best in my father. It showed him to be a person with a sense of integrity, a principled man. Even under the monstrous conditions of the death camp, he managed to hold on to his values and inner freedom. Ironically, his finest moments seem to have taken place in those tragic times. Undoubtedly my father was a complex individual; my feelings toward him were ambivalent. Although I could respect and admire his strength of character, I resented his coldness and apparent lack of feelings for me. In my eyes, he had failed as a father. Spyros's sensitive and loving ways with Lina were a constant reminder of the fathering that had been missing in my own life.

After my father's death, when we visited my mother in their Jackson Heights apartment, his absence was barely noticeable. He had been so withdrawn during his lifetime that I had to remind myself that he was not in the next room. Mother sometimes spoke with tears in her eyes and a quiver in her lips of missing him, but, in truth, she seemed more alive and free without him. It was her guilt that gave her the most trouble. She reproached herself for not having been a good-enough wife, for having pursued her own pleasures while he suffered with his depression. She felt that she had abandoned him when he needed her.

As for me, I did not have a strong reaction to his death. I knew that it was a momentous event to lose a father; but only the idea of it saddened me, not the reality. I had lost my father even before I knew him. The most meaningful bond that my father and I had ever shared was Lina, the grandchild that was his link to the future and his connection to the past. We never spoke of it, but Lina's likeness to Jasia, his favorite lost child, was unmistakable. My father cherished Lina in a way that he had never been able to feel about me. Lina was my gift to him. One day, after he died, I suddenly realized that my daughter's name was actually quite similar to my father's. I suppose that if I had chosen a name to memorialize Leon, Lina would have been a logical choice. The unconscious works in strange ways!

Chapter 16

The Hour of the Wolf

As I entered middle age, I found myself in a good psychological place. I felt secure and satisfied with my life. Marriage, motherhood, and my work were all immensely fulfilling. I couldn't imagine being in a better place either personally or professionally. Mother, who herself was always poised for disaster, warned against expressing such sentiments out loud. She was one of those people who quickly knocks on wood after an utterance of good fortune so as not to tempt the fates.

When Lina was born, we were amused to see that both grandmothers, hailing from totally different cultures, made the same little gesture over the body of the newborn, a magical incantation designed to keep the evil spirits away. They pursed their lips and spit three times—pu, pu, pu.

Angelina went even further to discourage the evil eye. When Lina was a toddler, and strangers stopped to admire her on the street, my mother-in-law lied about the child's age, making her seem slightly older so that she would appear less precocious and therefore be less likely to incur the envy of admirers.

Although these magical maneuverings made me smile, for I was never superstitious, I realized that I too worried that my happiness was a tenuous state. The wolf of my childhood had cast a long shadow over my life. Mother's warning had become an apt metaphor for living with a sense of impending doom. It was as though the dreaded creature was always nearby lying in wait for the moment to pounce. In the summer before my fiftieth birthday, just when I felt most confident and happy, the wolf made its appearance.

In the 1980s, we had purchased a country house in the Pocono Mountains. It was our weekend retreat, a place to escape the tensions of city life. At that time, New York City had been undergoing a depressing change. It seemed dirtier and noisier than in previous years. Maybe I was more sensitive to it because I had a young child, or maybe in middle age I was less tolerant of assaults on my nervous system. The house was the first that either of us had ever lived in, let alone owned. Spacious and comfortable, it was a relief from cramped city living. Architecturally, it was known as an upside-down house, referring to the fact that the bedrooms were located downstairs while the living room space and kitchen were upstairs on the second floor.

The house was part of a planned, family-oriented community, a feature that guaranteed a lively social life for our child as well as ourselves. Almost every weekend during the year we packed our Honda Civic wagon and headed for Hemlock Farms. Each year we took our summer vacation there as well.

In the summer of 1990, we looked forward to a restful vacation. Lina was attending day camp, Spyros had brought up his treasured computer, and I was looking forward to catching up on reading. Late one stormy July night, we prepared for bed. Lina was already asleep in her room, with her dolls Sara and Amy tucked securely beside her.

Earlier that evening, I had decided that the oven could use a good cleaning. I set the timer on the self-cleaning cycle and went to bed. We were in the middle of passionate lovemaking when we were interrupted by a loud sound: a thunderous clap, an explosion that seemed to come from the bedroom closet. We got out of bed warily and peeked into the dark closet. Everything was in its place. The house was still. Perhaps it had been just a clap of thunder on this rainy night, we rationalized, eager to return to our fervent embrace.

Afterward, Spyros went upstairs to turn off the lights and close up the house for the night. Suddenly, I heard him scream my name. I jumped out of bed and ran upstairs in dread. When I reached the top of the stairs that led to the living room and adjacent kitchen area, I found myself in the midst of a heavy fog that seemed to hang over the entire area. How did the fog get into the house? I wondered, confused. I could barely make out Spyros's form; he was in the kitchen with his back to me. Then, I saw the flames shooting out of the wall oven. This was not fog; it was smoke: the oven was on fire! Spyros, who had weathered several restaurant fires back in the days when he worked as a waiter and short-order cook, was desperately trying to contain the flames. When he realized that it was impossible, he shouted, "Get Lina out of the house; I'll call the fire department!"

My heart pounding, I ran downstairs to wake Lina. I heard Spyros's frantic voice on the phone in the background. I rushed the groggy child out through the sliding glass door of her room to the driveway. She was barefoot. I ran back in to get her a pair of shoes and a jacket. I knew my life was in danger; I was aware that there was only a small window of time before the fire would reach the lower level. I grabbed the first pair of shoes I could find, the black patent-leather ones she wore to parties. No matter! Time was of the essence. In my panic, it did not occur to me to grab my purse or any of our valuables. The only thing that Spyros saved was some of the computer discs lying on the dining room table.

When we reached the street, we heard a horrific explosion. The gas grill on the deck had exploded and shattered the plate glass sliding door that separated the deck from the house. Seconds before, on the urging of our neighbor, Spyros had gotten our car out of the driveway. The former's presence of mind had saved our car from the same fate as that of our barbecue.

By the time the fire trucks arrived, not much of our house was left. The wooden structure had burst into flames like a matchbox and was consumed within what seemed to be a matter of minutes. The entire second story was reduced to a mere shell. The huge wraparound deck that had been a recent addition to the house was totally gone—gone before we even had a chance to send the final payment to the builder for the work.

Fortunately for our neighbors, the previous days had been rainy and the dampness stopped the fire from spreading. It took several hours and more than one fire department to bring the raging monster under control. Lina and I shivered in the street. I held her close to me, her head buried in my body. I tried to keep her warm and to protect her from the terrifying sight. I knew that the imprint of that moment would remain with us for the rest of our lives.

Neighbors and friends came to our aid. During times of tragedy, we learn who our friends truly are. Mrs. Allen* from across the road gave us shelter till morning. We never expected such kindness from a neighbor whom we barely knew and didn't much like. We had always been critical of the Allens, for they were loud and seemed oblivious to the impact of their noise on the peaceful surroundings. They showed no interest in their neighbors and kept to themselves. Yet in

*Name changed.

our hour of need, one couldn't ask for a more generous, sensitive person than Mrs. Allen. We were ashamed of the way we had prejudged her.

The next morning, the air was clean and fresh, a beautiful summer day after the storm. Only the mangled skeleton of our house and a few scorched trees on our property remained as evidence that the nightmare had been real.

In an attempt to normalize life as much as possible, we sent Lina to day camp as usual. She still remembers the humiliating reception she got on that morning. At first, the other ten-year-olds laughed at the sight of her in her black patent-leather shoes and a pair of shorts and a T-shirt borrowed from another child, but when they heard about the fire, they were contrite. The bunk took up a collection to buy her some gifts to make her feel better. Her dolls Amy and Sara had been lost in the fire along with the rest of her toys.

When I entered the ruins of what had been our beautiful home, my nostrils were assaulted by the musty, acrid stench of smoke. It permeated the air, making it difficult to breathe. A blanket of gray ash covered everything, giving it a colorless, ghostly cast. What was left of the furniture was in total disarray. I searched through the rubble but found little that could be rescued. What had not been destroyed by the fire was ruined by the water used to douse it.

The fire marshal offered to help Spyros enter the precarious portions of the wreckage to search for whatever photographs and mementos could be salvaged. Later, we sat in the driveway with friends who helped us sort through the charred remains of the albums. Only a small number of photographs could be saved. A few had been miraculously preserved behind the plastic sheets of the albums, but most were burned around the edges and discolored. They left black soot stains on our fingers as we handled them.

The fire inspection revealed that the cause of the fire was faulty electrical wiring, not a defective oven as we had initially thought. We were told that the house had been a time bomb waiting to go off. The intense heat generated by the self-cleaning cycle was merely the trigger for the conflagration. The smoke alarm hadn't gone off, probably because the battery inside was dead.

In retrospect, the mystery of the loud burst coming from the bedroom closet was solved. The electrical panel for the entire house was located inside that closet wall. It was the sound of the circuit breaker snapping that had interrupted our lovemaking. Inflamed by our own passions, we had been oblivious to the imminent danger.

When I felt despair about our losses, I reminded myself that, under the circumstances, we were extremely lucky to be alive. If we had gone to sleep a half hour earlier, we probably would not have awakened in time to save ourselves.

Our brush with death left its mark on us. At first, we were in a state of shock and disbelief and did not experience the anguish that we would have expected to feel. Both Spyros and I found ourselves reviewing the events of that fateful night again and again, as if to understand exactly what had taken place. One of us would begin describing what had happened and soon the other would join in with additional details. This telling and retelling of the traumatic event was comforting. Perhaps we were validating each other's reality of an extraordinary event that seemed unreal.

The psychologist within observed these posttraumatic symptoms with some detachment. I recognized the classic signs. We had trouble sleeping. Lina, who had always been an excellent sleeper, experienced insomnia for the first time in her life. I had frequent nightmares and, while I had never dreamed of fires before, from that day on, the image of fire became a recurrent symbol in my dreams. We were on edge and especially nervous around flames. Lina had become so sensitized to the danger of fire that she could not tolerate lighted candles on a birthday cake for years to come.

In his characteristic way of coping with anxiety, Spyros took action. He put all his energy into dealing with the insurance company to recoup our financial losses. We busied ourselves with making lists trying to account for every missing item of clothing, furnishing, jewelry, etc. It was difficult to face our losses squarely in that way, but it helped us to recover from the disaster without financial repercussions.

The greatest losses, however, were those irreplaceable treasures from the past—the old photographs, the childhood diaries, the paintings—that we had stored in our country house. Prewar photographs that had survived the Holocaust because my mother had entrusted gentile friends with them before we went into hiding were forever lost.

For years, I had little interest in the memorabilia buried at the bottom of my closet. I barely glanced at them. Recently, however, my attitude had begun to change. I developed an interest in my personal history and with it a growing appreciation of these objects from my past. In fact, just two months before the fire, I had been interviewed on videotape by an organization dedicated to the preservation of the memory of the Holocaust. In preparation for that interview, I had rummaged through old papers and photo albums, selecting those I felt would best document my experiences. Diaries from my teenage years and school compositions provided me with some valuable insights into myself as a child and an adolescent.

What a bitter turn of events. Just as I realized the value of these old things, they literally went up in smoke. My only consolation was that at least I had a chance to reread some of my early writings before they were destroyed forever and that some of the photos that perished had fortuitously been captured on videotape.

Chapter 17

Out of Hiding

During the 1980s and 1990s, society was flooded with Holocaust materials—memoirs, films, educational programs. Holocaust awareness in America reached such great proportions that it captured the interest of psychohistorians eager to explain this phenomenon. Most theories were of a psychological nature. Thus, it was pointed out that sufficient time had elapsed after the trauma to allow both survivors and society at large to face the Holocaust. The curtain of silence had begun to lift in the 1970s; now, with dwindling numbers of survivors, there was a sense of urgency about getting the story from the last witnesses. Survivors who had been discouraged during the postwar years from talking about their traumatic experiences were now encouraged to share the most minute details about their wartime drama.

Some commentators, critical of what they perceive to be an obsession with the Holocaust in contemporary American society, maintain that there are political rather than moral or psychological reasons for that preoccupation. In this view, the public has been manipulated by special interest groups who use the memory of this catastrophe as a symbol to advance their own political agendas.

Although there may be some truth to these allegations, personally, I am less concerned with the question of why more than fifty years after it took place in Europe the Holocaust has such a prominent place in the American psyche and more interested in how the current receptive climate impacts the healing process. Unquestionably, we the survivors are the beneficiaries of the general changes in attitude toward the *Shoah*. The public fascination with the subject lessens our sense of shame, the trauma survivor's lot. When people feel that what they have to say is valued and that they are making an important contribution by sharing it with others, then a sense of pride develops. What was once considered a stigma to be hidden comes to be seen as a badge of courage to be worn proudly.

In the 1990s, those of us who had been children during the war were now entering middle age, a time for reflection and evaluation, a last opportunity to address the unresolved issues. For me, it was the impetus to come to terms with a fragmented and confusing past. The fact that I was settled and at peace in the here and now of my life gave me the strength to face my demons.

When I was invited to testify by the Fortunoff Video Archive for Holocaust Testimonies at Yale, I agreed to be interviewed. Mother had given her testimony about six years earlier to the same organization with much ambivalence. It took courage to revisit those terrifying times, but she felt a responsibility to do it. She had just turned eighty-one and knew that it was now or never; she wanted her grandchild to have a personal record of our family's history. We were fortunate that in her eighties, Mother's mind was still sharp and her memory excellent. Her testimony was clear and moving.

Like my mother before me, I reluctantly agreed to be a witness. My own hesitation had to do with a concern that I would not have enough to say. For many years, my wartime experiences had been minimized to the extent that I did not even feel like a legitimate survivor. I was very young during the war years; my memories of that time consisted of no more than a handful of images. My parents' injunction, "You were too young to remember," rang in my ears. How could someone too young to remember have a story to tell?

Yet deep down I knew that no matter what my parents or others said, those early years in the cauldron of death did affect me deeply and had made a lasting impact on my life. I hoped that the interview would help me integrate some of the fragments of memory that remained. I anticipated that it would be difficult to express myself—it always was without a written text—but I was not about to allow anxiety to rule my life. I was determined to tell my story in spite of it. Both of my parents had the courage to share their painful experiences with the world. Now, it was my turn. Giving testimony was an important step along the journey out of hiding. The night before the day of my interview, I broke out in hives for the first time in my life.

What surprised me most about the experience was the realization that I had plenty to say. In fact, when the interview was brought to a close after about one hour, I was left with the uneasy feeling that the session was ending prematurely. The extent of my disappointment was not clear to me at the time so I said nothing about it. Typically, I have a delayed reaction to unpleasant feelings. I suppose it is a protective mechanism, another form of inhibition. When the interviewer telephoned me several days later (a standard procedure to make sure that the survivor had not been unduly disturbed by the experience), I told her that I had felt cut off abruptly. She gave me the opportunity to return and continue my testimony, which I did.

The desire to speak out was in stark contrast to my usual reticence when it comes to sharing details of my life. But an internal shift was beginning to take place, a shift that was stimulated by both personal and social events. I was emerging out of hiding slowly but steadily.

The process of coming out was so gradual that it's difficult to pinpoint exactly when it started, although I consider the publication of my father's book in the mid-1970s a marker of its beginning. Symbolically, Father emerged from the attic once again; he came out of hiding into the open and let me and the rest of the world know what had happened to him in that hell called Janowska. His self-disclosure paved the way for my own.

At around the same time, I found myself in a stable, loving marriage that provided the security I needed to face the internal censors head-on. Sometimes people are afraid that if they dwell on painful things, they will get lost in them; the pain will become too great to bear, and they will sink helplessly into bottomless despair. I had my own antidote to depression—it was Spyros, the man whose hearty laugh could be heard across a room. His sharp sense of humor never failed to provide comic relief in times of sadness. I knew that he wouldn't let me take myself too seriously or dwell too long in the shadows of the Holocaust.

Another major catalyst for change was Lina's birth. Bringing a child into the world heightened the desire to know my roots and have a clearer sense of my own identity. The branches of my family tree, broken during the war, now had new growth.

Living with a child also put me in touch with my own lost childhood. Joyous Lina, who squealed with laughter and played with abandon, bore no resemblance to her physical clone, Zosia, the serious, frightened little girl who lived through the *Shoah*. Looking at Lina when she was a toddler, I was filled with awe to think that such a little person could be entrusted with such a big secret. The idea is almost incomprehensible, yet I know from my reading and from my work with survivors that children in hiding were capable of amazing behavior—their lives depended on it.

I delighted in my daughter's ebullient personality and at the same time mourned the loss of my own childhood. The mourning process that is so crucial in working through trauma was facilitated by the changes in the atmosphere around me.

My own drive to come to terms with the past was mirrored in the experience of countless other child survivors. In May 1991, the First International Gathering of Children Hidden During World War II was organized by an organization of former hidden children. I attended the weekend conference with Spyros at my side. It was a moving experience for both of us. A few hundred people were expected at the gathering; instead, more than 1,600 from all over the world showed up. Among them was my friend Irena from Sweden. We had known each other for over thirty years, meeting from time to time when she visited her aunt in America, but until that weekend, we had never spoken of our common history. As it turned out, we were born in the same region, one week apart, and we had both survived in hiding as Christians. It was remarkable to see how many of the issues I had struggled with were shared by others. Part of the program featured workshops that met in smaller groups. So many of the offerings were relevant to my personal experience that it was difficult to choose one. Just a few of more than a dozen titles were "Who Am I, Christian or Jew?" "Lost Childhood," "Still Hiding After All These Years," and "Understanding the Hiding Experience." Spyros went to the one for spouses of hidden children.

The event was profoundly healing. For so many years, my experience had been undermined and invalidated. We, the children who escaped death, had constantly been reminded of our good fortune. We had survived against great odds and were indeed lucky to be alive, but our trauma needed recognition. The fact that we lost our childhood, the reality of living with damaged parents suffering from a posttraumatic disorder, the confusion with regard to our identity—all of these consequences of having lived through the war were ignored, denied, or at best merely minimized. Finally, we were united with others who had lived through the same tragedy and shared our struggles. The designation "hidden child" acknowledged our special and unique identities. Just having a term to describe who I am gave me a sense of relief.

When the conference was over, some of us felt the desire to continue meeting with one another on a regular basis. I organized a small group that met weekly in my New York office for about six years.

We were a heterogeneous group in all respects but one: our hidden childhood. We were of different ages; we all had different professions. I was the only psychologist in the group for most of the years that we met together. The specific hiding experiences of the members varied considerably. Some, like myself, were hidden in plain sight under a false identity; others were hidden from view in cramped quarters. One woman had lost both parents in Auschwitz and had spent her early years in a French orphanage with her older sister. Another had been placed in her infancy with an infertile Polish couple who raised her as if she were their own child. A third had been hidden in a forest with a ranger and his family. All but me had been separated from their parents at some point during the ordeal. In that respect, I was the most fortunate. Presumably for that reason I experienced less separation anxiety and fear of abandonment, common symptoms among hidden children.

Despite our differences, the similarities were striking, particularly when it came to how we responded to the trauma. Most of us had minimized the effects of the war on our lives; some had actually denied it. One of the members, who was orphaned at the age of two, used to tell people that she had had a happy childhood without any awareness that she was lying to herself.

Coming out of hiding was a new experience for all of us. Among us, we had many years of psychotherapy, most of them disappointing, with therapists who were insensitive to the special problems of survivors. We all shared the feeling of never having truly belonged anywhere. The majority struggled with intimacy; most of us had been divorced.

Irrational fears were common among us. For instance, my fear of hunger and my habit of traveling with provisions, odd quirks that Spyros had often teased me about, were paralleled in the experience of other child survivors. At last, I understood that my panicky feeling about being caught without access to food was rooted in the war years when hunger was an ever-present reality.

Another reassuring observation was that I was not alone in my fear of driving. A number of my peers expressed the same anxiety. In trying to understand how such a phobic response could relate to our common background, I speculated that driving a car is the one activity in our current lives that has the potential of bringing us in contact with sudden violent death. The fact that on the road one wrong move can result in death makes it an apt symbol to express the terror of our past.

It was interesting to see the different ways in which we handled our emotions. For years, I had noticed that when I made reference to the Holocaust, a word or thought would trigger unexpected tears. I tended to be disconnected from my feelings and experienced the eruption as strange but not disturbing or unwelcome. I accepted those emotions without judgment and came to think of them as part of a mourning process going on outside of my awareness.

Another group member, Eva, had the same reactions; but when she was flooded with such feelings she became embarrassed and disturbed. She told us that her therapist had labeled her behavior immature, had urged her to get control over her feelings and leave the past behind. In contrast, Rena, who had spent three years in isolation in the forest, was numb and unable to mourn. For her, tears were a welcome sign of the return of her blocked feelings.

Although we were all bound by our common history, we did not all want to focus on the past. As trauma survivors, hidden children are suspended between remembering and forgetting; each individual has to come to terms with a balance. Some of us were intent on revisiting the past while others were more interested in focusing on the present and moving on.

I was one of those who wanted to discuss the past to better understand my present. In starting the group, I had not sought support or psychotherapy. I was basically content with my life, yet I was aware that, under the surface, troubling issues existed which had their roots in my childhood. I felt that I needed to go back to move forward.

One of the areas that troubled me most was my speaking inhibition. In groups, no matter how small or supportive, I felt inarticulate and blocked, unable to say what I thought and felt to my satisfaction. I had difficulty formulating my thoughts and finding the right words to express myself. Consequently, I tended to stay in the background and say little. From the feedback that I received over the years, it was evident that most people did not think of me as inarticulate or notice my struggle. My discomfort was well hidden.

The hidden children's group seemed to be an ideal place to confront and work out that particular problem. However, I was only mildly successful in that endeavor. A disadvantage of being the only psychologist in the group was the fact that other members looked to me for leadership. As a leader, I could help others with their struggles and keep my personal concerns in the background. My years as a group therapist had made me aware that expressing myself in that setting was less of a problem than speaking with peers. Perhaps the responsibility of acting as a facilitator overshadowed my discomfort or maybe having the mantle of authority gave me the security to speak my thoughts.

There were other puzzling aspects to the inhibition. For instance, I noted that unlike most people with public speaking anxiety, I was never uncomfortable speaking in front of an audience, no matter how large, as long as I had a written text in front of me. Presumably, in those circumstances, I could totally control what came out of my mouth. There was no danger of allowing something regrettable to slip by my internal censor.

The anxiety that I experienced in situations that called for oral participation was troublesome but not debilitating. It made my life more difficult but did not seriously interfere with it—that is, until the licensing exam fiasco.

In the summer of 1991, a year after the fire had destroyed our country retreat, we sold our New York apartment and purchased a house in the suburbs of New Jersey. Shortly after the move, I took the necessary steps to begin a private practice in my new home state. Lina was eleven years old; I wanted to work closer to home and keep my commuting into New York to a minimum. I planned to continue my New York practice on a part-time basis. It was well established. I had been licensed there for over twenty years, and I had good sources of referrals.

The two states had a modified reciprocal arrangement so that I did not need to retake the written portion of the exam to become licensed in New Jersey; I did, however, have to sit for the oral part—a requirement that most states do not have.

With almost thirty years of experience in the mental health field as a private practitioner, supervisor, and teacher, I was in a different league from the average psychologist who takes a licensing examination shortly after graduation from a PhD program. In fact, I had more credentials than most of the members of the New Jersey Board of Psychological Examiners.

There was no doubt in my mind that I was competent enough to pass a licensing examination designed to "demonstrate a minimal degree of competency to practice psychology independently." Still, knowing how difficult it was for me to answer questions orally, I faced the exam with some trepidation.

My worst fears came true. During the two-hour examination, I struggled to express my thoughts on the case that I had prepared as a sample of my work. The patient was the son of Holocaust survivors, a relatively high-functioning individual who suffered from a pervasive, underlying depression that rendered him unable to enjoy his life and his accomplishments. Of the many possible cases I could have chosen to present, I had decided on this one because of my special interest and familiarity with issues of second-generation survivors. Also, I felt proud of the work we had done; the patient had come a long way in therapy.

One of the two examiners seemed particularly challenging. I had the feeling that he was critical of my psychoanalytic approach and that I was not providing him with the sound bites that he was looking for. My attempts to explain complex therapeutic interactions were falling on confused and irritated ears. I'm sure that my halting speech and stumbling words did not help the matter. The other examiner had a more receptive attitude and actually seemed interested in what I had to say, but her positive evaluation was not enough for me to pass the exam, since a unanimous decision was required.

I was devastated. My work had always been the one area in my life that I could count on for success. It was hard to believe that I had not passed; yet, at the same time, I was not really surprised. It seemed to be a confirmation of what I had always believed, namely that under questioning, I was unable to adequately communicate what I knew. Spyros, who had sat for the same exam several weeks after me and passed with no difficulty, was in shock. He was fond of publicly boasting, "Sophia is the most talented clinician I know," and could not believe that I had failed an examination meant to test for minimum, entry-level clinical skills.

The situation was terrible. It became even worse when I learned that the temporary permit that had allowed me to practice provisionally was automatically revoked. The ultimate purpose of licensing is to protect the public against incompetent professionals. Now that the New Jersey Board of Psychological Examiners considered me a danger to the public welfare, I was ordered immediately to cease all practice in the state and to transfer my patients to another psychologist. What an absurd and humiliating position to find myself in! On the basis of a subjective test procedure of questionable validity and reliability, I was suddenly deemed unfit to practice my profession on the west side of the Hudson River.

Determined to right the situation, I submitted an extensive written appeal to the Board. Quoting from a transcript of the taped examination, I was able to show that I had answered all questions posed to me by the examiners well enough to demonstrate sufficient proficiency, but because of a bias against my psychoanalytic orientation, my responses had been misunderstood. The examiners were not sufficiently knowledgeable about the psychoanalytic model that informed my clinical work to be able to evaluate me fairly.

In the appeal, I also acknowledged my responsibility for failing to give a seamless oral performance. I included a short statement about the effects of my hidden childhood, "I learned early in life that the less I said, the safer I was. Consequently, in stressful situations, when I am questioned orally about what I know, I sometimes experience emotional blocking and I have difficulty verbalizing my thoughts fully and clearly."

I won the appeal and was given another opportunity to repeat the examination using the same case but with two different examiners, one of them an experienced psychoanalyst. This time, I had no difficulty passing. A license was granted shortly thereafter.

Between the first and the second examination, I signed up for an oral-exam workshop to make sure that I would not make the same mistakes the second time around. The instructor provided us with a written list of suggestions. Number one on the list was the injunction, "Be humble." I wondered, in retrospect, if I had made the mistake of relating to my examiners as colleagues rather than as irrational authorities with power over me. It seemed pathetic that, at that level of professionalism, passing a licensing examination would depend on a show of humility rather than a demonstration of competence.

Several years after the licensing exam fiasco, I confronted a similar situation. I had an opportunity to become Board Certified in Psychoanalysis by the American Board of Professional Psychology, a clinical credential that represents the highest distinction awarded by my profession. It required an oral examination. I decided that I would not allow my anxiety to hold me back. I also thought of it as a chance to prove to myself that the original licensing exam had been truly a travesty and that, when evaluated by my peers, I am judged competent.

I presented the very same analytic case to the three senior psychoanalysts on the examination committee. They passed me unanimously and praised me for my work. After the examination, one of them commented that he had been somewhat surprised at the level of my competence, because I tended to downplay it. Another instance of the hidden child keeping a low profile, I thought to myself.

It was time to face these troublesome issues squarely and return to analysis. There was no doubt that Sabe, the analyst I had worked with seventeen years earlier, was the person I trusted with my psyche. His existential orientation was compatible with my own worldview. I was drawn to the existential philosophy with its emphasis on freedom, responsibility, and authenticity. As a survivor, I could relate to the idea that our ultimate human concerns have more to do with fear of death, isolation, and meaninglessness than with repressed instinctual drives, as posited by some theories.

Sabe's phenomenological approach to therapy was also consistent with my belief that to understand a person, one must enter his or her frame of reference and refrain from imposing one's own preconceived theoretical ideas. He was no expert on the Holocaust, but he knew me well, and I trusted him. I believed that his presence and wisdom would help me to clarify some of the more elusive connections between the past and the present of my life.

Chapter 18

Secrets and Secretions

For many years, I had an unwelcome nightly visitor, a recurrent dream that puzzled and disturbed me. I had talked about it countless times in therapy with Dr. Bunsen and with Sabe as well, but it continued to elude my understanding. Although the specifics of the dream changed from one night to another, the essence was always the same.

I'm in a public restroom; it is a dark, unpleasant, disgusting place. There are other people around. I have to defecate or urinate, and I can't, no matter how hard I try. Caught between the urgency to relieve myself and the inability to do so, I am frustrated. Finally, I wake up out of the dilemma.

A version of that theme occurred endlessly. The details of the place varied, the people in it differed, but the basic theme remained the same. Always a public restroom, always a frustrated need.

Psychoanalysts are interested in dreams. We see these nightly productions as the "royal road to the unconscious," a way to provide the dreamer with insight into his or her deepest concerns. I realized that my "toilet dream," as I referred to it, was an important communication to myself. But what did it mean?

When I returned to analysis to address my unresolved childhood issues, the dream finally became clearer. I came to see it as a metaphor for the familiar struggle between the desire to speak and the prohibition against it. In a creative way, the dream expressed both the urge to bring the internal products into the outside world, i.e., to speak the thoughts, and the injunction against making public what was private. I longed to relieve myself, but I was blocked in my effort to do so.

Why a public restroom? A dark, disgusting place with no privacy? Is sharing private thoughts in a public place a shameful act, like revealing secrets that are not meant to be seen or heard? As I pondered these questions, one day I came across an interesting reference in a journal dedicated to the theme of knowledge of the Holocaust. Theodore Jacobs, a well-respected psychoanalyst, had observed that the words "secret" and "secretion" have the same root and concluded that, because of the secretive nature of intimate bodily processes such as elimination, the idea of a secret is often associated with the private secretions of the body. My toilet dreams seemed to support his idea that, on an unconscious level, secrets may be linked with issues of sphincter control.

Dream images are often multiply determined; they stand for more than one idea. As I struggled to understand the toilet dream in the context of my childhood experience, more connections became apparent. One of my earliest childhood memories dating back to about two years of age was the moment of terror when the attic door opened and a strange figure emerged, as I sat on my little potty on the verge of having a bowel movement. It was not the dreaded wolf, but it was a stranger. The toilet dreams seemed to capture the traumatic moment when a natural body process was suddenly interrupted.

My subsequent childhood experiences with public toilets in the slums of Paris may have been reminders of the original trauma and provided me with the disgusting images that later found their way into my toilet dreams.

My mother's preoccupation with elimination probably had something to do with that theme as well. When I was barely able to sit up by myself, she diligently placed me on a potty, center stage on the kitchen table, where she could keep an eye on me hoping that sooner or later the urge would come and that I would create the desired product. Her technique eliminated the need for diapers. I presume it was a fairly typical approach to toilet training in her day. But maybe her preoccupation went further than that of her contemporaries. In later years, she delighted in mimicking my baby words, *najcio koupki,* a phrase meant to communicate that I had to use the potty. She managed to capture and save a photograph of me at about eighteen months standing stark naked next to my little *najcio* in the garden in front of the house in Zimna Woda. That photo was destroyed in the fire.

Mother was as preoccupied with secrets as she was with secretions. She was a talented dissembler who had mastered the art of changing reality to fit her notion of the way things ought to appear. When I met other members of her family, I learned that she was not unique in that regard. She came from a family where hiding was a way of life.

It was 1970 when I first met my cousin Tomasz. The fourth of Uncle Manek's five children, he was the first son to leave Poland in search of a better life. A charming young man, bright and educated, with a wife and two young children, he came to America at my mother's invitation. Once here, he decided to stay and eventually brought his family over. That was no simple matter, but Tomasz was ingenious and determined; he came up with a solution. He divorced his wife, found her an American husband to provide her with U.S. citizenship, and proceeded to remarry her after the required time period following her second divorce.

I admired Tomasz's ingenuity and perseverance. Of all of my cousins, he was my favorite. After knowing him more than a decade, I was surprised to learn that he was born in the little town of Oswiecim in 1946. "Isn't that Auschwitz?" I asked incredulously, shocked that he was born in that infamous place. "Yes," he said matter of factly. "I think that's another name for it." I wanted to understand what would bring Uncle Manek to that place of death after the war to raise his children, but I knew that in discussing that subject I was in dangerous territory. Tomasz's wife was sitting by his side, and I had been warned that she knew nothing of his Jewish roots. In fact, he himself had only learned about them some years earlier when he first came to America.

At that time, Tomasz had been staying with my mother until he could find a place of his own. One day, she was attending to some correspondence and had written her maiden name, Weiss, on a document. "How come your name was Weiss, and my father, who was your brother, was named Bialowski?" he asked her. Cornered, she stammered and blushed; she realized that she could no longer hide the truth from him and told him that Manek had converted to Catholicism in the early 1920s when he was a young man, and that he had changed his name to Bialowski, a proper Polish name. Uncle Manek had taken the secret of his Jewish identity to his grave. His wife Marysia had promised him that she would never let the children find out about their true heritage, and she had extracted a similar promise from my mother, his only living sister. Tomasz was distressed. He knew his father as a taciturn individual who kept to himself, but he never suspected that he was the carrier of such a secret.

In deference to his parents, or perhaps for less noble reasons, my cousin decided to continue to hide the truth from the rest of the family, even from his own wife. His brother Stefan had to wait until my mother's funeral to discover that his Aunt Dorothy was a Jew and that his own father had lied about his roots.

The same pattern of secrecy and denial was evident among other family members whom I visited in Ukraine several years later. My cousin Irena, who had survived the war with her Christian Ukrainian mother after her father was murdered, had married a Ukrainian and had never told her children that their maternal grandfather had been a Jew.

What prevented these relatives from leading more authentic lives? Did they feel guilty that they survived while others close to them perished? Were they afraid that admitting to a Jewish heritage would expose them to persecution? Or did they themselves harbor anti-Semitic feelings? Since the subject was not open for discussion, I could only speculate. I believe that some variation of shame and fear motivated the creation and maintenance of these family secrets. I think that shame was a big part of my mother's experience. Her attempts to maneuver reality so that she could look "good" spoke of her lack of self-esteem. Regrettably, that remarkable woman did not appreciate herself.

I admired her more with the passing of time. She aged gracefully, without any decline in her sharp intelligence or her zest for life. In her late eighties, she did not allow anything to hold her back from living life as fully as she was able. Although she suffered from angina and could barely walk one city block without popping a nitroglycerin tablet in her mouth, she managed to go wherever she chose. In the style that was typical of Eastern Europeans of her generation, she refused to waste money on taxis and insisted on taking public transportation.

Unlike my father who could never face his impending death—he had once stopped talking to me for months when I had commented that he was not going to live forever—Mother faced her own death with the same courage with which she faced life. Her determination to control her own destiny was evident even as she prepared for life's end. After her death, I discovered an incredible stash of sleeping pills in her apartment. I presume these medications, collected and hoarded over the years, were to be agents of a merciful death in the event that infirmities of old age rendered life intolerable. If she could not live life on her own terms, Dorothy was prepared to end it.

People wonder how survivors who narrowly escaped death during the war can take their own lives years later. Some of our most productive and creative individuals—Paul Celan, Tadeusz Borowski, Jerzy Kosinski, Primo Levi—to name just a few, have shocked the public with their suicides.

It doesn't surprise me, however, that a person once so brutally deprived of freedom values the right to choose the manner and time of his or her exit from life. Under some circumstances, suicide is an act of affirmation and empowerment rather than merely a sign of despair.

Fortunately, Mother never had to make that difficult decision, for death took her by surprise in her eighty-ninth year while she still had the energy and vitality to participate in life. Less than two months before her death, she tackled the long trip from her apartment in Queens to the high school in Montclair, New Jersey, so that she could hear Lina sing in the holiday concert. The fact that it meant traveling for hours on trains and buses with her weakened heart condition was, for her, only a minor inconvenience well worth the joy of listening to her granddaughter's voice.

Toward the end, Dorothy seemed acutely aware that any day might be her last. There was a special look in her eyes each time we parted after a visit. The look said: This may be the last time we see each other, and I want to etch your faces in my mind forever.

Her greatest pleasure was entertaining her family. By the mid-1980s, Uncle Manek's oldest son Stefan had arrived in America with his wife and three children, and Mother became the matriarch at the center of what was left of her original family. She longed for all of us to be close, but that was not our natural inclination. Besides, she seemed to set up situations that created competition among us.

Over the years, resentments had build up between cousin Martin and myself. I never forgave him and his family for their callousness in our hour of need, when our country house burned down. Distant acquaintances had been calling with concern and offers of help. Martin and his clan were silent. Not a single phone call or acknowledgment of our trauma. I had long suspected that the country house had stirred up feelings of envy in them. Their house gift to us on the occasion of their first visit to Hemlock Farms had been a carefully gift-wrapped secondhand toaster, broken beyond repair.

Mother refused to hear any criticism about her beloved nephew, who was the son she did not have. At the same time, she never tired of bragging to him about her amazing granddaughter and her accomplished son-in-law. When Spyros received his PhD, Mother gave a party in his honor and invited her nephews and their families. I know that Martin and his wife Olga tired of hearing about how special we were. In those subtle ways, Mother created and encouraged a kind of sibling rivalry between us. The competitiveness and resentments came to a head after her death.

My fifty-first birthday came quietly in the middle of the workweek in January 1992. Mother had invited me to lunch. She made it convenient for me by coming to my office during a break, between patients. She arrived a little out of breath, after having sat for over an hour on a bumpy bus from Jackson Heights, but smiling and cheerful in her typical way. In her arms, she carried a beautiful bouquet of pink carnations, the flower of my birth month. She said those flowers were hardy and fresh and predicted that they would last. Sadly, those carnations outlived her. She brought them on the twenty-eighth of January; by February twentieth, she was gone. Yet her magnificent carnations were still alive.

The exact time of her death and the exact cause of her death were not known. During the night or early morning hours of February twentieth, I awoke with a strange dream. It was a dream about a toilet, but not one of my typical toilet dreams. In fact, it did not seem to be a dream at all but merely a vivid image in my mind's eye. It was a toilet bowl with three pieces of excrement floating in the water. I had no idea what to make of it. I dismissed it and fell back to sleep.

The next morning, while I was at work, Spyros phoned with tragedy in his voice. He had received a telephone call from Irena, the cleaning lady who worked for us and for my mother as well, with the news of my mother's sudden death. Irena had gone to the apartment and opened the door with her spare key on the urging of a concerned neighbor who could not reach my mother by phone. She found Mother in her nightgown lying on the floor in the small hall connecting the bathroom and the bedroom. When she realized that Mother was dead, Irena rushed out of the apartment in terror and called Spyros.

When we arrived at my mother's apartment, we saw that she had fallen directly outside of the bathroom. I could see from the corner of my eye that there was something in the toilet; it had not been flushed. I looked more closely. I was shocked; there, in the toilet, floated three pieces of excrement.

I have never been a believer in telepathy or other parapsychological phenomena. When it comes to such matters, I maintain a skeptical attitude. I don't believe in astrology. I have never been to see a fortune teller. Nor do I believe in an afterlife. Yet there was no denying that something extraordinary had taken place, something that was inexplicable by natural laws. There was no possible way of accounting for the dream image of those three pieces of excrement and their real presence in my mother's toilet. I can only come to the conclusion that a powerful connection existed between my mother and myself that transcended the bounds of time and space. At the moment of death, she had somehow reached out to me, waking me out of deep sleep. If I had not shared my dream with Spyros that very morning when I woke up, I might have wondered if I had imagined the whole thing. But there was no denying that the dream was as real as the evidence in my mother's toilet before Spyros flushed it away.

I was not the only one to have a clairvoyant experience with Dorothy's death. Lina had her own version. The afternoon preceding her *babcia's* (Lina's name for her grandmother) death, Lina had written a sad song with death as its theme. My eleven-year-old had never written a song before, and its depressing theme was inconsistent with her ebullient personality. Perhaps Lina had a premonition that her grandmother was about to die. She sang that song at Mother's funeral. Everyone cried.

There was no autopsy performed on Dorothy; it was assumed that she had died of heart failure during the night. She was in her eighty-ninth year and had a merciful death—at least I like to think so. She was vibrant and productive to the end. We found a library book on her dining room table that she had been reading. After her cataract surgery a couple of years before, she had thrown away her glasses and had better vision than I. In the kitchen sat a tray full of *rugelach* that she had baked the previous day. We went back to her place after the funeral and ate those delicious cookies.

I appreciated how lucky I was to have had my mother for so many years and that her sudden passing spared me the pain of watching her deteriorate. Many of my contemporaries who must cope with aging parents are not so blessed.

I also considered myself most fortunate in having had the chance to learn more details about my early childhood before Mother died. In the last decade of her life, she had spoken more openly about the war years and responded generously to my questions. In addition to her videotaped testimony, she had provided me with handwritten notes of her memories.

Before her death in February, I had been scheduled to present a scholarly paper on the Holocaust at a psychoanalytic conference in the spring. I was in the process of writing that paper when Mother came to Manhattan to celebrate my birthday. At our lunch, I took the opportunity to ask her some questions about the chronology of events, specific dates, and the names of our rescuers. She held back her tears. I suspect that she may have known how little time she had left in this world and responded lovingly to my need to know more of the facts before it was too late. It was her final gift to me.

As I mourned the loss of my mother, I became aware of a strange phenomenon. Mother was not one person to me, but many different individuals coexisting side by side. When I grieved out loud, calling *Mamusha* in the privacy of my shower, it was the mother of my baby years that I was mourning, the one I could not imagine life without, the face with the large, sad dark eyes who smiled at me and made everything all right.

I did not miss the mother of my adolescent years, the one who was critical and controlling. That was the woman who admonished me for wearing my eyeglasses when I came to meet her after work one day. "You know how much better you look without your glasses. Did you wear them just to embarrass me in front of my friends?" she had asked in accusation. I was as angry with her as she was with me. "How did you expect me to find you without my glasses on?" I had retorted.

The mother who was preoccupied with the way things looked to others was the one I resented the most. That was the same mom who embellished the truth and created her own version of the world. I hated her lies and exposed them at every opportunity.

In later years, another mother emerged for me—a woman of substance and courage. I was proud to be the daughter of such a person, one who embraced life and acted on the world.

Spyros's relationship with Mother had started on shaky ground but had grown stronger and better with time. In some ways, she was able to make up for the things he could not get from his own parents. Their lack of education made it difficult for them to understand his achievements. My mother truly appreciated his intellectual gifts and celebrated his accomplishments. He grew to love her deeply. Half jokingly he sometimes said to our friends, "When I first met my mother-in-law, I thought that she was the personification of evil. Eventually, she turned out to be one of my favorite people in the world." He knew the best and worst of my mother.

The side of Mother that appeared after her death was not the most favorable, at least as far as I was concerned. I was in for some bitter surprises when it came to her financial affairs.

Apparently Mother had given a good deal of thought to her estate. She had revised her last will and testament only a few years before her death and had kept the document in a safe deposit box. Once she had asked me to accompany her to the bank and had shown me the document but quickly put it aside without revealing its contents. Her secretiveness did not surprise me; it certainly was characteristic of her. What I was not prepared for was the size of her estate and the convoluted way in which she had decided to divide it up.

Upon her death, the estate was worth more than $350,000. Both of my parents had worked very hard during their lifetimes; they had lived modestly and denied themselves all but the basics of life. In addition to their earnings, they had collected a substantial pension from the German government. I was vaguely aware of that pension, but, as with other money matters, it was made clear to me that the subject was none of my business, so I never knew any of the details.

The subject of restitution had come up in the hidden children's group. There, I was surprised to learn that every member of the group but me had received money from the German government, either in the form of a lump-sum settlement or a lifetime pension. In most cases, it was their parents who had applied on their behalf because my peers were minors at the time. It was most puzzling to me that my parents, who had always been so savvy about money matters, would have neglected to submit an application for me. Of course, there was always the possibility that they had applied but the application had been rejected.

After my mother's death, I decided to hire an attorney and inquire into the matter. Eventually, documents arrived from Germany indicating that not only was an application submitted in my name by my mother in the late 1950s, but that I had supposedly received a settlement of DM 3.450—the equivalent of approximately $3,000. It was shocking for me to learn that my parents had appropriated the entire amount, without a word to me about it. I was especially bitter when I realized that the money must have been received around the time that I was struggling to pay college tuition. In those days, such a sum would have easily covered the cost of college and made it unnecessary for me to work or to take out a loan.

It is difficult to reconcile the mother who professed to love me with the woman who watched dispassionately as I worked long hours and assumed heavy financial debts, all the while knowing that she withheld the means to ease my burden. It was a mockery to realize that, at the time, I was immensely grateful to Mother for agreeing to co-sign my student loan application. As always, Dorothy managed to look like the supportive caring parent.

I am certain today that my parents rationalized their actions so that they felt entitled to keep the money that had been awarded to me. After all, in their eyes, I was not truly a "survivor." Their perception of me was consistent with their denial. They saw me as a well-adjusted child, unaffected by the Holocaust. They probably reasoned that, since they were supporting me financially, they needed the money more than I did. As far as college was concerned, I could have a free education. If I chose to go out of town to school, it was my responsibility to find a way to finance it. Besides, ultimately, their money would be mine since I would inherit it upon their deaths.

In actuality, my inheritance turned out to be a much more complicated matter. When Father died, he left his entire estate to my mother. I presume he expected that she would do the same for me when her turn came. Apparently, however, that was not Mother's intention.

Mother left behind a financial morass that I, as the executrix of her will, had to sort out. In her desk drawer, I found an elaborate list of at least twenty separate bank accounts. Each account was in the form of a certificate of deposit held jointly with the relative of her choice. I suppose that her rationale for disposing of her money in that manner was to outsmart the government in the matter of inheritance taxes on her property. Also, I assume that by distributing all of her money in that way, she remained in control of it even after her death. As her only child, I probably would have automatically inherited what she left behind. But the way she arranged things, she made certain that her nieces and nephews would receive more than one-third of her estate.

Mother's favorite nephew, Martin, and his wife, Olga, were the recipients of the largest sum of money and were named in the will as heirs to two-thirds of her jewelry and assorted valuables. Every item of value was specifically listed in an addendum to the will. In what seemed to be a strange oversight, nothing was left expressly for her beloved granddaughter. I was confused and deeply hurt.

The hurt feelings intensified when, among Mother's papers, I found a document that gave my cousin Martin power of attorney for her health care. It was a blow to learn that she chose to entrust her nephew with crucial medical treatment decisions rather than her own daughter. Did she mistrust my judgment? Or was this a manipulative maneuver? I speculated that perhaps it was her way to try to keep her nephew close by so that he would be present at her life's end. She had, in fact, been sadly disappointed when he had moved to Florida several years prior to her death.

Grief gradually gave way to bitterness and complicated the mourning process. The financial mess had to be sorted out, as well as my feelings of confusion and anger. I had no problem with the amount of money that she had left me; in truth, I had inherited more than I ever expected to. What I resented was the way in which she had maneuvered her estate and the competition she had set up between my cousins and myself. Mother had left a mess for me to clean up. Was the unflushed toilet a message from the grave? I wondered.

Chapter 19

The Wolf Strikes Again

My very first memory is that of Mother's warning about the wolf in the attic. She lied about the wolf, but her message was sincere. "Be careful; don't get too comfortable or complacent, for tragedy can strike when you least expect it." At the same time she espoused a contradictory philosophy. "Everything usually works out for the best." After all, we had been lucky in our misfortune. Dorothy alternated between an optimistic and a catastrophic position and seemed not to be bothered by the inconsistencies in her worldview. She acted as if being prepared for disaster would somehow help her control it.

But, of course, one can never really be prepared for tragedy. When it occurs it is shocking. When it happened to us in January 1995, Spyros and I said to each other, "It's a good thing that Mother is no longer alive. If she hadn't died, the news surely would have killed her." We comforted ourselves with the thought that Dorothy had been spared the misfortune that befell our family. Yet, at the same time, I missed the possibility of finding comfort in my mother's strength. I longed to hear her melodious voice uttering the familiar reassuring words, "Don't worry, Sophinkou, everything will be all right"—words that had given me comfort in times of despair.

But even Mother's optimism would have been no match for the calamity that we faced, particularly since it threatened the most important person in her life, her precious granddaughter.

Lina was Dorothy's miracle grandchild, born in the twilight of her life, just when she was beginning to doubt that she would ever be a *babcia* (grandmother in Polish). At the age of seventy-seven, Dorothy fell in love. When Lina was a toddler and Mother came to visit, it was clear that she had eyes only for her grandchild; no one else seemed to exist. She ignored the person who opened the door and lunged at Lina with such enthusiasm that the small child had to protect herself. Lina learned to defend herself from *babcia's* overpowering love by grabbing a toy before the door opened and holding it out in front of her grandmother like a cross before Dracula.

This early sign of Lina's skill at managing people was borne out as she developed into a young girl. She was not a person to be controlled or intimidated by anyone. She had a strong sense of herself and had no difficulty asserting herself in difficult situations. She had grown up feeling cherished by all the significant adults in her life and consequently appreciated and respected herself.

As an only child and an only grandchild on both sides of the family, Lina was cherished just for being there. But, in truth, Lina came into the world with special gifts. She was intelligent and talented. When she was three years old, she was given an intelligence test as part of the selection process for Hunter elementary school, a public school for gifted children in New York City. Testing revealed that our child had an incredibly high IQ—so high that it was off the charts. We were told that it was 160-plus, a figure that could only approximate the true level of her intelligence.

Although we had known that she was bright, we did not expect her to do so well on a standardized measure of intelligence. Unlike many of our contemporaries, who were preoccupied with developing their children's minds by constant teaching and coaching and turning every situation into an academic learning experience, we tended to let Lina develop at her own pace. My personal experience with my controlling parents had left me with an aversion to intruding on my child's natural development.

From the start of her life, Lina displayed an unusual responsiveness to music. The nurses at the hospital where I gave birth told me that they had observed that whenever Lina fussed, the radio in the nursery had an immediate calming effect on her. I noticed that the musical mobile on her crib had the same effect. As a toddler, Lina had become so familiar with the mobile's tune, a Brahms lullaby, that when the music stopped, she continued to hum the melody to herself until she fell asleep.

She used music as a transitional object—a psychological term to describe a comforting object like a blanket or toy that helps the child make a transition from the mother, something that gives her a sense of security. Lina did have a special blanket, but music also seemed to serve a soothing function for her. When she was just over a year old, we were vacationing in Cape Cod. I was away for part of the day at a professional conference in the area. During my absence, Spyros noticed that Lina would sometimes sit by the door with her thumb in her mouth looking a little forlorn. One of those times, he heard her hum the theme from *Sesame Street,* her favorite television program. It was amazing to hear how clearly she replicated the sound of that fairly complicated tune.

We felt privileged to have such a musical child. Music was an important part of our lives, but neither of us had any real talent in that direction. Spyros congratulated himself for having played beautiful music for Lina in utero. Maybe his efforts had paid off, but it was more likely that our child had inherited the musical talent of members of my mother's family. Her sister, my Aunt Jadzia, was known to have a beautiful voice—silenced by the Nazis before I ever had a chance to hear it. It was thrilling to know that it lived on in Lina.

Before her eighth birthday, Lina was accepted into the Children's Chorus of the Metropolitan Opera. Her second-grade teacher, Mr. Zucker, an opera buff whose idea of a school play was to put on an opera, discovered her remarkable talent and urged me to contact the Met for an audition.

The day that I contacted Elena Doria, the director of the Children's Chorus, was the afternoon of the day that I heard the incredibly powerful voice of my seven-and-a-half-year-old filling the school auditorium with an aria from the obscure Russian opera, *The Tale of the Tzar Sultan.* When Ms. Doria said curtly, "We don't need girls in the chorus, but tell me about her voice anyway," I responded with enthusiasm and described the voice that had filled the large auditorium with its magnificent sound. "Okay," she said, "I'll hear her out. Bring her in."

On the day of the audition, Lina developed a cold, and I considered canceling the appointment but decided against it. My phone conversation with Ms. Doria had given me the sense that this was to be our only chance and we were lucky to have it. So, the three of us headed to the Met. Spyros always made it his business to be present at all of the significant events in Lina's life.

In the elevator, Ms. Doria announced again, "We don't need girls." Spyros said, "Well, this one is special." Then, he added, "She has a cold today; she may not be in her best form." "Don't worry, she won't be singing any arias," Ms. Doria said wryly. "Maybe not tonight!" Spyros retorted.

We followed Ms. Doria through a maze of corridors until we arrived at a classroom. We sat on the side. Ms. Doria, at the piano, instructed Lina to sing "Happy Birthday" in many different ranges and styles. As Lina sang, Ms. Doria became visibly more enthusiastic. Before long, it was clear that Lina was going to join the Children's Chorus, even if they didn't need girls. Spyros was so excited that he could barely contain himself; he phoned Mother with the news from the Met cafeteria. They cried together with joy.

For four years, I enjoyed the role of "stage mother" as I brought Lina to the opera for her many performances. It was exciting to run into people like Placido Domingo in the halls of the opera house and to know that my child was sharing the stage with the likes of Pavarotti.

Lina's career came to a premature end when she outgrew the costumes designated for children. She developed earlier than her peers. She continued to study privately with Elena Doria who appreciated Lina's talent. "Her voice is able to reach extraordinary heights," she had once said to me. "She sounds more like a woman than a young girl," was her comment at another time. But Elena was a demanding teacher and became critical of what seemed to be a lack of self-discipline on Lina's part. Lina looked forward to her lessons but did not practice much on her own. She had difficulty remembering words to songs, and Elena concluded that Lina was not serious enough about music.

Elena was also critical of Lina's weight gain. She perceived it as a character flaw, another sign of Lina's lack of self-discipline. As a young child, Lina had a perfect little body, but, before her tenth birthday, she began to put on weight. It was somewhat puzzling to me because she didn't overeat. Although I wasn't happy about her weight, I did not become unduly concerned. We called it "baby fat" and assumed that she would outgrow it by adolescence. However, it bothered Elena enough to say, "Lina has a beautiful voice, but it's in the wrong body!" At the time, we had no idea how prophetic Elena's remark would turn out to be.

Elena was not the only person to be frustrated with Lina's apparent lack of motivation. Her teachers in middle school were beginning to complain. Her academic performance was gradually deteriorating.

We did not understand what was going on. After all, we knew how bright Lina was, and she had been a very good student during her elementary school years. She had attended a gifted program in public school and, with the exception of spelling which had always been difficult for her, everything else seemed to come easily.

In truth, however, we had noticed over the years that Lina did not live up to the promise of her intellectual potential. For instance, she did not enjoy reading and seemed to avoid it. That was a surprising behavior for a child who had learned the word "boo" for book before she could walk and who could recognize written words by age two.

As it became evident that Lina's schoolwork was deteriorating, we became more and more concerned, and the psychologists within us proceeded to weave one theory after another to explain what was happening.

At first, we thought that the move to New Jersey and a new school system was responsible. She was not used to the more rigorous expectations of the middle-class community that was now our home. Then, we reasoned that my mother's death was traumatic for her and made it difficult for her to concentrate on schoolwork. Then I blamed myself for my laissez-faire attitude in bringing her up and my failure to insist that she develop good study habits. Then Spyros blamed himself for his bad temper and his explosions, which were becoming more frequent as she brought home failing grades. Her response to our confrontations supported the idea that it was willful behavior on her part. She stubbornly insisted that since she planned to become a singer, all this academic work was irrelevant and she had no interest in it.

Another theory we leaned toward was that this was Lina's way of trying to distance herself from us. What better way was there for a child with highly educated parents to reject parental values than to fail in school? Another version of the same theory was that because Lina looked so much like me—in fact, we were occasionally mistaken for one another—she needed to separate from me and choose a nonintellectual path for herself. There was no end to our theories.

Every time we met with friends, most of whom were psychologists like ourselves, the subject of Lina would inevitably come up in conversation, and more theories and suggestions would be offered. In the meantime, nothing changed; Lina's grades got worse and worse. By her last year of middle school, her English teacher, who had known her for three years, told me at a parent-teacher conference, "I stay up nights trying to figure out what's wrong with Lina, and I'm completely baffled."

Lina avoided schoolwork as much as possible. She was constantly visiting the school nurse with vague complaints. At first, the nurse took her seriously, but, since no malady was ever found and since we all knew how much Lina wanted to be out of the classroom, eventually, like the child who cried wolf, Lina's complaints were ignored and she was summarily sent back to the classroom.

The only area that Lina continued to be interested in was music. She auditioned for the school play, *The King and I,* and managed to land one of the star roles. The teacher in charge was aware of Lina's academic difficulties and told her that unless she passed all of her courses the role would be taken away from her and given to an understudy. We supported the idea of making Lina's performance in the play contingent on her academic work, for we knew that if anything would motivate Lina, it would be an opportunity to sing in the school play.

As it turned out, even the threat of losing what she most wanted had no effect. Lina was devastated when the role was taken away from her and given to the understudy. Nothing seemed to make a difference—none of our theories, interventions, not the many hours of tutoring after school, or the psychotherapy sessions that we were providing.

Her psychotherapist, a warm, competent professional whom we trusted, met with Lina regularly. Lina loved the experience; she finally had a chance to see firsthand the kind of work that her parents did behind the consulting room door. She looked forward to her therapy sessions, but treatment had no impact on the behavior that we were concerned about. Lina's therapist had no more idea than we did about what prevented Lina from functioning in school.

Our next step was to arrange for psychological testing. We hoped that through an extensive battery of tests we would learn more about what was going on emotionally and cognitively with our child.

What we learned was shocking. But it was to be the first of many shocks to come, like the aftershocks of an earthquake. After many hours of testing, the psychologist concluded that Lina had a learning disability in reading and in writing. Her intelligence quotient was found to be low-average, over sixty points lower than when she had been tested previously. It was highly unusual to find such a staggering drop in IQ in a measure reputed to be stable over time.

The diagnosis of a learning disability made no sense to me. It did not describe my child who at birth was highly developed neurologically, who reached every developmental milestone earlier than expected. We were told that her visual memory was impaired, and I remembered the child who beat us all at the Memory Game when she was only three years old.

I began to put other pieces of the strange puzzle together. We had been witnessing the gradual unfolding of various physical abnormalities. A number of years earlier, the toes on Lina's right foot had started to curl under. We had consulted physicians from different disciplines—a podiatrist, and an orthopedist—and both had concurred that Lina had hammer toes, a condition that was not very serious and could be corrected with surgery. They had recommended an MRI scan of the lower spine, just to rule out neurological involvement. When we followed up, no abnormalities were found.

We observed that Lina's walk was changing. She had developed a slight limp and her gait was becoming strange. We assumed that the hammer toes were affecting her walk. Then we noted that she seemed to have difficulty holding a pencil with her right hand. The grip was awkward, and it affected her handwriting.

Another concern that I was beginning to have was that, despite early puberty, Lina was not yet menstruating. Although fourteen is not late for the onset of a girl's first period, her physician had prepared us for an early menses because she was highly developed. I took her to my gynecologist who gave her a routine examination, said everything seemed fine, and told her that she could expect her period any day. But nothing happened.

I began to have the uneasy feeling that all of these disparate symptoms were in some way connected. During our second visit to the psychologist who had tested Lina, I described them and asked her, "Is it possible that there is a degenerative disease that's causing the learning disability that you identified?" She looked at me skeptically, "What kind of degenerative disease? Do you mean something like a brain tumor?" That was the first time the words had been said out loud. "Yes, maybe something like that," I answered. She thought for a moment, then said, "No, I don't think so. But you can check it out if you're worried."

Well, we were worried—very worried. Soon, a new symptom appeared. Now, the fingers in Lina's right hand went into spasm, curling up like her toes had done several years before. It was clear that something was happening to the right side of her body. It was time to visit a neurologist. Why had we waited so long?

On New Year's Day, we were invited to our friends' house to celebrate the start of 1995. The hosts, Martin, a neurologist, and his wife Norka, a radiologist, were good friends who had known Lina since she was a small child. During the party, I took Martin aside, described Lina's numerous symptoms, and told him of my concern. "Bring her in to the office next week, and I'll examine her," Martin said.

His examination did not reveal much. He recommended an MRI of the brain as soon as possible. Unfortunately, the timing was not good. Spyros was scheduled to leave for Greece the following week on professional business. He asked if he should cancel his trip or if the MRI could be scheduled after his return, seven days later. Martin hesitated for a moment, then said, "Sure, we'll do it after you get back; we probably won't find anything anyway."

Spyros left on Saturday. His trip was the dream of a lifetime come true. With my encouragement, he had created the opportunity to meet and interview his hero, the Greek composer and political activist Mikis Theodorakis, with the intention of eventually writing a biography of that great man. We were worried about Lina, but Spyros was not going to be away for long. He was due to return the following Friday, and, after all, Martin did not seem overly concerned about Lina's condition.

During Spyros's absence I felt suspended in time, waiting to learn what horrible disease had crept into our lives. I invoked my usual coping strategy at such hapless times. If I could know more about what we faced, I would feel less helpless. I immersed myself in medical books trying to match Lina's symptoms with those I found in the section on disorders of the nervous system.

Spyros called daily from Greece. He was on Mount Olympus. I could hear the excitement in his voice. His research was going very well. His excitement was tempered by the knowledge that all was not well at home. We shared that sense of being suspended in time, an unreal state that could not last.

On Wednesday, two days before Spyros' return home, Lina awoke during the night with an intense headache that she located directly behind the bridge of her nose and her eyes. She had been complaining of headaches on and off, but this one was unbearable, worse than any other. Then, she vomited. I invited her into my bed and, as we waited for dawn to come, she fell back to sleep.

In the morning, I sent her to school as usual while I went off to work in New York. I had hesitated about letting her leave the house, but she insisted that she was feeling better, and I wanted to believe it. It would have been helpful to talk it over with Spyros, but, as luck would have it, for the first time since his departure he didn't call. There was no way I could reach him.

When I got to my office, I turned to the medical textbooks again. Headaches and vomiting were among the classic signs of a brain tumor. I hoped against hope that the suspicion that was forming in my mind was wrong. On numerous occasions, Spyros had accused me of dramatizing; friends had implied that I was overreacting; my therapist had said that I was beginning to sound hysterical; and Martin had not seemed alarmed when he examined Lina.

But now I had new data. I called Martin to tell him about Lina's brutal headache and her night of vomiting. This time he did sound alarmed. "Get her to the hospital immediately!" he said. When I called the school, the nurse told me that Lina had felt so sick that she had been sent home in a taxi. I felt a pang of guilt: what kind of mother was I to have sent her to school that morning? I fought off the feeling of panic that was washing over me. I called every friend I could think of who lived in our community to drive Lina to the hospital. No one was around. Finally, Martin went to pick her up himself.

After canceling my afternoon appointments, I called a car service to take me to the Neuroscience Institute at JFK Medical Center in Edison, New Jersey, with which Martin was affiliated and where he had taken Lina. Our friend Barbra, who had promised Spyros before he left for Greece that she would look in on us, happened to call as the crisis was unfolding and insisted on canceling her own patients and accompanying me to the hospital. I welcomed the support. Barbra was an "up" person, the kind one needed at a time like this. As we sat in traffic on the long ride to the hospital, she used all of her considerable therapeutic skills to calm me and to distract me. We had not been close friends—she was more Spyros's friend than mine—but after that shared experience, Barbra came to hold a special place in my heart.

It was Barbra who was the first person to hear from me that indeed Lina had a brain tumor. We both knew by the look on Martin's face that what he had seen on the CAT scan performed before we arrived was bad news. Lina could tell as well; she saw the tears in Martin's eyes, even though he tried hard to hide them.

As Barbra sat with Lina in the waiting area, Martin took me into a small room where several physicians were looking at the scan of Lina's brain. He introduced me to a young woman physician, a pediatric neurosurgeon, Dr. Rosemaria Gennuso. I did not know at the time how important that woman was to become in our lives. She explained that Lina had a tumor the size of an orange deep within the brain. There was no way of telling exactly what kind of tumor it was, or if it was benign or malignant, until a biopsy would be performed at the time of surgery. Its immense size suggested that it had been there for a long time and was probably benign. She pointed to a dark spot on the scan and said that the tumor was blocking the third ventricle, one of the four cavities of the brain through which cerebrospinal fluid circulates. Because of the blockage, the liquid that cushions the normal brain was not draining properly and was creating a serious condition called hydrocephalus. If not operated on soon, Lina could go into a coma. She needed to remain in the hospital, and surgery should not be delayed more than a few days.

The next step was an MRI scan of the brain to give us a clearer and three-dimensional picture of what the CAT scan had revealed. As Lina lay motionless in that monster of a machine that clanged and made unearthly sounds, I tried to process the events that had just taken place. I was in shock; I was numb, but my mind was clear and sharp. My emotions seemed frozen. I recognized the state; it was all too familiar—a defense that had served me well in the past.

During the night, both Lina and I lay sleepless in the hospital room we shared with an insomniac teenager with Crohn's disease, who was intent on watching television throughout the night. After Lina finally dozed off, I wandered through the halls to the nurses' station. When I shared my despair about Lina's condition, they told me we were lucky that the tumor was operable. It was hard to feel lucky about anything. During that long night, I thought of Spyros in flight on his way back to New York. There was no point in trying to reach him, I said to myself. There's nothing he can do but worry, and there will be enough time for that when he returns.

The next morning, when the nurses came to draw blood and poked mercilessly at my child's arm in search of a vein, I fainted. Several nurses rushed to my side. Embarrassed, I began to laugh. Suddenly, the laughter changed to crying. I could not stop sobbing. The floodgates were wide open; my frozen emotions were finally beginning to thaw.

Lina was controlled—perhaps she was in shock. Dr. Gennuso, or Rose, as we came to call her, had explained to her that a lesion in her brain (a term less scary than the word tumor) was causing the problems that had been plaguing her for so long. No doubt Lina was partly relieved that, finally, a clear explanation was found for all her mysterious symptoms. "You see, it wasn't my fault!" she exclaimed at one point. Yes, she was right, and I felt terrible for all the years of blaming her for her supposed lack of motivation. It was hard not to feel guilty, even though, rationally, how could we have known?

Spyros arrived on Friday evening. His best friend Sam met him at the airport and broke the bad news. In that moment, Spyros came crashing from the heights of Mount Olympus to the depths of Hades. They drove from JFK Airport to JFK Medical Center—no relationship between the two, only an odd coincidence. Before they left the airport, Spyros called Lina in her hospital room. He had a hard time forgiving himself for not being there when she had needed him most. She, in turn, harbored some angry feelings toward him for his absence during the greatest crisis of her life, but all she said at the time was: "Daddy, I have a brain tumor, and you have to sign the papers so that I can have the surgery as soon as possible." No frills, just the facts. She faced the calamity that had befallen her without flinching.

Lina's courage was amazing. She endured whatever needed to be done without complaining or bemoaning her fate. She even managed to hold on to her sense of humor as she teased me about taking center stage away from her when I fainted. "I was the sick one, and you got all the attention; they dropped me and ran over to you." She feigned indignation.

At fourteen, Lina seemed wise beyond her years. Overnight, she had lost the omnipotence of adolescence, the illusion that one is invincible. A few days before the surgery, she took me aside and said, "Mom, I've been thinking a lot about this. If something goes wrong with the surgery, I don't want to be kept alive on machines. Promise me that you'll do as I wish." Later, I learned from Spyros that she extracted the same promise from him.

Because of the nature of the crisis, we did not have much time for second opinions. We trusted Martin, who had highly recommended Rose Gennuso. He said he would want Rose to perform the brain surgery if it were his child. They had trained together at Mount Sinai in New York before joining the staff of the Neuroscience Institute.

Surgery was scheduled for Monday morning, only three days after Spyros's return. He spent the night with Lina in the hospital, and I stayed at a hotel nearby. Early on Monday morning, we stood by her side as she waited to be admitted to the operating room. The night had been difficult and restless. Spyros had held and comforted her, but now, as she was being wheeled into the operating room, she seemed strangely calm. She clutched a well-worn teddy bear that had been given to her by a caring cousin after the fire in Pennsylvania. Mr. Teddy, as she called him, was going to be present in the room during surgery. Also at her side was a CD player with the score from *West Side Story,* one of her favorite musicals. The nurses had told her that she could listen to music as she was being prepared for surgery. In her inimitable fashion, she entered the operating room humming "America" from *West Side Story.*

As she disappeared through the double doors of the operating room, Spyros and I held each other and took a deep breath. It was to be a long day—at least we hoped so. We had been told that the longer the surgery, the better the prognosis, because it meant that more of the tumor could be removed.

We wandered about the hospital corridors like two lost souls. Fourteen years earlier, in another hospital, Spyros had gazed into the eyes of the newborn he cradled in his arms, moments after her birth, and had made her a solemn promise: "Lina, I will always love you and protect you and when you are ready to spread your wings, I'll applaud you." Those words rang hollow now. We were powerless to protect our child from the fickle, faceless enemy that had invaded her body. My mother had shielded me from death when I was a child, but I could not do the same for my own daughter. I could only wait and hope.

In the early afternoon, we were joined by Barbra and Sam, our dear friends committed to helping us through this most difficult day of our lives. These two psychologists who had never met before shared a wonderful sense of humor. Amazing as it seems, they managed to make us laugh and help the time pass more quickly. I don't remember what we talked about for so many hours, but one comment stayed with me. "Think of how good her college essay is going to look," Barbra said. "How many applicants can say that they have sung at the Metropolitan Opera and survived a brain tumor?" It was clever of them to focus on the future to keep us from dwelling on the terrifying present.

Periodically, a nurse came out of the operating room to inform us of the progress of surgery. During one of the visits, she told us that a preliminary biopsy revealed that what we were dealing with was a type of astrocytoma, an optic nerve glioma. Its location identified it as a chiasmatic/hypothalamic tumor. It was on the left side of the brain in the optic chiasm, the area where the optic nerves meet, adjacent to the hypothalamus.

The good news was that it was benign; the bad news was that it was life threatening because of its location. The tumor had become intermeshed and shared blood supply with the hypothalamus, a vital center that controls the pituitary gland and many involuntary functions, such as sleep, appetite, body temperature, and emotions. It could not be fully removed without damaging the hypothalamus and threatening to leave our child in a vegetative state. Dr. Gennuso, assisted by two other neurosurgeons, was removing as much of the tumor as possible without damaging the hypothalamus or the surrounding healthy cells. Unlike more aggressive neurosurgeons who are willing to sacrifice certain functions to remove a greater portion of the tumor, Rose was mindful of the effects of her interventions on the subsequent quality of life of her young patients and had a more conservative approach to surgery. We appreciated her philosophy.

Once we knew the kind of tumor we were dealing with, the four of us headed to the hospital library to learn as much as we could about it. The dense material on tumors of the optic chiasm extending into the hypothalamus was not encouraging. It was a relatively rare tumor; the prognosis was not good.

Surgery took fourteen hours. It was late in the evening when Dr. Gennuso appeared before us, still wearing her surgical garb. Spyros kissed her hand; she looked embarrassed by his show of emotion but smiled and said that the surgery had gone well. She had removed about seventy-five percent of the tumor, and now Lina was resting in the recovery room. Our friends went home.

When we saw Lina later that night, she seemed fragile and vulnerable in her white turban-shaped bandage but slept peacefully and appeared to be physically intact. We were warned that in a few days there would be swelling and that she would look much worse. Indeed, she did.

She lay in a private room in the intensive care unit, attached to many machines. She was not conscious. Her face was puffy, her eyes closed, and occasionally I could see a small tear trickling from the corner of her eye. I wondered if she was crying in her sleep. We were encouraged to speak to her even if we were uncertain whether she could hear us. By the afternoon, she was taken off the respirator and seemed to be regaining consciousness. Spyros leaned over to her and said, "Lina, you did very well. I'm so happy with the way the surgery went, and Mommy is happy too." Lina, in a barely audible voice, uttered her first words. "Is Rose happy?" Her question made us laugh with delight and relief. It was clear from those words that her intelligence was intact. She was quite right, whether Mommy and Daddy were happy was less relevant than whether her neurosurgeon was pleased. "Yes, Lina, Rose is very happy," Spyros answered. Rose, who was in the room, smiled and assured her that the surgery had gone very well.

We left her sleeping peacefully late that night and headed to our hotel room. Early the next morning, we returned to the intensive care unit to find a horrible sight, one we were totally unprepared for. Lina lay unconscious, thrashing from one side of the bed to the other, her arms tied to the crib-like bars of the bed to prevent her from pulling out wires. Her face was swollen beyond recognition, and there was foam trickling from the corner of her mouth.

No nurses were to be found. They were all occupied with other patients in the unit. I ran frantically to the nurses' station. A sullen-looking young woman behind the desk refused to let me use her telephone to reach Dr. Gennuso. "Parents can't use our phones. It's our policy." I did not waste time arguing with her. I headed for Rose's office in another part of the hospital. As I ran through the corridors, I heard Dr. Gennuso's name paged over the loudspeaker. By the time I returned to the intensive care unit, Spyros was pacing outside of Lina's room. His face was white, his voice tremulous. "While you were gone, she stopped breathing," he said. "The nurses brought her back to life. Rose is in there with her now. We can't go in yet."

He continued pacing. I went into the waiting area. A television set droned on. Two Indian women dressed in saris were conversing. I was barely aware of their presence until they turned to stare at me. I curled up in a vinyl chair in a fetal position and wailed, "My child . . . my baby is dying!" My usual self-control was gone; my defenses had left me bereft—no merciful numbness to protect me from despair. The two strangers came over. One held me in her arms as I sobbed. The other talked gently. I have no idea what she said, yet somehow their words and caring gestures provided comfort.

Lina was taken for a CAT scan. The doctors suspected that she had had a seizure. After the scan, they rushed her into the operating room to implant a temporary shunt to relieve the mounting pressure in her brain. The narrow piece of tubing inserted into the ventricle allowed the fluid in the brain to drain into a body cavity, where it could be absorbed.

While we waited for the surgery to be over, I continued to feel overwhelmed. The terror of losing my child was more than I could bear. I stopped wailing but now found myself rocking and pacing. The tension was so great that I could not keep still. I had never experienced anything like that before. Visions of mental patients in back wards of hospitals came to mind as I rocked. The stereotypic motion seemed strange and out of my control. Mysteriously, it eased the tension.

Friends and relatives came to sit with us as we waited. We convened in the hospital chapel, not to pray, but to find refuge from the glaring lights and institutional atmosphere of the hospital waiting areas. Spyros's brother, Anastasi, pleaded, "Talk to your mother, Sophia; pray to her. You know how much she loved Lina. She'll hear you." I wished that I could believe that prayer would help, that I could turn to God or my dead mother to intervene in our behalf to protect our child. But I had no such faith. Some say that there are no atheists in foxholes or in the intensive care waiting room. They are wrong. We turned to friends for our solace.

Lina came out of surgery and rallied. The danger had passed. I was so relieved that I didn't even mind the strange tubes coming out of the top of her head—these were the external shunts that kept the pressure from building. The temporary shunt released the intracranial pressure; Rose hoped that eventually Lina would not need to depend on those tubes and they could be removed. The next few days would be telling.

Unfortunately, Lina did need a permanent shunt, and, once again, she was wheeled into the operating room for her third surgery in eight days. This time, however, it was not an emergency, and we handled it with our more usual calm and resignation. My composure had returned; my defenses were back; I was ready to deal with whatever came our way. It was as though there had been a brief episode where I faced the abyss with full awareness, and now, mercifully, I returned to a state of suspended concern.

Our child had faced death and survived—for now. We had read the medical journals in search of hope for her future, but the statistics on survival rates gave us no comfort. Rose was disturbed when she heard that we had investigated the literature. She knew that it would not give us the hope that we searched for. She said that the type of tumor that Lina had was so rare that, since the 1950s when such cases were first reported in the literature, one could find no more than thirty the world over. The research was therefore based on very few samples and did not adequately reflect the revolution in medical technology of recent years. In the past, Lina's tumor would have been inoperable. Now, with the advent of equipment such as operating microscopes and MRI (magnetic resonance imaging), it was possible to intervene successfully.

In cases such as Lina's, radiation is often recommended as a follow-up to surgery, to further reduce the size of the residual tumor. Rose, however, felt that the beneficial effects of radiation for this type of tumor were not substantiated. Instead, she recommended a wait-and-see approach with regular monitoring. We were in accord, relieved to spare Lina any additional insults to her body.

The ravages to her mind and body were multiple. The tumor had been there for a very long time, perhaps from birth, said Rose. Few of Lina's symptoms were obvious at first glance. To the outside world, Lina did not look like a brain-damaged child. The spasm in her right hand and foot dramatically improved as a result of the surgery. The tumor had been pressing on the basal ganglia, a network of nerve cells in the brain that controls movement. After the operation, her hand appeared normal and, with the physical therapy that followed her release from the hospital, the toes of her right foot gradually also returned to normal.

Improvement in other areas was less obvious. Lina had sustained neurological damage that affected her learning abilities. Some of the problems were caused by hydrocephalus and cleared up immediately after insertion of the shunt, but others, such as her short-term memory deficits and her reading disability, were irreversible. She would have to submit to repeated neuropsychological testing to determine the extent of her learning disabilities.

We were thankful that her beautiful singing voice, the source of joy and self-esteem in her life, was spared the devastation. It was a blessing that the tumor, located on the left side of the brain, did not interfere with music, a right-brain activity.

The effects of that tumor were far-reaching and insidious. Lina had suffered a visual loss that we first became aware of during hospitalization. Her excellent visual acuity had misled us into thinking that her vision was perfect, but, in fact, she had lost a considerable portion of her peripheral vision from the pressure of the tumor on the optic nerves. A visual field test revealed that the peripheral vision in both eyes was significantly and permanently damaged.

Pieces of the puzzle fit together. Now we understood why Lina had not begun to menstruate. The pituitary gland normally receives messages from the hypothalamus. A tumor in the area can interfere with the production of hormones and create a hormonal imbalance. The endocrinologist on the team reassured us that in time, menstruation could be induced, and, eventually, Lina could probably bear children.

We learned that Lina's weight gain was also directly related to the effects of the tumor on the hypothalamus. Appetite control is one of the functions of that structure. When the hypothalamus is compromised, anorexia or obesity can be the consequence. I was warned by Rose before Lina went into surgery that it was possible that Lina would suffer from obesity for the remainder of her life. The chances were high that she would develop such a condition, and, in that case, nothing could be of help in preventing or ameliorating it. No medications, no amount of dieting, no behavioral weight-loss programs, no counseling would make a significant difference in stemming the tide of physiologically based obesity.

Only time would tell the extent of the damages. Right after the surgery there were more questions than answers. The most troubling question of all was whether or not the tumor would continue to grow. After all, that's what tumors do. The future was uncertain. The one thing that we could be sure of was that life would never be the same again.

Chapter 20

Invisible Scars

Lina was released from the hospital on January 29, 1995, seventeen days after her admission. We settled into life in the shadow of tragedy, the legacy of brain tumor survivors and their families. Sometimes it felt as if we were living with a time bomb. The frightening prospect that the tumor might grow was always with us. The surgeon hoped that, by removing a large portion of a benign tumor, the remaining part would wither away. In Lina's case, however, the amount removed turned out to be considerably smaller than initially believed. Several months after surgery, the most optimistic estimate was that about 50 percent of the original mass remained.

Our fourteen-year-old understood the tenuousness of her life. We lived from one MRI to the next. With each positive report—no change in the tumor—we relaxed; a few weeks before the next MRI, we were tense again. Between the MRIs, we lived with a heightened awareness of life's fragility and preciousness. Lina had been given "the gift of time," a term borrowed from Dr. Fred Epstein, the famous neurosurgeon who works with children who have life-threatening brain and spinal-cord tumors. According to him, for these children recurrence is always a possibility, and so is death. It is the quality of the time in between that is of importance.

Each day, Lina marked an X on her calendar to keep track of the passage of time. On January 16, 1996, the first-year anniversary of her surgery, she wrote in bold letters: "I'M ALIVE!" She did not take life for granted. My heart ached for my child who had to deal with issues that no teenager should have to face.

After surgery, Lina's trauma was not visible to the outside world. Only her mutilated hair stood as the symbol of the massive attack on her body. One of Lina's best features had always been her magnificent head of hair, thick, long, rich brown curls framing her round face. For the operation, her head had to be shaved beyond the top of the skull where the incision was made to enter the brain. She was given a choice of cutting the rest of her hair short to minimize the contrast with the baldness, but she insisted on keeping as much of it as she possibly could.

Our first glimpse of Lina without her bandage on was in the hospital, as her dressing was being changed. A strange and disturbing sight met our eyes as we peeked through a slightly lifted shade on her room door. There she lay, looking vulnerable and weird, as if from another planet. Her white head was shaved to the top of her skull and the new hair line began behind a huge jagged wound. What was left of her beautiful mane hung down several inches beyond the stitched wound. I dreaded the thought of her looking in the mirror and facing the bizarre image. I also worried about the reaction of others to her appearance.

Upon her return from the hospital, she wanted to show her grandparents and Uncle Anastasi what had been done to her. "Do you want to see the scar?" she asked. "No" was the answer. She did not remove the scarf from her head. The hurt in her eyes was clear.

After several months of physical and occupational therapy and home instruction, Lina was ready to return to school. By that time, her hair had regrown a couple of inches, but did not yet cover the jagged scar that extended from one ear to the other. The first few days, she wore a scarf to classes, but she soon decided to remove it. "I'm not going to hide the way I look. That's me, and if it bothers anyone, it's their problem!" was her expressed opinion.

She accepted the stares of others as inevitable and ignored the occasional insensitive remarks. Once in a while, she responded with anger. Because of her learning disability, certain adjustments were made in her learning and testing. For example, she was entitled to have extended time for tests and allowed to use her notes when answering questions, so that she did not have to rely only on her memory. When another student expressed envy of the special treatment that she was receiving, she snapped, "How would you like to have a brain tumor?"

For a brief time after the surgery, Lina was depressed and bitter about what had happened to her. We were alarmed to hear from one of her teachers that she was questioning whether her life was worth living. With us, she downplayed her despair, wishing to spare us further torment. We later learned that she had been feeling guilty about the impact of her illness on our lives.

Unlike many adolescents who are uncommunicative with adults, Lina had an unusual capacity to connect with people. Like her father, she was outgoing and self-assured in most social situations and seemed to be comfortable with others regardless of their age or status in life. She had developed strong bonds with several of her teachers and was able to turn to them for support during her recovery period. Her courage in the face of tragedy earned her the respect and admiration of many of her peers and the adults in her life. Her voice teacher expressed the sentiment of many when she wrote, "Lina is an inspiration to the rest of us."

Lina found in poetry a voice for her pain and confusion. At the height of her illness, as the tumor had attacked her body and her mind, she had turned to poetry to express her troubled feelings. Neither her writing disability nor her awkward pencil grip had discouraged her from creating these poems. Even when her words were barely legible, twisted, and tiny, and her hand hurt from the strain of writing, she had fervently continued to put her feelings onto paper. Two months before she was diagnosed with the tumor, she wrote the following poem:

Darkness

My heart glistens
in the open
sun.
The beauty that surrounds me
is closing in.
A painter paints my picture
but he does not know what's inside
my soul.
I blink and
darkness surrounds my body
Everything turns into
dust.

(November 1994)

In this and other poems of that period, Lina had expressed her feeling of vulnerability. Apparently, she had a sense that something was going wrong inside her that was not visible to others. During the recovery period, her poetry reflected the healing process. This piece, written six months after surgery, while we were vacationing on the island of Ereikousa in Greece, is a testament to her resilience.

Untitled Poem

A young girl
sits outside a home
far away from her problems.
A relaxing breeze
cools her head
and the
music that is played
calms her.
Pussy willow flows in the
wind.
Everything is
calm.
The song may stop
but the music still
continues.

(July 1995)

In time, her optimism and enthusiasm for life returned. I believe that these qualities actually helped the healing process. It is a known fact that the human spirit plays an important role in recovery. Lina had inherited her grandmother's indomitable spirit.

In May 1995, only four months after her release from the hospital, Lina decided that our street should have a block party. She organized the entire event and worked indefatigably to make it happen. We were acquainted with few of our neighbors, but Lina seemed to know everyone on our street. She was so gregarious and friendly that people responded to her in kind. They had prayed for her during her illness and sent cards and gifts. I think the block party was her way of saying thanks and also announcing to the neighborhood that she was alive and well.

With extensive tutoring and hard work, in spite of her learning disabilities, Lina managed to become a straight-A student in the last two years of high school. It was a remarkable achievement for a child who had to struggle against the ravages of a brain tumor. With great pride, we watched her claim her diploma on graduation day, wearing the special mantle that marked her as an honorary member of the National Honor Society.

High school graduation was followed by college. Lina was accepted to the school of her choice, Westminster Choir College, a small college in Princeton, New Jersey, dedicated to the study of vocal music. Here she could pursue her talent and passion.

Now, five years after surgery, Lina is in a very good place. To the outside world she seems to have fully recovered; even her physicians pronounce her case a success story. But to those of us who witness the endless struggles, the picture is more complicated. When friends ask with a hint of trepidation in their voices, "How is Lina doing?" we hesitate before answering. Do we give the optimistic version or the other one? Is the proverbial glass half empty or is it half full? It is a matter of shifting perception. Both versions are true.

The big picture is wonderful: Lina is doing remarkably well. When Dr. Jeff Allen, her neuro-oncologist, looked at her latest MRI (now performed on a yearly basis) he told us that her case is humbling to the medical profession. Despite the fact that only a relatively small percentage of the tumor was removed, and without any additional medical interventions, the tumor has not grown—in fact, it is shrinking.

But life is not easy for Lina; it never will be. She is plagued with medical problems, learning problems, social problems, and other consequences of being a tumor survivor. There are many physicians in her life: neuro-oncologists, endocrinologists, neuro-ophthalmologists, and numerous other "ologists."

Despite countless interventions, nothing seems to stem the tide of her growing obesity. As the steady and unrelenting weight gain disfigures her once lovely body and face, we worry about the impact on her health and on her self-esteem. Lina's engaging and outgoing personality facilitates friendships, but her physical appearance makes dating more difficult.

Learning continues to be a challenge for her. Her disabilities affect her performance even in the study of music, where deficits in associative and symbolic memory make it difficult for her to master subjects such as music theory. Many professionals that we come in contact with, including some learning disabilities specialists, are naive about the hard-core effects of brain damage and, adding insult to injury, imply that if Lina only tried a little harder, she could succeed.

It is an ironic fact of my life that my child is a survivor of trauma in her own right. Although hers and my traumatic experiences were of a completely different nature, some of the issues that we have struggled with are similar.

The trauma each of us experienced in childhood has left a mark that separates us from the rest of humanity. For survivors, the trauma becomes a defining event, an identity that sets one apart and makes one feel different, like an alien in the world. It is a difference born of tragedy and associated with suffering and shame. We are members of a special club that no one wants to join. The only comfort of being on the inside is the feeling that one is not alone.

During her period of recovery, while she was still in high school, Lina joined a support group composed of youngsters who had survived brain tumors. Just as I had found a sense of belonging among hidden children whose experiences paralleled my own, Lina also derived strength from her association with peers who had lived through similar assaults on their bodies and their minds. These children found comfort in sharing their pain and their triumphs with others who understood their struggle.

Lina felt very fortunate in the presence of these peers. The surgery had left many of them with visible and extensive damage. Some had had malignant tumors that required a more aggressive surgical approach compromising healthy tissue and function to destroy the cancer. Often surgery was followed by radiation which further devastated their bodies. Most of these children could not live without medication for the remainder of their lives. In contrast, Lina was in good shape. To the outside world, she was just another overweight adolescent. If she chose, she could hide her tumor from the world. That presented her with a dilemma.

When she entered college, a new environment where no one knew of her history, she was faced with the question of whether or not to tell people about her brain tumor. Adolescents don't like to be different from their peers; they want to fit in. Telling people that you have a brain tumor, like saying that you are a Holocaust survivor, is a conversation stopper. In general, people feel uncomfortable when they encounter victims. They don't know how to respond, what questions to ask, or how much to probe. They want to say something helpful, but they don't know what to say. Often their own fears of vulnerability get in the way and make them anxious.

It was tempting to say nothing. But not telling people who are close to you is problematic as well. If she said nothing, she was keeping a secret that could become a barrier to intimacy. Lina chose to be selective about whom she would tell. She mentioned it to her closest friends at college but decided to withhold the information from boys whom she dated, fearful that it might prejudice them against her. She put off the inevitable until the relationship had passed the test of time.

Like Lina, I have always had a choice about whether to disclose my personal history. I have no accent; I don't look like most people's idea of a survivor. As I age, I have the good fortune of looking younger than my years, so that the most frequent reaction I get to my revelation about being a Holocaust survivor is, "How is that possible? You're too young to be a survivor." In response I say wryly, "Looks can be deceiving; during the Holocaust I passed as a Christian; now, I pass as a younger woman!"

It would have been simple to remain in hiding—simple, but cowardly, the cost to myself too dear. The desire to be authentic would not be stilled in me. What had begun as tentative steps out of hiding back in the 1970s and picked up in tempo over the next two decades has now become a driving force to emerge into the open. Today, I feel a responsibility not only to myself, but also to those millions who perished, to be honest about my Holocaust past when the subject arises. I have also come to see it as an opportunity to educate others about this dark period in our history and its pervasive effect on generations of survivors.

Stereotypic notions about trauma survivors exist not only in the general population but among mental health professionals as well. For instance, well-respected psychoanalysts Leon and Rebeca Grinberg write: "It has been said, and it would seem to be true, that survivors of massacres such as the Holocaust and the atomic explosion of Hiroshima inevitably become so disturbed that in their mental states they are like people from another planet." Such pronouncements tend to perpetuate misconceptions. A narrow view that presents survivors as either permanently damaged or amazingly resilient doesn't do justice to complex human beings struggling to come to terms with the effects of devastating traumas. Whether one perceives survivors as either damaged or resilient depends on one's perspective rather than on any objective reality. Is one looking through the lens of pathology or of adaptation? The survivors I have known, myself included, have permanent scars from wounds that are forever in the process of healing. These scars, not always visible, do not stop us from living productive and, in many cases, rich and fulfilling lives.

Survivors, like others, are complex individuals who are not affected in the same way by their experiences. Any attempt to draw simple conclusions about what survivors are like is doomed to miss the essence of the individual. My parents provided me with a picture of different possibilities and different roads to healing. My mother remained full of life and hope; my father was bitter and pessimistic. On the surface, it would seem that he was more damaged by his experiences. Yet I could see how each was affected by trauma and how each coped in his or her own way.

Dorothy, who lived in dread of discovery during the war years, made secretiveness a part of her very being and continued to hide her true thoughts and feelings even after the danger had passed. Leon remained bitter and cold toward people, behaving as if he still existed in the hostile environment of the concentration camp. Both parents reenacted their wartime trauma until the day they died.

Yet they found a measure of happiness in life. My father turned to intellectual and creative endeavors for solace; my mother found hers in relationships. As for me, I considered both essential to my own healing.

For many years, I had concentrated on my psychology practice without giving much thought to painting, the interest of my youth. Then, one day in the early 1990s, I signed up for a painting class. When I entered the art studio, I felt moved by the sight of easels and the smell of oil paint; it was like meeting an old friend after a long separation. But I had changed and grown and could bring something new to the friendship. I was no longer interested in merely replicating the still life I saw before my eyes. Now I wanted to reach inside and find something of meaning that could express my personal experience.

After Lina's illness, I created a painting that reflected the tragedies of my life, past and present. The painting titled *Hidden Traumas: Zosia and Lina* portrays Lina as a thirteen-year-old on the threshold of adolescence looking serene and pretty in her red velvet dress. In the background, behind ominous barbed wire, stands Zosia, my childhood self, at the time I went into hiding. Both children are captured in their innocence as they pose for a photograph unaware of the tragedy that is lurking and will transform their lives forever. A reproduction of the painting is featured in a book by Nelly Toll, *When Memory Speaks: The Holocaust in Art.*

By finding the parallels between the trauma of childhood and the trauma in my current life and expressing it visually and symbolically, I found a way to transform the pain inside into a tangible creation that could be shared with others and at the same time provide me with a sense of satisfaction and self-esteem.

One does not have to look hard to find testaments to the healing power of creativity. The abundance of artistic productions rising from the ashes of the Holocaust is noteworthy. Whether well-known or not, talented or not, survivors driven by a desire to express the unimaginable, to make sense of it, to communicate it to others, and to preserve it for posterity, are turning to the arts.

For many survivors, memoirs are a particularly significant form of self-expression because they encourage the creation of a cohesive, integrated narrative of life while at the same time serve a crucial witnessing function. Bearing witness to the suffering of others is a driving force behind most Holocaust memoirs. The author of a memoir experiences the healing power of witnessing on two levels. First, the writer as witness fulfills a responsibility to those murdered who cannot speak for themselves. Then the reader as witness provides the writer with an affirming, understanding presence.

For me, personally, the memoirs of other survivors have been invaluable, for through them I have gained a better understanding of the events that shaped my own life. After the death of my parents, I searched for more information about the world that I had come from. The memoirs written by survivors of the Janowska camp were of particular interest for me. Among them Simon Wiesenthal, the famous Nazi hunter, and Helene Kaplan, who spent several months at Janowska before she went into hiding as an Aryan. The title of Dr. Kaplan's memoir, *I Never Left Janowska,* was especially intriguing for it communicated the profound and long-lasting impact of the concentration camp on her life.

Like a detective in search of the tiniest clues, I read many autobiographical accounts and sometimes contacted the authors. In this way, I got to know many survivors and their unique ways of coping with the same tragedy that had befallen my own family.

It was through such detective work that I met Frank Stiffel, or Franek, his Polish name. In the process of cleaning out my mother's apartment following her death, I came across an old program of a benefit performance for survivors of Lwów. In the playbill, I found the telephone number of one of the organizers. A call led me to his widow, who in turn put me in touch with Franek, her brother-in-law. Franek had been in his twenties when the Nazis invaded Lwów. He had survived several concentration camps, including Auschwitz. Like my father, he had written a memoir about his wartime experiences, *The Tale of the Ring: A Kaddish*. But, unlike my father, he gave me a copy of his book without expecting payment in return.

Besides his generosity, Franek had other characteristics that distinguished him from my father and from others of his generation whom I have met. He had a wonderful sense of humor, was open, and interested in other people. Unlike many older survivors whose idea of a conversation is a monologue, Franek was pleased to participate in a real interchange of ideas. Once, when I called him at his home, not wanting to intrude, I asked "Can you talk?" "Yes," he answered, "and I can listen!"

Knowing Franek gave me a better perspective on my father. I had always wondered if my father would have been a more loving individual if he had not been exposed to such dehumanization in the concentration camp. Was he irreparably damaged by his wartime experiences, or did his suffering merely exacerbate his natural tendencies? Franek's capacity to love seemed intact. His daughter, born shortly after the war, was the fortunate recipient of that love. To me, Franek was living proof that one could suffer the indignities and torments of concentration camp life and still emerge a vital, caring, loving person.

By the time I met him, Franek had come to terms with his Holocaust past. He told me that after the war he was as filled with hate and a yearning for vengeance as any other survivor, but, years later, he made the conscious decision to forgive those who had hurt him. "A person is born today; he or she dies tomorrow. Whatever is between those two principal points in the geography of existence is all we have." He realized that whether to love or hate, to forgive or seek retribution was his choice to make.

Franek re-created himself as a person without hate, bitterness, or anger. Personally, I don't share his aversion to these human emotions. I do, however, appreciate his recognition of how brief life is and the importance of choosing how one lives. Growing up in the shadow of the Holocaust influenced my perspective of time—past, present, and future. The past was a dark place one should not dwell in, the future is uncertain, and only the present can be counted on. Lina's illness underscored my conviction that life is to be lived in the moment as fully as possible. So while other parents worry about their children's careers and their futures, I find myself more concerned with the quality of Lina's life in the here and now.

Researchers are becoming increasingly aware of the intergenerational transmission of trauma. My parents' worldview was shaped by what they lived through, and, for better or for worse, it was conveyed to me long before I had a chance to develop my own critical judgment. Either implicitly or explicitly, my parents communicated some of the following:

The world is not a safe place; people are capable of anything; so, be careful whom you trust. Don't expect much, and you won't be disappointed. Life is tenuous and uncertain, tragedy may be lurking just around the corner. At its best, life is difficult; it is up to us to overcome the obstacles we find in our path. Some people may try to help, but ultimately we are responsible for ourselves and cannot rely on others to rescue us.

When I went through my mother's desk after her death, I found a scrap of paper on which she had copied a quotation from Jean Paul Sartre, the existential philosopher. It read: "Man can . . . count on no one but himself, . . . he is alone, abandoned on earth in the midst of his infinite responsibilities, without help, with no other aim than the one he sets himself, with no other destiny than the one he forges for himself on this earth" (*Being and Nothingness,* 1943).

Independence was a virtue in my family. Sometimes it bordered on an "each man for himself" philosophy and contributed to my feeling of being a burden on my parents. Apparently, I transmitted the same value to my child, with similar negative and positive consequences.

An image of Lina shortly after surgery comes to mind. She had been home from the hospital for only a day or two, still too weak to manage the stairs in our house. I called out to her, "I'm coming up to change your bandage." "I've already done it myself," she said matter of factly. This was classic Lina, self-sufficient, competent, and mature beyond her fourteen years. I worried that sometimes she did not feel sufficiently nurtured by me, but at the same time I knew that her ability to take care of herself was a strength that would serve her well in life, particularly in view of her disabilities.

The fundamental attitudes and beliefs transmitted by my parents were helpful in coping with the crisis of Lina's illness. Having been raised to anticipate the possibility of doom, when catastrophe actually struck, I never raised my arms to heaven crying out "Why me? Why our family?" I accepted the fact that life had dealt us a bad hand, and it was up to us to make the best of it. Behind me was the image of my parents, who had encountered tragedy with courage and a determination to survive. I admired their sense of personal agency, and the active stance they took toward life. Their inner strength was my model.

It was heartening to hear Lina express a similar idea several years after her diagnosis. In 1998, I was interviewed by the Survivors of the Shoah Visual History Foundation. Toward the end of the meeting, both my husband and my daughter were invited to join me. When the interviewer asked Lina if she wanted to say something to me, she answered:

> Yes . . . I went through a traumatic experience also and I think that the reason I was so strong in dealing with it was because of my mother and the kind of life that she led and the kind of childhood that she went through.
>
> I'm glad that she's able to come forward about it and talk about it because a lot of people hide their feelings or hide the fact that they were Holocaust survivors, and I'm glad that she's not one of them . . . I'm just glad that she's a strong person.

The philosophers say that courage is the capacity to move ahead in spite of despair. I have seen that quality in my child as well as in my parents, and I have seen it in other survivors who after living through devastating events have managed to create lives with meaning and hope.

Chapter 21

Coming to Terms

My healing journey out of the Holocaust was a long one. It began slowly and gained momentum over the years. My goal was to get to a place where I would feel a sense of integration and continuity in my life and, ultimately, to experience a greater freedom from the inhibitions that had been the legacy of my hidden childhood. Many different roads led me to that place. The major one was my personal analysis. When I first began reconstructing my past, Sabe was my invaluable guide along the way. His empathy and understanding created the safe atmosphere that enabled me to put the fragmented pieces of my early childhood into a coherent whole. With memory images, occasional dreams, and bits of information gleaned over the years, we reconstructed the events of my past. Creating a coherent narrative is a healing experience for any trauma survivor. In my case it was especially important and especially difficult.

As a very young child, I experienced the Holocaust in a way that made it almost impossible to integrate and make sense of the experience. For me, there was no life before the war, no secure early childhood to hold in mind, no context in which to place what was happening to me and around me. The Holocaust was in the air that I breathed daily for the first four years of my life. I took it in deeply without awareness or critical judgment. I ingested it with the milk I drank from my mother's breast. It had the taste of fear and despair.

Erik Erikson, the eminent psychoanalyst, wrote about the stages in the development of a person as a social being. The earliest stage from infancy to about eighteen months is the time for the development of a sense of trust. It is during this period that infants develop their earliest internal models of relationships. During that critical period of development, I lived in the most hostile environment imaginable. I was carefully taught to mistrust others. I could feel my mother's intense anxiety as strangers approached.

According to Erikson, the second stage occurs during the second and third years of life when the toddler begins to experience himself or herself as an independent source of will and power. In hiding, I did not have the freedom to explore my environment or assert myself. Our living circumstances forced me to control any spontaneous impulses and stay very closely tied to my anxious mother. When autonomy does not develop as it should, shame and doubt are the consequences. My recurrent toilet dreams seem to be graphic expressions of a disturbance at this stage of development.

One of the major tasks that confronted me as a toddler was to make sense of the strange and confusing things going on around me. I watched Mother for clues, but sometimes her reactions perplexed me even more. Like the morning in Zimna Woda when there was a knock at the door and Daddy jumped into the wardrobe to hide. Mommy's look of terror was instantly replaced by a friendly smile as she opened the door and faced the stranger.

A three-year-old is old enough to notice such bizarre goings-on, but too young to find meaning in the situation unless the adults provide it. My parents did not explain anything. It was their way of ensuring our safety.

The 1999 Academy Award-winning Holocaust film directed by Roberto Benigni, *Life Is Beautiful,* deals with this theme in a creative and poignant way. A child, who is incidentally around the same age as I was during my hiding years, is given outlandish explanations about the events taking place in the concentration camp where he is hidden by his father. In an attempt to protect his son, the father turns reality on its head. Audiences laugh hysterically at the father's antics and outrageous fabrications, but I relate to the struggle of the young child who is desperately trying to understand what is going on around him. I know firsthand about the long-term impact of such mystification on a developing mind.

Memories of a hidden childhood are fragile and easily challenged; children are vulnerable to what adults want them to think and remember. My parents were intent on perpetuating the myth that I would not remember what I was too young to understand. Consequently, my memories lived on inside of me as isolated images and sensory impressions disconnected from time and place. Fortunately for me, when my parents decided to record what had happened to our family during the war, I was finally able to anchor and validate some of the elusive images in my head.

But the profound confusion of my childhood had a long-term effect. The need to understand turned out to be a pervasive theme in my life. I believe that it influenced my choice of profession, among other things.

As a psychologist, I am committed to understanding human behavior and motivation. It is my job to help people make sense of what is puzzling in their lives—their symptoms, their unexpected reactions, their troublesome feelings. Much of the work of analysis involves sorting out what is real from what is imagined or fantasized.

It is no accident, to be sure, that I have chosen to dedicate myself to a healing profession. In my consulting room, I encounter people who struggle to make a better life for themselves. Some of my patients have been victims of trauma while others have lived in hiding without any shadow of the Holocaust in their lives.

The work often brings me face-to-face with the core issues of my own life. Psychoanalysts are the keepers of secrets. Patients express their private thoughts and feelings and know that the analyst, bound by confidentiality, will never reveal their secrets. By sharing their innermost thoughts, patients feel less alone.

Helping others to overcome their suffering is a healing experience for the analyst as well. It is immensely gratifying to feel deeply connected with another human being. Through the process of identification, the struggles as well as the victories are shared and both parties in the dyad are enriched by the experience. Yet the relationship is one sided to the extent that the focus is exclusively on the patient; the analyst's personal life remains hidden—a safe and familiar place for me.

My profession has been a tremendous source of gratification and healing for me. But it is in my adult relationships that I have found the greatest opportunities to make up for what was missing in childhood.

Psychologists use the term "corrective emotional experience" to describe the process by which a new relationship repairs the damage done by previous dysfunctional ones. The concept is usually used in connection with the therapist-patient relationship, but I believe that in life many opportunities occur for such corrective experiences.

Marriage provides such an opportunity for healing, particularly if it is a good marriage. But even a bad marriage can be a chance to learn more about oneself and one's needs. Both times, I married men whose spontaneity and playfulness were in striking contrast to my own seriousness. Being "good" as a child meant keeping a low profile, not attracting attention to myself, and, most important, controlling whatever came out of my mouth. I had learned these lessons so well that they became second nature. My capacity for spontaneity was buried and split off. It is no accident that I found myself with husbands who expressed themselves with little inhibition.

Their lack of control had a darker side as well. Both of the men I married, like my father before them, had explosive tempers. Freedom of expression sometimes turned into uninhibited fury. In childhood, I had felt victimized by my father's explosive temper, yet in adulthood I found myself once again, this time by choice, living with men who had difficulty controlling their outbursts of rage. My first husband lost control to the point of violence. Spyros is less destructive but nevertheless intimidating in his rage.

I suppose that part of my unconscious attraction to these men is their freedom to express their anger so directly. I had been well trained to hold back aggression. A child in hiding cannot safely express anger or any strong emotion. I had learned to inhibit my negative feelings to the point of sometimes not even being aware of them in myself. The outbursts of the men in my life put me in touch with my own denied emotions. Through my union with them I could feel connected to those parts of myself that had gone underground in childhood.

The fact that my partners resembled my father in this respect gave me a chance to work through the unfinished business of childhood. It was a familiar situation, but this time I had more power and options at my disposal; I did not have to be a victim. My father's anger was not tempered by love. His rages would end in withdrawal and interminable silence. In contrast, Spyros's bursts of temper are short lived and part of his mercurial nature. He can go from intense anger to equally intense affection within minutes.

My second marriage provides me with many opportunities to make up for deprivations of childhood. My husband's generosity is in direct contrast to my father's stinginess. Whether it comes to material things or to his emotions, Spyros always gives freely and never keeps score. He comes from a family and a culture where generosity is the norm. Greeks are a hospitable people who treat strangers with warmth and generosity. The value that they place on hospitality has even found its way into the language where the word for guest and the word for stranger *(xenos)* are one and the same.

In my experience, the commonly held notion that Greeks are a passionate, emotional people is not merely a cultural stereotype. With few exceptions, I have found Greeks to be intense and full of vitality. At functions such as weddings and baptisms, it is common to find more people on the dance floor than seated at the tables. Even the old folks who can barely get around manage to gather up enough energy to join the endless circle dances. The life-affirming spirit that surrounds me in my new family is a welcome contrast to the depressive overtones in my family of origin.

Everyone on the little island of Ereikousa where Spyros's family has their roots is related to everyone else. He boasts that he has about 300 close relatives, most of them living in America. Finally, through marriage, I have found the extended family that I had so longed for in my childhood. With my Greek name (Sophia is a common name in Greece) and my limited knowledge of the language (I learned the basics so that I could communicate with my in-laws), I fit into the world he came from with unexpected ease.

In fact, I used to worry that I could get absorbed in his culture and lose my own in the process. Spyros's strong ethnic identification overshadowed my tenuous connection with Judaism. My concern was not about losing my religion but rather my shaky cultural identity.

On the subject of religion, Spyros and I are perfectly compatible. He had been brought up in the Greek Orthodox tradition, but, by the time I met him, he had abandoned his church, no longer believed in God, and completely rejected any religious affiliation. His antireligious feelings were as strong as those of my father's.

Unlike many interfaith couples who are faced with the decision of how to bring up their first child, we never considered it an issue. We celebrate all holidays as if they were secular events. At first, Spyros's family tried their best to imbue Lina with religion but couldn't get too far. Each time they brought Lina a small gold cross to wear around her neck, it disappeared into a little box hidden away in my dresser. Mother did her share to bring Jewish awareness into Lina's life; after all, she had the influence of the 300 Greek Orthodox relatives to counterbalance.

When Lina was four or five years old, she drew an interesting picture that revealed some of her own struggle with her cultural and religious identity. The drawing in colored pencils featured a large anthropomorphic smiling heart with the word LOVE printed boldly in its center. Her name, LINA ORFANOS, printed directly above the heart conveyed that it represented herself. At either side of the heart in the lower right and left quadrants of the page respectively, she drew the symbols of Hanukkah and Christmas, a menorah on one side and a carefully decorated Christmas tree on the other. The drawing seemed to be a perfect integration of her separate identities, yet something troubled her. She spontaneously ripped off the lower right hand corner, the one with the menorah, then Scotch-taped it back on. Was she ambivalent about the Jewish side of her? Did her ambivalence reflect my own confusion about my Jewish identity?

My Jewish identity had been figuratively ripped off and then subsequently reattached in an awkward way with the result that I never felt like a real Jew. I always had difficulty keeping track of the Jewish holidays and their significance. The first menorah I ever owned was the one that my mother brought for Lina when she was a toddler. In the last years of her life, Dorothy seemed to reclaim her Jewish identity. After Leon died, she joined Hadassah, the women's Zionist organization, and became an active, devoted member. Dorothy, who had never shown an interest in Israel before, now found a sense of purpose and community in the organization dedicated to the development of Israel. She was recognized as a leader and honored with an award for her service. She left Hadassah a generous contribution in her will. Dorothy had come a long way since the day in 1936 when she had renounced her Jewish identity to meet my father's condition for marriage.

It is interesting that Spyros and I, who originally came from such different backgrounds, ultimately had more in common than many couples who seem better matched. We shared many basic values about life. In time, we also came to share the same profession. When our paths first crossed in that Greek coffee shop in the summer of 1972, I would never have predicted that the young waiter who flirted with me would become my partner and soulmate and, eventually, a highly successful professional in my field.

After obtaining his PhD from NYU, Spyros followed the same path that I had taken some years earlier and earned a certificate in psychoanalysis from the NYU Postdoctoral Program. A skilled clinician, he has a thriving independent practice, but that is only one of the many diverse activities that fill his days. He teaches, writes, codirects the Manhattan Institute for Psychoanalysis, and is actively involved in professional political activities. He has earned the respect and admiration of his peers both in the Greek-American community and the world of psychoanalysis. The numerous teaching awards granted by both communities attest to his talent and scholarship.

Spyros's charismatic presence makes him a natural leader. I marvel at his sense of ease in large groups and his skill in "working the room." With a grin, he tells me that he developed this talent during his days as a waiter. I think his leadership abilities were bequeathed to him by his passive, ineffectual parents who assigned him the role of caretaker when he was still a boy.

As with many individuals who are used to taking responsibility for others, Spyros is very good at it but also resents the role he seems compelled to take on. I suspect that part of his initial attraction to me was my independence and competence—qualities that reassured him that he would not have to take care of me. The ten-year age difference between us also contributed to the sense that I was a woman of the world; perhaps he secretly hoped that he had found someone to mother him.

His perception of me collided with my own agenda, hidden from myself as well as from him at the time, namely that, at last, I had found a loving man who was nurturing and generous and, unlike my parents, would not resent taking care of my needs. I was drawn to his strength and assertiveness and his ability to handle situations that tend to overwhelm others. Occasionally, it crosses my mind that if there were another Holocaust, we could count on Spyros's ingenuity and courage for protection.

Our marriage is satisfying in many ways, yet both of us sometimes find our deep need for caretaking frustrated. When overburdened with work responsibilities, Spyros resents the inevitable demands of domestic life, and, once again, I find myself with someone who experiences my needs as burdensome. It is this theme, more than any other, that is the subject of our marital battles, particularly as his professional life moves forward with incredible momentum.

As the years passed, Spyros distinguished himself in the psychoanalytic community. Colleagues were drawn to his enthusiasm and limitless energy. In 1998, he was elected president of the Division of Psychoanalysis of the American Psychological Association, one of the largest organizations of psychoanalysts in the world. My husband was a rising star, and I basked in his light. It was wonderful for me to be at the center of cutting-edge developments in my field without having to be on center stage—an anxiety-producing place for a hidden child. Vicariously, I enjoyed his successes.

Spyros, in turn, applauded my growth. He watched my transformation as I moved from a place of denial and numbness to an acceptance of my suppressed past. His steadfast support and encouragement made it easier to pursue my quest. When I considered writing a memoir, his enthusiasm propelled me forward. He believed in the project and understood its importance in my life. Like a dedicated promoter, he constantly talked about it with friends and anyone else who would listen.

I had read countless memoirs, but now the time had come to tell my own story. With my daughter away at college and my husband involved in the demands of his work, I had the time and space in my life to devote to such a consuming undertaking. Once I made the decision to write, a sense of urgency and excitement took over. Sometimes I had the feeling that I entered a trance-like state, effortless and automatic, as if guided by a force from within. It was as though the creative process took over and I merely had to avoid standing in its way. When I began the project, friends said, "You have to make time for writing; build it into your life." But as it turned out, it was the rest of my life that I had to make time for.

The experience changed me in unexpected ways. I felt more energy and vitality. Friends reacted to the changes, commenting that I seemed different somehow, more lively and self-assured. I had found my voice, and it was an exhilarating and freeing experience.

The process of self-exploration involved in writing the memoir was exciting. I was surprised to discover that recording the narrative on paper provided me with a depth of understanding that went beyond what I had learned in years of analysis. By examining my life in its totality, I was able to recognize the intricate patterns in its fabric.

Coming to terms with a traumatic past is a lifelong endeavor. Wounds may heal, but scars remain. There are constant reminders of the past in the present. For instance, I cannot attend a funeral today without the dark thought that the individual lying in the coffin is fortunate to be the recipient of such pomp and circumstance. It is a stark contrast to the fate of my thirty-five blood relations who, with millions of other unfortunates, were dumped into nameless graves or had their ashes scattered over unknown towns in distant places.

Occasionally, my unconscious plays tricks on me reminding me that, under the surface, I am still that little child with the big secret. On the fiftieth anniversary of the liberation of Lwów, the son of one of my mother's close prewar friends who had survived in hiding arranged a reunion of survivors from our town. We each told our story of survival. When my turn came, I talked about how my mother and I had lived as Christian Poles in Zimna Woda; I talked about my father's year in the concentration camp and about his daring escape. When I finished, I realized that I had totally forgotten to mention the fact that for almost two years, we hid my father in our attic. "After all these years, you're still hiding your father!" Sabe had said to me when I recounted the experience.

Other signs of the past alive in my present are more disturbing. They are the paranoid thoughts that linger and cannot easily be dismissed. For instance, when I was recently interviewed by the Survivors of the Shoah Visual History Foundation, I had the fleeting thought that perhaps it was dangerous to be identified as a surviving Jew. After all, it could happen again. Then, like my relatives before me who registered with the *Judenrat* (Jewish council), I would become an easy target for those who wanted to destroy me.

In a world where Holocaust deniers are a creeping malignancy, it's important to educate future generations to what actually took place and what could happen again if we don't remain alert. It is the responsibility of those of us who lived through the events to share our stories with others who did not experience them firsthand.

In the past few years, several schools have invited me to speak about my hidden childhood. The students listen attentively to what I have to say, and many ask questions that reflect their struggle to grasp the enormity of the Holocaust. Following a visit to a fifth-grade class, I received a packet of letters written to me by the children. Here is an example of one ten-year-old's simple yet profound attempt to understand the incomprehensible:

Dear Mrs. Sophie Richman
    Thank you for coming and talking to us we really appreciate you explaining your view of what happened to Jews during the

holocast [sic].

What I liked best about your talk was when you told us the title of your fathers book; Why? I have often wondered why myself; Why would any one want to exterminate a people just because of there [sic] religion? Why us? Why was my family and your'se [sic] killed? and most of all why did this happen at all?

It is good to know that this won't happen again, that the human bill of rights will not again be violated and that none of us ever again will have to ask why.

Sincerely,
Erica

Erica, the grandchild of European Jews, grapples with the essential questions that face generations of atrocity survivors. "Why us?" she asks. The arbitrary nature of tragedy shakes the human faith in a just and predictable world order. Erica needs to understand why her family has suffered, but there are no adequate answers to such questions. She then reassures herself with the idea that it will never happen again. Regrettably, the happy ending in her letter reflects a wish rather than a reality. We don't have to look very far to see evidence of genocide in different parts of the world today.

To face a better future, we need to address the hatred that is at the core of our inhumanity to one another, and we must find ways to turn intolerance of differences into acceptance and respect. Perhaps education is the key to these goals.

The story of my life represents a tiny portion of the large tapestry dedicated to the preservation of the memory of this dark period in modern history. I hope that in its own way, it serves to illuminate the long-term impact of the Holocaust. For me personally, the journey has been a major step toward healing; through it, I have gained a greater sense of wholeness and integration. The existential philosopher Kierkegaard wrote: "Life can only be understood backwards; but it must be lived forwards." Understanding where I've come from gives me a clearer perspective on where I'm going. The road ahead is uncertain, but my footing is sure. I face the future with cautious optimism.

Epilogue: Ghosts of Galicia

After Mother's death, my desire to know my roots became more intense. I wanted to learn as much as possible about the culture I was born into and the events that had shaped me. During Mother's lifetime, I had heeded her injunction to stay away from Lwów, the graveyard where our past was buried. Her death freed me to learn more about my origins, yet paradoxically robbed me of the most important link to the past. No one was left to validate my discoveries.

Perhaps my quest was an expression of the human propensity to desire what is no longer within reach, or maybe it was a way to hold on to my parents after their deaths. Whatever fueled me, there was no doubt that a trip to my hometown was important to me. In 1993, Spyros and I set out for Eastern Europe.

The city of my birth was now called Lviv by its Ukrainian inhabitants. This once-beautiful cosmopolitan city was a shadow of its former prewar vibrant self. Time seemed to have stood still under the many years of Soviet rule. With the recent collapse of the communist regime, the city was desperately trying to regain its balance. It was dirty and neglected; layers of grime covered its majestic buildings. People struggling with poverty lined up in the streets for bread, their faces depressed or expressionless.

After our visit, Spyros jokingly referred to Lviv as "the armpit of the world." When, six years later, I proposed that we return for another look, he was adamantly against it. He didn't feel safe there and was too protective of me to agree to let me go on my own. There were rumors of rampant crime in the poverty-stricken region. One morning, Spyros pointedly handed me an article from the front page of *The New York Times*. It began: "LVIV, Ukraine—The citizens of this graceful but impoverished city have a message for the West: Hand over your money, or we'll shoot" (February 26, 1999).

But I would not be deterred. My initial return to Lviv had been enlightening but a bit overwhelming. This time, I knew much more about my personal history, so my research could be more focused. My memoir was in its final stages, almost ready for publication. The trip represented a last opportunity to check my facts, get more details, and integrate some of the memory fragments into a coherent picture of my early years. Retracing the steps of my refugee journey was like connecting separate dots on a page to form a meaningful image. So in the summer of 1999, we headed for Ukraine, Poland, and France. This time around, Lina, who also wished to know more about her maternal roots, joined us.

To our surprise, Lviv was no longer the dingy, depressed place we had encountered six years earlier. It seems that a few weeks before our visit the historic city was host to a summit conference of leaders from Central and Eastern Europe. As a result, Lviv was treated to a facelift. Buildings within view of the center of town were cleaned and restored to their former glory. Those that were not visible from the town square were ignored, but even without a coat of paint they seemed brighter somehow. The bread lines were gone, and store shelves were now stocked with food and other goods.

Regardless of the changes, one fact remained the same—a striking absence of Jewish life in Lviv. The city that had once been home to a thriving Jewish community had lost its ethnic soul. Hitler had succeeded in his goal of a *Judenrein* (cleansed of Jews) Galicia. Those who had escaped murder had emigrated shortly after World War II. The few Jews who remained were now old and dying out. Also gone were most of the Poles who had dominated the region for four-and-a-half centuries. The Ukrainians, the most avid Jew haters and Nazi collaborators, now had their day; Lviv, the capital of Western Ukraine, belonged to them.

It was eerie to enter a world where the buildings stood in their old majesty, many completely unchanged, while the life and the spirit that had filled them was now gone forever. The magnificent Lviv Opera house, built in the style of the one in Vienna, had been restored to its former grandeur. One hour before show time we were able to get the best tickets in the house for the equivalent of two dollars and fifty cents, about the price of a soft drink in town. There were many empty seats as the residents of Lviv seemed more interested in gathering outside on the square on this Sunday evening in June. They sang nationalistic songs in groups that formed spontaneously, or they listened to the sounds of English rock blasting from neighboring cafés.

As we sat enthralled listening to *La Bohème,* I was aware of the ghosts in the opera house, the former inhabitants of Lwów who had once enjoyed the same exquisite musical score in that same beautiful building, before they were murdered or driven away. As I looked out from my loge into the orchestra, I could picture my young mother sitting in the audience, as she had so many times before the war. I was deeply moved by the music, by my associations, and my memories. *La Bohème* was not only Mother's favorite opera but ours as well, for Lina had appeared in it for three consecutive seasons at the Metropolitan Opera in New York.

Before we left Lviv, we visited the one remaining synagogue. In contrast to the magnificent churches that abounded in Lviv, the Jewish house of worship was in a sad state of disrepair. As we approached the gate, a small group of boys exited from the building each wearing a baseball cap on his head. "Probably covering a yarmulke" observed Spyros. To be sure, in a place where Jews are a tiny minority, a young Semite would not want to be so conspicuous.

We entered and looked around. I have always felt like a stranger in a Jewish temple. Yet here I experienced a greater sense of belonging than in the rest of the city. We introduced ourselves to the young woman in the office who seemed to be in charge. Her face lit up when she heard that I was a Jew born in Lviv and living in America. She readily answered my questions. Yes, this was the only surviving synagogue in Lviv. The boys we had seen on our way into the building had been taking a computer class at the school. Few Jews resided in Lviv; the congregation numbered about three hundred and she was not familiar with many of the older members.

In response to my question about Jewish life in Lviv, she took out a package of photographs. "Last week I got married here in this synagogue; perhaps you would like to see the pictures." Both Spyros and I were moved to tears as we looked at photos of families celebrating the joyful event, as it had been celebrated for centuries. These Jews of Lviv, dwelling among the echoes of their vanished brethren, were affirming life.

The scarcity of Jews was even more striking in other parts of Galicia. Of course we didn't expect to find any in Zimna Woda, the little village that had been my hiding place during the war, but we were surprised that so few Polish families were living there. From the residents, we learned that immediately after the war, the area had undergone a major population shift. The majority of Poles emigrated west into Poland, and Ukrainians from the east were transplanted into the territory to replace them. Even the Catholic church where my sister and I had been baptized had been transformed into a Ukrainian church. Sadly, these changes made it impossible to find out any information about my hiding place or the people who had known my mother and me.

When we took a side trip to Tluste, the little *shtetl* where my father was born at the turn of the century, we found no sign of Jewish life there either. An old timer pointed to the spot where the synagogue had stood before it was destroyed by the Nazis, then directed us to the Jewish cemetery on the edge of town. That was the only trace of the large Jewish community that had existed there before the Second World War.

It was this infamous cemetery that Martin Gilbert, the renowned historian, made reference to when he wrote:

> Most of those marked out to die in Galicia were now (during May and June 1943) taken, not to one of the death camps, but to local forests or gravel pits, or as at Tluste, to the Jewish cemetery. Here, the executions were carried out with savagery and sadism, a crying child often being seized from its mother's arms and shot in front of her, or having its head crushed by a single blow from a rifle butt. Hundreds of children were thrown alive into pits, and died in fear and agony under the weight of bodies thrown on top of them.

The old burying ground that had been the site of such brutality was strangely peaceful and deserted on this clear June day in 1999. Two unattended white goats roamed about and grazed on the tall grass. The place had a haunting quality; the large expanse of land was dotted with countless rows of tombstones in various stages of deterioration. Some were relatively intact and stood tall; others, weighted down by the ravages of time, leaned toward the earth. Despite the overgrown weeds climbing up the headstones, one could make out Hebrew letters, beautiful intricate carvings, and, in some cases, family names and dates. Several of the headstones were punctured by bullet holes, a reminder of the carnage that had taken place on this spot fifty-six years earlier.

In one corner of the cemetery stood a modest monument with a plaque memorializing the massacre of 1943, when the last Jews of Tluste were herded into this place and brutally murdered one by one.

With horror, I realized that one of those victims whom Gilbert wrote about was my own cousin, Uncle Zygmunt's eldest daughter, who had remained in the village until the very end. Her father had perished in Janowska six months earlier; her mother and four siblings had been murdered as well, and now her turn had come. She was thrown into that mass grave along with her baby and the last Jews of the *shtetl*.

The old graveyard that had been witness to such sorrow was neglected but not vandalized as our Ukrainian guide and interpreter pointed out. He commented that it is unusual to find a Jewish cemetery in such good condition around these parts. In other villages, people demolish the gravestones and use them for construction. Here, not only were they left undisturbed, but a memorial had been erected to the memory of those who perished. I left Tluste feeling grateful that the townspeople had not destroyed the last sign of Jewish life in their midst. How odd to be grateful for such a small bit of humanity!

There was not much else for me to see in this sad village. I was disappointed that no one living there today had ever heard of my father's family. The Reichmans had lived in that *shtetl* for many generations, yet I could find no trace of them, not even a gravestone to mark their existence and their passing.

As for my mother's side, the Weiss family, it was a different story. Two sets of relatives had remained in Eastern Europe. One in Warsaw, Poland, the other in Kołomyja, Ukraine, a small town south of Lviv at the foot of the Carpathian Mountains.

My Aunt Marysia, the matriarch of the Polish family in Warsaw, was the widow of my Uncle Manek, who had converted to Catholicism and fled to England during the war. Her two daughters, Marta and Sabina, lived nearby, and she was surrounded by grandchildren. The other branch of the family consisted of my cousin Irena and her two adult children, Oksana and Oreste, their spouses, and many grandchildren. Irena, also widowed, was the daughter of my Uncle Izio, my mother's favorite oldest brother, murdered at the start of the war. Izio's wife, a Ukrainian woman, had raised Irena as a Greek Catholic, one of the sects of the Christian religion in Ukraine.

On our first trip to Eastern Europe, I had met cousins and children of cousins whom I never even knew existed. In both Warsaw and Kołomyja, the reception was friendly but at the same time somewhat formal and distant. In Kołomyja, where Ukrainian was spoken, I had hired an interpreter; in Warsaw, I managed with my imperfect Polish.

The conversation remained superficial. While the language barrier could have accounted for some of the awkwardness, I had the distinct feeling that something else was blocking communication.

Before long, I learned that the younger generation of relatives had no knowledge of their Jewish connection and both matriarchs wanted to keep it that way. In Warsaw, there was a cover story: my poor mother had married a Jew and put her own life in danger as a consequence. In Kołomyja, there was merely a shroud of silence. "We don't talk about such things," my cousin Irena had said when I asked if her children knew about their Jewish roots. Now, I understood their discomfort with my presence; I held the power to destroy the family myths and expose the fact that the grandfathers had been born Jews, a fact that had been carefully hidden from several generations.

After my initial visit to Eastern Europe, I had maintained contact by telephone. Aunt Marysia was my oldest living relative, a contemporary of my parents. Her ninety-year-old mind was amazingly sharp and clear, so I appealed to her for information about the family. She responded to my questions with a long letter translated into English. It began "Dear Zosia, you do not have to go to Poland as I can answer in English the questions asked for by phone." It was only later, when I visited her in Poland, that I realized that the opening paragraph was actually an entreaty to stay away.

I was grateful for Aunt Marysia's letter because it clarified certain ambiguities about my mother's relationship with Tadeusz Witwicki, the friend who had been so helpful to us during the war. At the same time, however, I realized that Aunt Marysia had rewritten history to avoid any mention of my family's Jewish roots. According to her version, my father had been arrested by the Germans because of his political affiliations, and my mother, fearful of being arrested too, had appealed to her to provide us with false documents.

At the end of Marysia's long, carefully written letter, there was a note in Polish scribbled in her own handwriting. Since I don't read Polish, I could not make out a word of it and resolved to ask her about it on my next visit.

As soon as we arrived in Warsaw, I called Aunt Marysia. She seemed less than eager to meet but agreed to have us over the following day. I had the sense that something was troubling her; finally, she got to it. It was about the "big family secret." She had promised her husband on his deathbed that the children would never know that their father was born a Jew, and now, to her dismay, one by one they were discovering the dreaded truth. She told me that Sabina, her youngest, knew nothing of Manek's Jewish identity and implored me to keep silent.

Apparently, it was this same warning that she had tacked on to her letter in Polish. Even the translator could not be trusted with such a secret. It occurred to me that there was something ludicrous in this situation. Here I was, determined to dig up my past, and there was my Aunt Marysia equally determined to keep it buried.

During this visit, I learned to what incredible lengths Aunt Marysia had gone to protect the lie that she and her husband had fabricated more than sixty years earlier. She was currently writing an autobiography totally devoid of any references to her husband's true origins. This memoir was her legacy to her children and grandchildren. She had also recently purchased a ring for each of her two daughters featuring the Bialowski family crest.

My uncle had taken the name Bialowski to replace the Jewish sounding Weiss. In a creative "sleight of hand," he had translated the German word "weiss" which means "white," into a name that sounded like the Polish word for white. Then he had added the suffix "cki" to complete it. In Polish, names that end in "cki" or "ski" denote a noble lineage. So Uncle Manek Bialowski assumed the identity of an aristocrat by creating this impressive name for himself. No doubt Aunt Marysia was thrilled to bear such a name and naturally expected that her daughters would wear their signet rings with pride.

After my phone conversation with Aunt Marysia, I called cousin Sabina. She sounded delighted to hear from me and immediately invited all three of us to visit with her and her nineteen-year-old son. Lina was excited to meet her cousin Kasper who was only six weeks older and spoke a bit of English.

I had met Sabina briefly on my last visit to Poland. At the time, I had been struck with the strong physical resemblance she bore to our Aunt Jadzia who had perished in the Holocaust. At the age of fifty, Sabina was a charming woman with a very successful career in fashion design. After her recent separation, she had moved into a beautiful apartment on the outskirts of Warsaw.

Our hostess was warm and entertaining, a great storyteller. At times, however, the conversation took some unexpected turns. She talked about how her two older brothers had exchanged identities at certain points in their lives. My cousin Julek, who was a better student than his brother, Stefan, had taken examinations for him, signing Stefan's name on the exam booklet. Stefan, in turn, had taken on Julek's identity recently when he filled out some governmental forms.

Sabina also told us an interesting story about how some years before she had spent a summer working in a hotel in the Netherlands. Since at the time, Poles were unable to legally work outside of the country, Sabina had assumed her friend Wanda's identity and borrowed her working papers. Wanda, who incidentally was Jewish, was married to a Frenchman and therefore eligible to work outside of Poland. Spyros and I listened to these stories about passing from one identity to another and knowingly glanced at each other. Why did Sabina's talk keep returning to the subject of false identity? Was the subject on her mind? As psychologists, we are aware that when people can't speak about something directly they will often make allusions to it. We began to wonder—Did Sabina know the family secret on some unconscious level?

We had our answer later that same evening. As we walked to the waiting taxi, Sabina took my arm and pulled me aside. She whispered: "Zosia, I learned something shocking a few months ago. A cousin told me that my father's name was not really Bialowski, but Weiss. Is it true? Was he really Jewish? Do you know anything about this?" Her voice trembled slightly. Then without waiting for an answer she continued. "I told my sister what this cousin had said. Isn't it ridiculous? I said to Marta, how can she say such stupid things? And then Marta told me that it was true, and that she herself had known about it for some time." Sabina looked ready to cry. "I can't believe everyone lied to me. Why would they keep something like this secret?"

I didn't hold back my own tears. "Sabina, I want to tell you everything but I don't feel free to talk about it." I was torn. How could I betray Aunt Marysia? But why should I participate in a deception that I truly wanted to expose? And, anyway, Sabina already knew the truth. The taxi was waiting. I agreed to meet with her at another time to continue our talk privately.

Later that week, at an outdoor café in the quaint Old Town in Warsaw, I heard the whole story. Sabina recounted how, six months earlier, she had visited a distant cousin who blurted out the carefully guarded family secret. It all began when Sabina innocently showed off her new ring.

The old lady challenged her. "Do you really have the right to wear this ring?"

"What do you mean?" Sabina had asked bewildered. "Bialowski is our name and this is our coat of arms."

"Oh, do you really think it's the family name?" the old lady had responded sarcastically. One question led to another and, before long, Sabina had heard the whole sordid story. It's my guess that the cousin was offended by the family's attempt to pass as Polish aristocrats while there was a Jew hidden in their closet.

After having exposed the family myth, the old woman feigned remorse. She apologized for her indiscretion saying that she had been under the impression that Sabina already knew the truth about her father.

When her sister Marta confirmed the cousin's story, Sabina was devastated. It was not the truth of her father's identity that troubled her, but the lies that had kept it hidden all these years.

It was truly ironic that the very precautions that Aunt Marysia had carefully taken to seal the lie ultimately backfired and exposed the bitter truth. As Marysia had feared, her daughter was furious with her. Sabina was convinced that it was her mother rather than her father who had the difficulty with his Jewishness and had gone to such great lengths to hide it.

I myself had begun to suspect as much when I had last spoken with Marysia. My aunt told me that she learned the truth about Manek's Jewish roots "right before the wedding when it was too late to back out." When I asked her how she felt about her husband having been born a Jew, she answered without hesitation: "I got used to it." But, evidently, she had not.

My talk with Sabina was the highlight of my return to Poland. In this cousin whom I barely knew, I discovered a friend that I could feel close to and who shared my values about openness and honesty. When she exclaimed "What's the point of a memoir based on lies? It's worthless!" she was expressing my sentiments exactly.

Sabina was hungry to know everything about her father's side of the family. She asked me where our grandparent were buried, how our aunts and uncles had perished, what were their names, who were their children. Happily, I shared whatever my own investigations had uncovered.

At one point in our conversation I experienced the sense of awe that comes over me from time to time when I encounter unconscious phenomena at work. Sabina told me how she had always had a great fascination with Judaism, which was puzzling in view of her Roman Catholic upbringing. As a young student, she had become actively involved in the struggle against the persecution of Jews in her country. Then, in college, she had been drawn to the study of Semitic languages. In fact, she had taken a double major: art history and Hebrew.

There seemed no end to the ironic twists and turns of this situation. Manek, a man who fled from his beleaguered Jewish identity, raised a daughter who embraced the culture he had abandoned. The fact that Sabina was indisputedly the favorite of his five children made me wonder if my uncle was secretly pleased that his Jewish heritage lived on in her. We will never know, for Manek is long gone.

Sabina decided to keep her discoveries hidden from her mother. She worried that the old woman would be destroyed by the news. It was not lost on me that Sabina was now doing to her mother precisely what her mother had done to her all these years and presumably for the same reason, namely to protect her. Nor was it lost on me that by my agreeing to keep silence about Sabina's knowledge, I was once again drawn into a web of deceit.

Whether we are aware of it or not, the long tentacles of the Holocaust have us in their grip and have left an indelible mark on us. Our heritage is a fact of our life; we cannot escape from it. Freedom of choice is in our attitude. Whether we see ourselves as damaged or as special because of the mark we bear is up to us. In the final analysis, our image of ourselves influences our decisions, our actions, and, ultimately, the person we become.

Bibliography

Bergmann, Martin S. and Milton E. Jucovy (Eds.), *Generations of the Holocaust.* New York: Columbia University Press, 1982.

Drix, Samuel. *Witness to Annihilation: Surviving the Holocaust: A Memoir.* Bellevue, WA: Brassey's, 1994.

Epstein, Helen. *Children of the Holocaust: Conversations with Sons and Daughters of Survivors.* New York: G.P. Putnam's Sons, 1979.

Frankl, Viktor E. *Man's Search for Meaning.* New York: Simon and Schuster, Inc., 1984.

Friedman, Philip. The Destruction of the Jews of Lwów, 1941-1944. In Ada June Friedman (Ed.), *Roads to Extinction: Essays on the Holocaust* (pp. 244-321). Philadelphia: Jewish Publication Society of America, 1980.

Gilbert, Martin. *Atlas of the Holocaust.* New York: William Morrow and Co., 1993, p. 160.

Gilbert, Martin. *The Holocaust: A History of the Jews of Europe During the Second World War.* New York: Holt, 1985.

Grinberg, Leon and Rebeca Grinberg. *Psychoanalytic Perspectives on Migration and Exile.* New Haven, CT: Yale University Press, 1989, p. 155.

Helmreich, William B. *Against All Odds: Holocaust Survivors and the Successful Lives They Made in America.* New Brunswick, NJ: Transaction Publishers, 1996.

Herman, Judith Lewis. *Trauma and Recovery.* Basic Books, 1992, p. 178.

Jacobs, Theodore J. Secrets, Alliances, and Family Fictions: Some Psychoanalytic Observations. *Journal of the American Psychoanalytic Association, 28*(1), 1980, 21-42.

The Janovska Camp at Lvov. Video. Ergo Media Inc., 1993.

Jewish Life in Lwów. Video. National Center for Jewish Film, 1991.

Kahane, David. *Lvov Ghetto Diary.* Amherst: University of Massachusetts Press, 1990.

Kaplan, Helene C. *I Never Left Janowska.* New York: Holocaust Library, 1989.

Kestenberg, Judith and Ira Brenner. *The Last Witness: The Child Survivor of the Holocaust.* Washington, DC: American Psychiatric Press, Inc., 1996.

Laub, Dori and Nanette C. Auerhahn (Eds.), Knowing and Not Knowing the Holocaust. *Psychoanalytic Inquiry, 5*(1), 1985.

Levi, Primo. *Moments of Reprieve.* Britain: Abacus, 1987.

Marks, Jane. *The Hidden Children: The Secret Survivors of the Holocaust.* New York: Ballantine Books, 1993.

Marshall, Robert. *In the Sewers of Lvov.* New York: Charles Scribner's Sons, 1990.

Peck, Jean M. *At the Fire's Center: A Story of Love and Holocaust Survival.* Chicago: University of Illinois Press, 1998.

Richman, Leon. *WHY? Extermination Camp Lwów (Lemberg) 134 Janowska Street, Poland.* New York: Vantage Press, 1975.

Stiffel, Frank. *The Oxymoron Factor,* Part 1. Xlibris Corp., 2000.

Stiffel, Frank. *The Tale of the Ring: A Kaddish.* New York: Bantam Books, 1985.

T-291, Richman, Dorothy R., Fortunoff Video Archive for Holocaust Testimonies, Yale University Library. Used by permission of Yale University Library.

Toll, Nelly. *When Memory Speaks: The Holocaust in Art.* Westport, CT: Praeger, 1998.

The Trial of Adolf Eichmann. Video, 1997. Produced by Great Projects Film Company Inc. for ABC News Productions. Used by permission of ABC News.

Wells, Leon W. *Janowska Road.* New York: Macmillan, 1963.

Wiesel, Elie. *All Rivers Run to the Sea: Memoirs.* New York: Alfred A. Knopf, 1995.

Wiesenthal, Simon. *The Sunflower.* New York: Schocken Books, 1970.

Wines, Michael. Struggling Ukraine Teeters Between East and West. *The New York Times,* February 26, 1999, p. A1.

ABOUT THE AUTHOR

Sophia Richman, PhD, is a survivor of the Holocaust who lived in hiding as a young child in Eastern Europe. Dr. Richman is a practicing psychologist and psychoanalyst licensed in New York and New Jersey. She is a Diplomate in Psychoanalysis of the American Board of Professional Psychology.

Dr. Richman has been a member of the American Psychological Association for over thirty years and has served on several section boards of the Division of Psychoanalysis. She is a fellow of the Academy of Psychoanalysis. In addition to her full-time private practice, she is on the faculties of the Institute for Contemporary Psychotherapy in New York and the Contemporary Center for Advanced Psychoanalytic Studies in New Jersey.

Dr. Richman is knowledgeable about the impact of the Holocaust both from her personal experience and her work with survivors and their children. She has lectured in schools, universities, and psychoanalytic institutes about her experiences during the war and has presented papers at professional conferences on the long-term impact of early childhood trauma.

Order Your Own Copy of
This Important Book for Your Personal Library!

A WOLF IN THE ATTIC
The Legacy of a Hidden Child of the Holocaust

_____in hardbound at $49.95 (ISBN: 0-7890-1549-8)

_____in softbound at $22.95 (ISBN: 0-7890-1550-1)

COST OF BOOKS_____

OUTSIDE USA/CANADA/
MEXICO: ADD 20%____

POSTAGE & HANDLING_____
(US: $4.00 for first book & $1.50
for each additional book)
Outside US: $5.00 for first book
& $2.00 for each additional book)

SUBTOTAL_____

in Canada: add 7% GST____

STATE TAX____
(NY, OH & MIN residents, please
add appropriate local sales tax)

FINAL TOTAL____
(If paying in Canadian funds,
convert using the current
exchange rate, UNESCO
coupons welcome.)

❏   **BILL ME LATER:** ($5 service charge will be added)
(Bill-me option is good on US/Canada/Mexico orders only;
not good to jobbers, wholesalers, or subscription agencies.)

❏ Check here if billing address is different from
shipping address and attach purchase order and
billing address information.

Signature_____

❏   **PAYMENT ENCLOSED: $_____**

❏   **PLEASE CHARGE TO MY CREDIT CARD.**

❏ Visa ❏ MasterCard   ❏ AmEx   ❏ Discover
❏ Diner's Club   ❏ Eurocard   ❏ JCB

Account # _____

Exp. Date_____

Signature_____

Prices in US dollars and subject to change without notice.

NAME_____

INSTITUTION_____

ADDRESS_____

CITY_____

STATE/ZIP_____

COUNTRY_____ COUNTY (NY residents only)_____

TEL_____ FAX_____

E-MAIL_____

May we use your e-mail address for confirmations and other types of information? ❏ Yes ❏ No
We appreciate receiving your e-mail address and fax number. Haworth would like to e-mail or fax special
discount offers to you, as a preferred customer. **We will never share, rent, or exchange your e-mail address
or fax number.** We regard such actions as an invasion of your privacy.

Order From Your Local Bookstore or Directly From
The Haworth Press, Inc.
10 Alice Street, Binghamton, New York 13904-1580 • USA
TELEPHONE: 1-800-HAWORTH (1-800-429-6784) / Outside US/Canada: (607) 722-5857
FAX: 1-800-895-0582 / Outside US/Canada: (607) 722-6362
E-mail: getinfo@haworthpressinc.com
PLEASE PHOTOCOPY THIS FORM FOR YOUR PERSONAL USE.
www.HaworthPress.com

BOF00